MILTON STUDIES
XXXIII

MILTON STUDIES

XXXIII ❧ *Edited by*
Albert C. Labriola
and Michael Lieb

The Miltonic Samson

UNIVERSITY OF PITTSBURGH PRESS

MILTON STUDIES

is published annually by the University of Pittsburgh Press as a forum for Milton scholarship and criticism. Articles submitted for publication may be biographical; they may interpret some aspect of Milton's writings; or they may define literary, intellectual, or historical contexts—by studying the work of his contemporaries, the traditions which affected his thought and art, contemporary political and religious movements, his influence on other writers, or the history of critical response to his work.

Manuscripts should be upwards of 3,000 words in length and should conform to the *Chicago Manual of Style*. Manuscripts and editorial correspondence should be addressed to Albert C. Labriola, Department of English, Duquesne University, Pittsburgh, Pa., 15282-1703. Manuscripts should be accompanied by a self-addressed envelope and sufficient unattached postage.

Milton Studies does not review books.

Within the United States, *Milton Studies* may be ordered from the University of Pittsburgh Press, c/o CUP Services, Box 6525, Ithaca, N.Y., 14851, 607-277-2211.

Published by the University of Pittsburgh Press, Pittsburgh, Pa. 15261

Copyright © 1997, University of Pittsburgh Press

Manufactured in the United States of America

Printed on acid-free paper

10   9   8   7   6   5   4   3   2   1

Library of Congress Catalog Card Number 69-12335

ISBN 0-8229-3949-5

US ISSN 0076-8820

A CIP catalog record is available from the British Library.

CONTENTS

INTRODUCTION
Albert C. Labriola

F OUNDED IN 1974–1975 by Thomas Kranidas of the State University of New York, Stony Brook, and Mario A. Di Cesare of the State University of New York, Binghamton, the Milton Seminar originally met in New York and its environs. Before they inaugurated that enterprise, however, Professors Kranidas and Di Cesare were, and continue to be, original members of the editorial board of *Milton Studies*, and both of them contributed essays to the first volume in 1969. For more than two decades, the two activities—the Milton Seminar and *Milton Studies*—have run parallel to one another, each in its own way providing a forum for distinguished scholarship on Milton. The present volume of *Milton Studies*, however, represents the first intersection, indeed collaboration, between the seminar and the series. Further commentary on the separate but parallel backgrounds of the seminar and the series will enhance our understanding of their present interrelationship.

In the years after it was founded, the Milton Seminar included approximately a dozen invited Miltonists. Increasing its membership to approximately twenty-five Miltonists and expanding its geographic horizons, the Milton Seminar eventually stretched from the Northeast to the South, Southeast, and mid-Atlantic region as some of its original members relocated elsewhere and more recent nominees for membership were elected. In fact, the Milton Seminar, which meets biannually (in the fall and the spring), was convened at Duke University in April 1994. I was the host of the next meeting, which was held on October 14–15, 1994, at Duquesne University in Pittsburgh.

Traditionally, the Milton Seminar meets on Friday afternoon and evening and in the morning and afternoon of the following day. There is an invited lecturer for Friday's session, after which discussion follows; and two other speakers are invited as the principal discussants—the one for Saturday morning, the other for the afternoon—to present their work-in-progress and to elicit reaction. The seminar becomes an open forum that involves all members in commentary, critique, and questioning. This openness informs the seminar, even to the extent that the lecturer on Friday and the principal discussants on Saturday may freely choose to comment on any works by Milton, on elements of his life and the era in which he lived and wrote, and on critical trends that assist in the process of interpretation. From conception to execution, diversity rather than uniformity is the norm that guides the Milton seminar.

In a similar manner, *Milton Studies* is an eclectic publication, a miscellany, its essays not acquired and organized according to a preconceived design, though each submission surely undergoes rigorous evaluation. About the time—in the mid-1970s—that the Milton Seminar was originated, *Milton Studies* VII (1975) appeared, with Michael Lieb and me as the guest editors. This was the first extra issue of *Milton Studies,* and it was published in addition to the regular issue in the same year. As early as 1975, the founding editor of *Milton Studies,* James D. Simmonds, foresaw the value of a periodic extra issue. Since 1975, four other extra issues have been published, along with the regular issues in those same years: 1978, 1983, 1984, and 1992. Each extra issue had at least one guest editor, sometimes two, and on one occasion three; and each extraordinary volume, in contrast to the miscellany published in the same year, was organized according to a preconceived design, whether topical or methodological. For the extra issues, most of the essays are invited, but the process of evaluation guarantees not only that the essays meet the highest professional standards but also that they conform to the organizing principle of the extra issue of *Milton Studies* wherein they will appear and, when possible, that they interact with one another.

The foregoing remarks concerning extra issues of *Milton Studies* provide the frame of reference for understanding the unique Milton Seminar that I sponsored in October 1994, which diverged from the traditional format in two ways: by establishing a focus on one of Milton's works, *Samson Agonistes,* and by inviting two speakers, not three, as featured presenters. Sharon Achinstein presented the Friday lecture, but also guided the open forum on *Samson Agonistes* on Saturday morning because I sought the fullest possible discussion of her innovative ideas. In the afternoon, John Shawcross led the open forum by informally presenting his views on Milton's dramatic poem, then by overseeing the discussion, which centered upon questions submitted in advance by members of the seminar or upon problematic passages in *Samson Agonistes* that members cited. Because the focus on *Samson Agonistes* generated such intense interest, keen analysis, and complementary discourse, the idea underlying the present volume was confirmed, an idea developed collaboratively by Michael Lieb, a guest at that Milton Seminar, and me. Thus, the Milton Seminar with its focus on *Samson Agonistes* and the present extra issue of *Milton Studies* with an identical emphasis are conjoined. And more than two decades after our collaboration in producing the first extra issue of *Milton Studies*, Michael Lieb and I are collaborating "yet once more," as Milton might say, on the sixth extra issue.

The present volume contains essays by five attendees at the Milton Seminar: Sharon Achinstein, John Shawcross, Michael Lieb, Norman Burns, and John Rogers. The other three contributors—Mary Beth Rose, David Loewenstein, and Janel Mueller—though not attendees at the seminar, were invited to compose essays because their research engages central, present-day topics of significance concerning *Samson Agonistes*. The Milton Seminar raised and the present volume is structured to reflect eight such topics: the deity of *Samson Agonistes*, Milton's appropriation and adaptation of scriptural analogues, the prosody of Milton's dramatic poem, concepts of heroism, the secret of Samson's strength, *Samson Agonistes* and Restoration drama of dissent, the bearing of the radical religio-political culture of seventeenth-century England on *Samson Agonistes*, and, finally, ways and means of misreading Milton's dramatic poem. If these topics seem familiar, they are. They are the inveterate topics that each generation of commentators has addressed, that our generation is engaging, and that future generations will continue to ponder.

In line with the foregoing viewpoint, a measure of the progress (or should one say "the difference"?) between an earlier and a later generation is the diverse treatment of the same topics. Or to put it differently, each generation must reformulate the questions that underlie the same topics. From this process of reformulation alone, some progress emerges. But in the present volume, each essay not only reformulates the questions but also substantively engages one of the eight topics enumerated above in a manner heretofore unrealized and with the greatest degree of revisionist thinking. Each generation, moreover, must write its own books; and our generation, represented by the contributors to the present volume, is writing its book on *Samson Agonistes*. While the present volume, from one perspective, comprises some of the pages in the larger work being composed by our generation, from our perspective the commentary herein will be among the most important and profoundly influential on what is being written by our generation and, I daresay, on what is not yet conceived and still to be presented by later generations. While such a claim is bold, the proof is in the essays that follow.

Leading off is Michael Lieb's " 'Our Living Dread': The God of *Samson Agonistes*," which astutely focuses on whether the deity is present in, or absent from, the dramatic poem. By reformulating the question above and rendering it as a paradox or, theologically speaking, a mystery—an absent but present deity—Lieb enters the critical debate concerning the "god of

Samson Agonistes." By surveying biblical passages, various seventeenth-century texts, Milton's other works (poetry and prose), and interpretive commentary, Lieb restructures our understanding of the deity "in" *Samson Agonistes* and even in Samson himself. What he concludes is that the *mysterium tremendum* is a godhead of dread, whose presence may be centered or embodied in Samson. Underlying the dramatic poem, therefore, is a theology of dread, whose basis is primitive and whose import is terrifying.

Complementing Lieb's approach is that of Norman Burns, who in " 'Then Stood Up Phinehas': Milton's Antinomianism, and Samson's" also cites biblical texts as analogues for understanding Samson's role as an agent of the godhead. Burns, however, develops an antinomian perspective on Samson's role, using Phinehas as a precedent to justify illegal acts presumably performed on God's behalf. If indeed Samson is inspired by God, then the freedom he enjoys as God's agent has both biblical and theological foundation, involving the interrelationship of faith, works, and the process of justification. Thus, Burns reformulates the questions concerning Samson's climactic action at the Dagonalia and superbly redefines the concept of God's faithful champion or, one might say, the hero of faith.

Engaging the contested topic of the prosody of *Samson Agonistes*, Janel Mueller in "Just Measures? Versification in *Samson Agonistes*" perceives a verse design more purposive and expressive than previous commentators have discerned. Encoded in the verse, in short, are interpretive signposts pointing to sites of stability, indeterminacy, or tension if not contention. With a subtlety and sophistication not readily found elsewhere, Mueller turns an acute eye and finely tuned ear to the principles and elements of composition, detecting patterns and violations thereof and assessing their bearing on interpretation and meaning in the dramatic poem, most notably with reference to Samson—the norm (in countless ways) against whom all other characters are measured.

Following Mueller's essay is one by Mary Beth Rose, who also perceives Samson as normative, as the frame of reference against which conflicting concepts of heroism are measured—by Samson himself and by other characters in the dramatic poem. Whereas Mueller with microscopic intensity turns her vision onto the verbal patterns in *Samson Agonistes*, discovering in effect a colossus in a cherry stone, Rose is telescopic in her outlook, juxtaposing in her field of vision Milton's dramatic poem and also two other Restoration texts centering upon heroism. In " 'Vigorous most / When most unactive deem'd': Gender and the Heroics of Endurance in Milton's *Samson Agonistes*, Aphra Behn's *Oroonoko*, and Mary Astell's *Some Reflections Upon Marriage*," Rose argues that all heroism is by definition problematic. Discussing the interplay of the heroics of action, male privilege, gender construction, and gender relations, Rose splendidly reformulates questions but substantively redresses our understanding not only of heroism but of its relation to slavery, marriage, and agency.

In "The Secret of *Samson Agonistes*," John Rogers approaches Samson's climactic action at the Dagonalia by indirection. Not unlike Polonius in *Hamlet*, who instructs Reynaldo that he should "by indirections find directions" out, Rogers incisively probes the secret "cause" of Samson's ultimate and consummate destructive act at the temple by investigating the circumstances and decision making surrounding the secret of Samson's strength. Precisely by reformulating the question in this manner—how does the earlier secret shed light on the later one?—Rogers breaks new ground in our analysis of *Samson Agonistes*. By situating Samson at the site of contradictory explanations of the secret of his strength—whether in his hair or diffused through his body so long as he maintains his Nazarite vow—Rogers launches into a study of the theology of the dramatic poem. Innovatively, he argues the case for an ontology of strength, for a "secret" connection between Samson's strength and his vow and for the godhead's mysterious role therein.

While Rogers's essay casts light on a curious Miltonic theology of strength, Sharon Achinstein in "*Samson Agonistes* and the Drama of Dissent" insightfully construes Samson as a moral agent performing acts of obligation. Her analysis, however, is framed within the Restoration context of dissent, obedience, and compulsion and coercion. By inquiring into the topic of moral action, though deliberately remaining outside the sphere of theology and even spirituality, Achinstein brings to bear on Milton's dramatic poem and Samson's conduct the distinctive context of local historical circumstances, notably Restoration political theory. In doing so, Achinstein defines Samson's experience as political.

In "The Revenge of the Saint: Radical Religion and Politics in *Samson Agonistes*," David Loewenstein, like Achinstein, situates the dramatic poem in the local historical context of the Restoration, though his critical lens brings into focus the revolutionary and radical religio-political culture in mid-seventeenth-century England. In effect, Loewenstein stresses the radicalism inherent in *Samson Agonistes*, not by pursuing so-called "source and influence" investigation but by comprehending the zeitgeist of ferment and upheaval—apocalypticism, concepts of militant sainthood, the operation of the Spirit, and the like. Accordingly, Loewenstein concludes that *Samson Agonistes* may be termed a radical Protestant drama.

Finally, John T. Shawcross, in a fitting conclusion to the volume, "Misreading Milton," proceeds from opening remarks on *Paradise Lost* to lengthy comments on *Samson Agonistes* in order to admonish readers against misinterpretation. Because such a caveat if presented abstractly has little if any applicability, Shawcross identifies numerous interpretive cruxes in Milton's dramatic poem in order to demonstrate correct, and to remonstrate against incorrect, readings. Such an outlook may appear naive or presumptuous. Upon closer inspection, however, one discovers that prudence, not presumptuousness, governs Shawcross's approach, which advocates liberty in interpretation while cautioning against license. If such a distinction appears Miltonic, this echo is deliberate on the part of Shawcross, whose emphasis on the text *qua* text of *Samson Agonistes* is crucial to correct understandings not only of the dramatic poem but of Milton's poetic oeuvre. If the essays in the present volume have adhered to a single principle, in line with Shawcross's guidance they have focused on the text. And in doing so, they have generated understandings that may be described as correct—and as corrective.

MILTON STUDIES
XXXIII

"OUR LIVING DREAD": THE GOD OF *SAMSON AGONISTES*

Michael Lieb

I

IN HER IMMENSELY influential and learned study, *Toward "Samson Agonistes": The Growth of Milton's Mind*, Mary Ann Radzinowicz argues that Milton's drama contains his most advanced theological outlook. Dramatizing this outlook, *Samson Agonistes* embodies a theology of "progressive revelation" through which one acquires an increasingly more enlightened understanding of how God's treatment of every man reflects his treatment of Samson. As a result of this understanding, one gains a freer and more rational conception of the nature of God. The movement toward God is the movement toward this heightened sense of rationality concerning God's ways. Rather than appearing on stage to foster this process of understanding, God makes his presence known in the human heart. He is revealed in every time and every place through the behavior of tested individuals who attest to him. By means of his free agent Samson, God manifests the renewal of freedom to all people. As a final demonstration of the importance of mind and will, "the good mind and the good will issue into an exemplary act which teaches how God gives freedom." God's "unsearchable dispose" is the bestowing of "new acquist of true experience" to individuals through the example of purposeful human beings. For Radzinowicz, the notion of God in *Samson Agonistes*, then, reflects Milton's essential stance both as a rationalist and as a moralist, one whose outlook endorses a progressive process of enlightenment for character and reader alike.[1]

As reassuring as this reading appears to be, it has come increasingly under scrutiny in recent scholarship on Milton's drama. In his powerful study, *Milton and the Drama of History*, for example, David Loewenstein calls into question the whole notion of a theology of "progressive revelation" based upon categories of rational and moral discernment: "Critics who argue that *Samson Agonistes* charts the linear course of its hero's regeneration or reveals the tempering of his passions," Loewenstein observes, "tend to smooth over the jagged emotional edges of Milton's tragedy, not to mention the disturbing implications of Samson's vehement iconoclasm." In place of the reassurances of Radzinowicz's reading of the drama, Loewenstein offers a reading that underscores the deeply troubled and conflicted dimensions of the drama. The effect of the drama is one characterized by a profound sense of anxiety and uncertainty about God's incomprehensible ways. For Loewenstein, the process of history in *Samson Agonistes* appears "ruptured and discontinuous, and God's purposes inscrutable." As a result of this vexed view of God and his ways, Milton's drama offers little to comfort or reassure us about the mysterious and indeed terrible actions of deity. All attempts to comprehend the mystery of God in history are repeatedly frustrated by the baffling nature of what transpires. Within this context, the drama culminates in the tumultuous events of its iconoclastic ending. In this theomachic encounter, the clash between God and Dagon becomes "a contest of dramatic spectacles, namely, the drama of Dagon versus the drama of God." Loewenstein sees in that terrifying enactment "something of a deep wish fulfillment on Milton's part: the impulse not only to remake and overturn history, but, in the process, to devastate one's enemies by means of a spectacular act." Rather than silencing the "cataclysmic devastation" associated with the account in Judges, Milton intensifies it.[2]

Although the two readings, that of Mary Ann Radzinowicz and that of David Loewenstein, could not be further apart in their respective assessments of the action and theological basis of *Samson Agonistes*, I think it essential to acknowledge the extremes these readings represent in order to gain an understanding of the current critical climate and of the choices one is faced with in coming to terms with what transpires in Milton's drama. As I have attempted to demonstrate in my own study, *Milton and the Culture of Violence*, I find the outlook reflected in Loewenstein's reading more nearly consistent with the spirit of *Samson Agonistes*.[3] Like Loewenstein, I too see the action of the drama as one that is infused with a heightened sense of personal wrath and frustration. For me, this is a drama that is far from reassuring in its outlook. Rather, it is a work of harsh and uncompromising violence, indeed, a work that exults in violence, while it gives expression to profound and deeply disturbing elements of vehemence and rage.

Focusing in particular upon the theological dimensions implicit in such a point of view, I wish to explore one aspect of it that has not received the attention it warrants. Arising from what Loewenstein sees as the profound sense of anxiety and uncertainty about God's incomprehensible ways in *Samson Agonistes*, this aspect manifests itself in the one name that is so aptly bestowed upon deity as a result of the cataclysmic devastation in which Milton's drama culminates. That name is "Dread"—"our living Dread," to be precise. The Semichorus gives voice to the expression of dread as an appellation of deity.[4] This appellation is bestowed immediately after the Messenger recounts Samson's destruction of the Philistines in the temple of

Dagon. Celebrating their destruction, the Semichorus declares of the Philistines:

> While thir hearts were jocund and sublime,
> Drunk with Idolatry, drunk with Wine,
> And fat regorg'd of Bulls and Goats,
> Chaunting thir Idol, and preferring
> Before our living Dread who dwells
> In *Silo* his bright Sanctuary:
> Among them he a spirit of phrenzie sent,
> Who hurt thir minds,
> And urg'd them on with mad desire
> To call in hast for thir destroyer;
> They only set on sport and play
> Unweetingly importun'd
> Thir own destruction to come speedy upon them.   (1669–81)[5]

At issue in this celebration of God's destructive power is the designation "our living Dread who dwells / In *Silo* his bright Sanctuary." To gain a sense of the meaning of deity in *Samson Agonistes*, one must come to terms with the full implications of a God who is not only dreadful but who is the embodiment of dread itself, indeed, whose very name is Dread. If, as Radzinowicz argues, *Samson Agonistes* reflects Milton's most advanced theological outlook, this is an outlook that certainly embraces some of the most disturbing elements that one is likely to discover in an encounter with his notion of deity. If Milton's drama moves progressively toward a more enlightened understanding of God and his ways, the culminating event of *Samson Agonistes* is one in which a God whose name is Dread manifests this quality in all its cataclysmic power. As a means of understanding the import of this idea, we shall examine in some detail the notion of dread as an appellation of God.

II

A consideration of dread as an actual name of God is best viewed from the overarching perspective of the phenomenon designated "the fear of God." According to R. H. Pfeiffer, this phenomenon is so crucial to the religious temperament reflected in Hebrew Scriptures that the earliest term for "religion" in biblical Hebrew, and in Semitic languages in general, is the phrase "the fear of God." In biblical Hebrew, there are many synonyms for the concept of fear, each with its own network of meanings and shades of nuance. One term alone (that of *yare*) occurs well over four hundred times in the depiction of the individual and his relationship to God. When it comes to "the fear of God," biblical Hebrew is terribly inventive. This fact only serves to reinforce the idea that at some archaic level God and fear are synonymous. In the range of meanings associated with fear, the most extreme form of that concept is what English designates as *dread*. Although biblical Hebrew has several terms that involve this meaning, *pachad* has the most direct bearing upon our undertaking. This term carries with it the notion of extreme terror and awe. So Job declares that "In thoughts from the visions of the night, when deep sleep falleth on men, fear [*pachad*] came upon me, and trembling, which made all my bones to shake" (Job iv, 13–14). Later, Job asks, "Shall not his [God's] excellency make you afraid? and his dread [*pachad*] fall upon you?" (Job xiii, 11). The *pachad* of God may fall upon an entire people in his anger (1 Sam. xi, 7).[6]

In Hebrew Scriptures, the term *pachad* assumes particular cogency because it is used as an actual name of God. So it occurs in Genesis with the remarkable phrase *pachad yitschaq* ("Dread of Isaac"). The phrase appears in Jacob's response to Laban's accusation that his son-in-law is responsible for the loss not only of Laban's daughters but of Laban's gods. Jacob declares indignantly: "Except the God of my father, the God of Abraham, and the fear of Isaac [*pachad yitschaq*], had been with me, surely thou hadst sent me away now empty" (Gen. xxxi, 42, 53). What one has here is a series of parallel phrases that define God not only by means of patriarchal relationship ("God of my father," "God of Abraham") but by means of attribute ("fear of Isaac"). In this rhetorical enactment, the patriarchal relationship culminates in the transformation of attribute into appellation. The God of the patriarchs is thereby redefined most fearsomely as very dread, indeed, dread deified. No wonder Laban is reluctant to pursue the matter further. Although the phrase *pachad yitschaq* has elicited a good deal of controversy concerning its precise meaning, the general consensus is that it is among the most archaic names of a God whose purpose is to sow terror among his enemies (compare Gen. xxxv, 5).[7]

Such is perfectly in keeping with formative notions of deity discernible in Hebrew Scriptures, notions that serve as the basis of the dread that surrounds what Rudolf Otto designates "the holy" (*das Heilige*).[8] What is true of Milton's epic is even more so of his drama. In my exploration of God as dread in *Samson Agonistes,* I think it appropriate to take account of Rudolf Otto's *The Idea of the Holy* once again.

Analyzing the nature of the holy, Otto makes a point of distinguishing between conceptions of God that define deity by the higher attributes of "Spirit, Reason, Purpose, Good Will, Supreme Power, Unity, [and] Selfhood," and conceptions of God that designate deity by the attributes that one might associate with a much more archaic view of religion. Such attributes are of a decidedly nonrational sort. The product of a "creature-feeling" in response to a power totally beyond the realm of knowing, these attributes are what characterize the notion of God as a phenomenon replete with the quality of *numen*. This quality imbues deity with a sanctity, indeed, a power, that renders it "wholly other" ("ganz andere"). Otto defines "wholly other" as "that which exists quite beyond the sphere of the usual, the intelligible, and the familiar, which therefore falls quite outside the limits of the 'canny', and is contrasted with it, filling the mind with blank wonder and astonishment." This for Otto is the experience of God in its most archaic form.[9]

As such, God is the embodiment of the "awefulness" that underlies what Otto calls the *mysterium tremendum*. A manifestation of the holy, the *mysterium tremendum* is characterized by "a feeling of peculiar dread." It is "peculiar" because it is a feeling quite distinct from the familiar emotion of fear. At the very least, it is the most extreme form of fear that one can imagine: fear divinized. By its very nature, the *mysterium tremendum* is that which is dreadful, that which causes the experience of being shaken by involuntary tremor. Both embodying dread in itself and causing dread in others, the *mysterium tremendum* manifests itself in an experience of deity that pours forth the dread that constitutes its essence. This dread can break out without warning and consume with paralysis all who encounter it. As a product of deity, it is associated with such qualities as the "Wrath of God," which Otto sees as "a unique emotional moment in religious experience, a moment whose singularly *daunting* and awe-inspiring character must be gravely disturbing to those persons who will recognize nothing in the divine nature but goodness, gentleness, [and] love."[10]

In keeping with his treatment of the "dreadfulness" of God, Otto offers one other attribute that he views as crucial to the holy. This attribute is what Otto calls God's "livingness," the fact that he is designated "the living God." For this, Otto cites Deuteronomy v, 26: "For who *is there of* all flesh, that hath heard the voice of the living God [*elohim chayyim*] speaking out of the midst of the fire, as we *have*, and lived?" As Otto is aware, there are many more biblical examples that might be invoked to support the notion of God's "livingness." Suffice it to say that it too is a crucial aspect of the *mysterium*. It is by his "life," Otto observes, that this God is differentiated from all concepts of rationality. By virtue of his "livingness," God becomes ultimately a "non-rational essence" that eludes all philosophical speculation. To appreciate the force of such a view of deity is to acknowledge "the non-rational core of the biblical conception of God."[11] For the Rudolf Otto of *das Heilige*, such a conception is what underscores any notion of God as the product of the *mysterium tremendum*. For our purposes, it is certainly what underscores the idea of God as dread, indeed, as "our living Dread."

Both from the Miltonic perspective and the milieu from which that perspective emerged, such an idea was hardly alien to seventeenth-century theologians and exegetes. So commonplace was the idea during Milton's own time, in fact, that one might even speak of a theology of dread as a dimension of coming to terms with the nature of godhead and as a means of understanding the relationship between the individual and his God. The seventeenth century in particular is replete with sermons and treatises that address the specific concept of dread as a divine attribute as well as a psychological response to that attribute. As one might expect, the concept falls under the general heading of the fear of God. In *A Christian Dictionary* (1622), Thomas Wilson, for example, defines dread or fear as both a natural affection in response to an impending danger and the danger itself as that which is dreaded or feared. In this latter sense, Wilson observes, God himself is called "the Fear of *Isaac*." Although Wilson does not hesitate to conjecture how the phrase came about, he concludes that it is a "Metonimie" for the name of God and cites several biblical texts to support his thesis. From this perspective, Wilson interprets "the Fear of *Isaac*" as "a metonimie of the effect for the cause." As such, it transfers the response to the object of fear onto the object itself. In the process of transference, fear involves "the whole worshippe of God" for those whose dread is an expression of devotion. In that capacity, it becomes a source of renewal, but for those who refuse to acknowledge the true significance of "the Fear of *Isaac*" and the worship it entails, it becomes a source of chastisement and even destruction. Such is Wilson's view of the notion of fear or dread as a religious phenomenon and as a divine attribute.[12]

Later in the century, John Bunyan produced a remarkable work of crucial import to the theology of dread. Examining dread as a fundamental manifestation of the religious experience, Bunyan's *A Treatise of the Fear of God* suggests the extent to which the notion of the *mysterium tremendum* represents a defining moment in seventeenth-century notions of deity. Bunyan is entirely aware that the phrase "fear of God" in the title of his work is as much a name *for* God as a response *to* God: "By this word FEAR," Bunyan observes, "we are to understand even *God himself,* who is the *object* of our FEAR." The Divine Majesty is known by this very name. Citing Genesis xxxi, 42, as the crucial text to support this contention, Bunyan says, "This name *Jacob* called him by, when he and *Laban* chod [contended] together on Mount *Gilead,* after that *Jacob* had made his escape to his Fathers house; *Except,* said he, *the God of Abraham, and the FEAR of Isaac had been with me, surely now thou hadst sent me away empty.*" Responding to this text, Bunyan declares that "*God* may well be called the FEAR of his people, not only because they have by his grace made him the object of their FEAR, but because of the dread and terrible Majesty that is in him." Imbued with this dread, the people of God worship him with godly awe and reverence of his majesty. *"Let him [God] be your FEAR, and let him be your dread,"* Bunyan counsels; "let his excellency make you afraid with godly fear." As a prime example of this quality of dreadfulness, Bunyan cites the Samson account in Judges, specifically the visitation of the angel of God to Manoah and his wife at the outset of the narrative (Judg. xiii, 22): "If *Angels,* which are but creatures, are, through the glory that God has put upon them, so fearful and terrible in their appearance to men," Bunyan observes, "how much more dreadful and terrible must God himself be to us, who are but dust and ashes?" For Bunyan, as for Milton, the key to the Samson narrative is the experience of a God whose very name is Dread.[13]

Exploring that name from a multiplicity of perspectives, Bunyan exhorts the faithful to engage in a proper worship of deity. Just as the presence and name of God are dreadful and fearful in the church, so is God's worship and service. Depending upon the nature of the individual (whether prince, lord, or parent) being worshiped, all manner of service involves dread and fear to a greater or lesser extent. So the divine worship due to God, who is so great and dreadful in himself and in name, is such that "his Worship must therefore be a fearful thing." Those who fail to worship God with the proper fear and dread that are due him are themselves destroyed by God's dreadful judgments. Bunyan cites several figures who, as a result of failing to accord Dread himself the rightful fear that is due him, are overwhelmed by the very fear they fail to acknowledge.[14] Although Bunyan does not single out the Philistines of the Samson narrative on this occasion, he would no doubt concur that they too qualify as prime examples of those who bring down their destruction upon themselves as a result of their disregard of the true significance of the God of the Israelites as the very embodiment of dread.

Within this context, Milton generates his own theology of dread throughout his works. In this respect, his *Christian Doctrine* is a case in point.[15] For Milton, as for a host of exegetes, any consideration of the nature of dread falls under the heading of the worship of God. So it is considered in the second book of *Christian Doctrine,* which in general is concerned with what it calls the *cultus Dei* ("Worship of God").[16] From the perspective of the *cultus Dei,* Milton examines those virtues belonging to "our duty towards God." Endorsing the need for a "devout affection" ("religiosus erga eum affectus") toward God in all matters of worship, Milton singles out the following virtues: "love, trust, hope, gratitude, fear, humility, patience, and obedience." These eight virtues constitute the foundation of the true worship of God (compare Deut. x, 12–13). Addressing the category of *timor Dei* ("Fear of God"), Milton observes that this virtue involves "reverencing God as the supreme Father and judge of all men, and fearing above all to offend him." To support this observation, Milton cites a host of proof-texts, among them, Deuteronomy xxviii, 58 ("fearing this most glorious and supremely reverend name, Jehovah your God"), and Psalm ii, 11 ("worship Jehovah with reverence and rejoice with trembling"). Clearly, for Milton, fear and reverence are synonymous affections: to violate one is to violate the other (CM XVII, pp. 50, 60–65; YP VI, pp. 656–57, 660–61).

Based upon a reading of *Christian Doctrine*, one is inclined to see in Milton the emergence of fear as an important constituent in any consideration of *cultus*. Under this heading, fear assumes a positive, indeed, a pious role in providing evidence of one's devotion to God. In its association with the virtues of love, trust, hope, gratitude, humility, patience, and obedience, the category of fear is charged with a kind of moral and spiritual valence that mutes any possibility of its association with the archaic dimensions of dread that distinguish the *mysterium tremendum*, as Rudolf Otto defines it. There is certainly no sense of it as a manifestation of the frightening qualities that we have come to associate with the notion of God himself as dread deified.

Nonetheless, this does not mean that the concept fails to materialize in *Christian Doctrine*. It does in fact emerge later in the second book of Milton's theological discourse, specifically in the chapter dealing with oath-taking and the casting of lots. In his discussion of oath-taking, Milton begins with the following observation: "When we TAKE AN OATH we CALL GOD TO WITNESS THAT WE ARE SPEAKING THE TRUTH, AND CURSE OURSELVES, EITHER BY IMPLICATION OR EXPRESSLY, IF WE SHOULD BE LYING." Moving from that observation, Milton maintains that "Both God's command and his example show that the taking of oaths is lawful." To that end, he cites, among other texts, Deuteronomy vi, 13: "Thou shalt fear the Lord thy God, and serve him, and shalt swear by his name." This passage is cited in the context of the admonition to fear God lest his anger "be kindled against thee, and destroy thee from off the face of the earth" (Deut. vi, 15). Already implicit in the act of swearing oaths in God's name is the fear that is associated with incurring his anger (CM XVII, pp. 118–21; YP VI, pp. 684–85). For Milton, the act of swearing oaths in God's name carries with it a sense of fear and anger implicit in the most archaic notions of deity.

It is here that the concept of God himself as fear or dread emerges in Milton's treatment. At issue is the unique phrase "Dread of Isaac" (*pachad yitschaq*), which Milton does not hesitate to invoke in his discussion of oath-taking. After citing examples in which not only humans but God swears oaths in his anger (Ps. xcv, 11), Milton avers that the taking of oaths is made particularly evident by the angels and saints of God. Among the proof-texts that Milton cites to support this statement of Genesis xxxi, 53: "Jacob sware by the fear of his father Isaac" ("iuravit Iacob per pavorem patris sui").[17] In his citation of this text, Milton renders "fear" not by its customary form *timor* but by the more nearly expressive form *pavor*.[18] Whereas *timor* does carry with it the notions of fear, dread, apprehension, alarm, and anxiety, it is more nearly associated in a positive sense with the idea of reverence and veneration earlier delineated under the heading of *cultus*. *Pavor*, on the other hand, carries with it the notions of trembling, quaking, and panting with fear. It is associated in particular with religious fear, awe, and dread, and it is even known to be personified as a god of fear.[19] This is the sense in which Milton no doubt understands it. For this reason, he explains the passage "Jacob sware by the fear of his father Isaac" by declaring quite unequivocally, "id est, Deum" ("that is, God"). The explanation is an acknowledgment of the remarkable force of the passage, the fact that it in effect *identifies* God with fear or dread. God not only inspires dread in others: he *is* himself dread. As Milton argues in this chapter of *Christian Doctrine*, the swearing of an oath is not something that one undertakes lightly. If one is to swear an oath in God's name, it had better be for a very serious purpose. Especially if one is to swear by the name known as *pachad*, or, to use Milton's term, *pavor*, one must exercise extreme caution (CM XVII, pp. 118–21; YP VI, pp. 684–85). Whether as *pachad* or as *pavor*, then, dread assumes an undeniable importance to the Milton of *Christian Doctrine*. What is true of his theological tract is no less true of his other writings.

His psalm translations are a case in point. If, as William Riley Parker argues, these translations reflect the spirit of *Samson Agonistes*, they likewise articulate a theology in which God is conceived in the most archaic terms as the source not just of wrath but of absolute dread. Here, one beholds dread deified. This is certainly true of the translations of Psalms lxxx–lxxxviii. At the very outset of the sequence, Milton imports the motif of divine dread into his portrayal of the psalmist's calling upon God to save the Israelites in their time of need. Whereas the first verse of Psalm lxxx in the Hebrew has simply "[you who] sit [between] the cherubim, shine forth" ("yoshev hacrubim hophiyah"), Milton transforms this rendering into an elaborate quatrain. Within this quatrain, the psalmist apostrophizes God as follows: Thou "that sitt'st between the Cherubs *bright / Between their wings out-spread*, / Shine forth, *and from thy cloud give light*, / *And on our foes thy dread*" (5–8). As Milton makes clear in the headnote to his psalm translations, his own additions are indicated "*in a different Character*," that is, in italics.[20] The additions to the original in the present quatrain are not only considerable but significant. Implicit in the original is the concept of God as a dwelling presence within the ark of the covenant. So conceived, God shines forth in his glory. Intensifying and elaborating upon this idea, Milton portrays the dwelling presence of God between the outspread wings of the cherubim as not only disseminating light but as overwhelming God's foes with dread. The divine theophany manifests its presence through the light that distinguishes its glory and through the dread that constitutes its divinity. In the juxtaposition that the quatrain structures, light and dread become corresponding entities in the portrayal of deity. Attributes of deity, both are imbued with a kind of materiality, a "thingness," that manifests the brilliance and power of God's dwelling presence. Disseminating its brilliance through the medium of light, that presence overwhelms all those who would violate its sanctity. This overwhelmingness assumes the form of dread.[21]

III

It is precisely this dread that overwhelms the Philistines in *Samson Agonistes*. Just when the Philistines are most elated by their conquest and blinded by their idolatry, we recall that God as "our living Dread" sends among them "a spirit of phrenzie" that urges them on with mad desire "to call in hast for their destroyer." The Philistines thereby unwittingly importune "thir own destruction to come speedy upon them." Such is the fate of those who, "jocund and sublime, / Drunk with Idolotry, drunk with Wine, / And fat regorg'd of Bulls and Goats," are filled with a kind of Dionysiac madness as they "chaunt" their idol (1669–81). The Semichorus's celebration of their destruction embodies a paradox that strikes at the heart of the concept of dread. Those who prefer the false god before the true God must experience the full import of dread as that which impels one unwittingly to effect his own demise. For such idolaters, the experience of dread is at once attractive and repulsive. The "spirit of phrenzie" that imbues the Philistines causes them to become increasingly consumed with a delight in the very thing that destroys them. Milton refers to this phenomenon in *Christian Doctrine* as a hardening of the heart (*indurando*) and a blinding of the understanding (*excaecando*) that consume the sinner and, at God's own prompting, impel him to bring his own destruction upon himself.[22]

In *The Idea of the Holy*, Rudolf Otto classifies the phenomenon "the element of fascination" (*fascinans*). If the numinous appears to the mind as an object of horror and dread, it is nonetheless that which allures its victim with a potent charm. Entirely intimidated and cast down, the individual who trembles before it has at the same time the impulse to embrace it, to make it his own. Although he may be bewildered and overcome by it, he experiences something that "captivates and transports him with a strange ravishment," rising to the pitch of a "dizzying intoxication." This is what Otto calls "the Dionysiac element" in the numinous. According to Otto, it is "at once the strangest and most noteworthy phenomenon in the whole history of religion." Otto is not alone in his account of the paradoxical nature of this phenomenon. In his treatise *The Concept of Dread,* Søren Kierkegaard considers what he terms "the dialectical determinants in dread." Constituting those determinants is the paradox by which dread becomes at once "a *sympathetic antipathy* and an *antipathetic sympathy.*" The individual is simultaneously drawn to it and repelled by it, that is, attracted to that which repels him and repelled by that which attracts him: "He cannot flee from dread, for he loves it," but "he does not love it, for he flees from it." Under this circumstance, dread becomes an "alien power" that lays hold of him and consumes him, as he sinks in the dread which he loves even while he fears it. Such is the quandary inspired by dread.[23]

As the Philistines of *Samson Agonistes* come to learn only too well and, of course, too late, this phenomenon in its divinized form culminates in their own undoing. "Drunk with Idolotry, drunk with Wine," they experience the full force of that which is at once the *mysterium fascinans* and the *mysterium tremendum.* Drawn to the first through a misplaced allegiance to an idol that ultimately fails them, they are destroyed by the second in the form of a power whose impact they never for a moment expected to encounter. Conceived as a "living Dread" that overwhelms them at the height of their frenzy, this phenomenon unleashes its cataclysmic forces in a manner that is all-consuming. Both the vehicle of that unleashing and the victim of that which is unleashed, Samson himself becomes the means by which God as dread manifests his power in the theater of Dagon's temple. What results in this Dagonalia is the spectacle of dread enacted in its most dramatic and catastrophic form. It is this enactment toward which the action of *Samson Agonistes* builds from its outset to its devastating conclusion.[24]

Early in the drama, Manoa himself delineates what will be at stake for his son: "This day," he says, "the *Philistines* a popular Feast / Here celebrate in *Gaza;* and proclaim / Great Pomp, and Sacrifice, and Praises loud to *Dagon,* as their God who hath deliver'd / Thee *Samson,* bound and blind into their hands." As the result of such a celebration, "*Dagon* shall be magnifi'd, and God / Besides whom is no God, compar'd with Idols, / Disglorifi'd, blasphem'd, and had in scorn / By th' idolatrous rout amidst thir wine" (433–43). The entire drama moves toward this moment, one in which the agon becomes a theomachic confrontation of momentous proportions. In response to his father's statement, Samson is painfully aware of the theomachic dimensions of the conflict. "All the contest is now / 'Twixt God and *Dagon,*" he declares; "*Dagon* hath presum'd, / Me overthrown, to enter lists with God, / His deity comparing and preferring / Before the God of *Abraham*" (461–65). Yet Samson has faith that God will prevail in this agon. "Thus provoked," God "will arise and his great name assert." In the assertion of that name, "*Dagon* must stoop," Samson promises; "and shall e're long receive / Such a discomfit, as shall quite despoil him / Of all these boasted Trophies won on me, / And with confusion blank his worshippers" (467–71). So Dagon will be overthrown in his cataclysmic event. It is what Milton himself in the argument to his drama calls the Catastrophe, which implies both a sudden and widespread disaster and in dramaturgical terms the "overturning" (*katastrophe*) that follows the climax.

As Samson is well aware, this will be the time when "the God of *Abraham*" will finally make his "great name" known. Implicit in the defeat of Dagon and his worshipers is the overturning of the bearer of the false name, that of Dagon, within the confines of his own temple.[25] In this act of overturning, the bearer of the true name reveals his identity. As the Semichorus declares triumphantly, that name is Dread. The name is apt, for, as we recall not only from the biblical sources but from the seventeenth-century commentaries on those sources, the one true name of "the God of *Abraham*" is Dread (*pachad*), the Dread of Isaac (*pachad yitschaq*), to be precise. Imported into the dramatic setting of the Samson narrative, this name might well be declared the Dread of Samson (*pachad shimshon*). Such a designation is only fitting considering the fact that the appointed bearer of this dread at the catastrophic moment that culminates the drama is none other than Samson. It is only fitting that he is ultimately the bearer of this dread, because he at one time bore that very name. So the Chorus avers that in better times the Israelites had once called Samson their own "great dread" (1474). As the bearer and embodiment of God's dread, Samson had assumed this name as a mark of his identity. If it is an identity he was more than willing to assume in a former life, the catastrophic denouement of the drama provides him the opportunity to assume it yet once more, even at the expense of his own life. The manifestation of the *mysterium tremendum* in all its terror, Samson as the heir of dread fulfills his destiny as the one through whom "our living Dread" asserts its awful power and reasserts its name as *pachad shimshon*.

Imbued with a sense of the destructiveness that such a destiny entails, Samson at the climactic point of his agon takes upon himself the task of implementing the full force of God's awesome power. So the Messenger who has escaped the cataclysm relates what transpired. Having satisfied his captors that he who was once "thir dreadful enemy" is now by Dagon made "thir thrall," Samson first performs great feats of strength before the assembled crowds. Thereafter, he is led between the supporting pillars of the theater, where, "with head a while enclin'd, / And eyes fast fixt he stood, as one who pray'd, / Or some great matter in his mind revolv'd" (1636–38). Then, raising his head, he cries aloud:

Hitherto, Lords, what your commands impos'd
I have perform'd, as reason was, obeying,
Not without wonder or delight beheld.
Now of my own accord such other tryal
I mean to shew you of my strength, yet greater;
As with amaze shall strike all who behold.   (1640–45)

This declaration differs markedly from the biblical source. There, Samson's final words are a simple and direct cry for vengeance: "And Samson called unto the Lord, and said, O Lord God, remember me, I pray thee, only this once, O God, that I may be at once avenged of the Philistines for my two eyes" (Judg. xvi, 28). What Samson seeks in the biblical account is retribution for his loss of sight. The Samson of the Miltonic account, on the other hand, is a much more mysterious figure. He is one who descends into the depths of himself, there either to pray or to revolve some greater matter in his mind.[26] This he does in preparation for an utterance that is as mysterious as the gesture that precedes it. The force of that utterance is such that it strikes with amazement all who behold what it occasions.

To understand the utterance, one must be attuned to the implications of the language in which it is cast. At issue is the phrase "of my own accord." Much has been made of the phrase. In his seminal study of Milton's drama, Joseph Wittreich, for example, has sought in effect to call into question the pivotal moment in which the phrase occurs by associating it with the discourse of false prophets: "*Of his own accord*," Wittreich observes, "is always used scripturally to mean by one's own initiative." At this moment in the drama, "it is used to imply a contrast between the false prophets who act of their own accord and the true prophets who act by divine commission."[27] For our purposes, however, an examination of the scriptural context of the phrase makes it abundantly clear that it is used in a technical sense as a formula for the swearing of oaths and that its employment is founded upon the discourse not of humans (whether in the form of false prophets or true) but of God.

Throughout Hebrew Scriptures, God acts "of His own accord" in the swearing of oaths. The phrase that appears time and again is *biy nishbati:* "by myself [or "of my own accord"] I have sworn." So Milton cites it repeatedly both as Old Testament and as New Testament topos in his discussion of oath-taking in *Christian Doctrine.*[28] There, one find such proof-texts as Genesis xxii, 16: "by myself have I sworn, saith Jehovah," and Hebrews vi, 13: "because he [Jehovah] could swear by no greater, he sware by himself" (CM XVII, pp. 120–21; YP VI, p. 85). Drawn from Hebrew Scriptures, the first proof-text concerns God's oath to Abraham that he will be blessed as the result of his obedience. Drawn from the New Testament, the second proof-text is in a sense a commentary on the first. God's acting of his own accord in swearing by himself to Abraham demonstrates the magnitude of the oath. In Hebrew Scriptures, the locution *biy nishbati* often appears in the denunciatory setting of prophecy as God swears of his own accord to destroy rebellious nations: "But if ye will not hear these words, I swear by myself, saith the Lord, that this house will become a desolation" (Jer. xxii, 5); "For I have sworn by myself, saith the Lord, that Boz'rah shall become a desolation, a reproach, a waste, and a curse; and all the cities thereof shall be perpetual wastes" (Jer. xlix, 13).[29] To invoke the phrase "of my own accord" or "of his own accord," then, is to align oneself with the discourse of God, who, more than anyone else in Scriptures, acts of his own accord (by himself) and customarily in the context of swearing an oath.

Thus when Samson declares "Now of my own accord such other tryal / I mean to shew you of my strength, yet greater; / As with amaze shall strike all who behold," he is adopting a locution that in its biblical context has all the denunciatory force of the swearing of oaths by an incensed God prepared to unleash his dread upon his desperate enemies. Rather than simply seeking to be avenged for the loss of his eyes in the manner of his biblical prototype, the Miltonic Samson in effect subsumes within himself the divine role implied by the phrase *biy nishbati* ("by myself I have sworn") and becomes that force, that *tremendum* through which "our living Dread" is made manifest. His assumption of such a role in the appropriation of divine discourse may have the ring of blasphemy to some. Suppose Samson is *not* divinely inspired to talk like God and thereby to assume that most archaic role of God as "our living Dread"? He does, after all, pull down the same destruction on himself that he metes out to his enemies. I think that such questions skirt the issue. The point is that Samson is able to talk like God because he is able to act like God. That is, he is empowered to be triumphantly destructive in God's cause. In this cataclysmic act, all sense of Samson's "beingness" is obliterated. With this obliteration, it is now his "livingness" that matters. He has become a force, a terror, and a dread: he exists totally within the context of this new role. That is his raison d'être. He is "our living Dread" incarnate.

IV

A figure so totally imbued with this dread that he effectively becomes it, Samson, like God, is *pachad*, dread itself. If God is known as *pachad yitschaq*, Samson fulfills his role as *pachad shimshon*. We recall that Thomas Wilson defined the phrase *pachad yitschaq* as a metonymy of the effect for the cause, a phenomenon in which the response to the object of fear becomes the object itself. So in Samson the metonymy is fulfilled: he becomes that very dread he unleashes. Wilson also maintained that in the metonymic process of transference, fear involves "the whole worshippe of God," an idea intensified by Bunyan's discourse on dread later in the century. Those who fail to worship God with the dread that is due him are doomed to experience the devastating effects of the very dread they disavow. Crucial to the concept of dread, then, is the element of *cultus,* placed within a terrifying context indeed.

That context is fully exploited in *Samson Agonistes.* Centered in the figure of Samson as the embodiment of dread, the overwhelming of the Philistines in the temple of Dagon assumes a decidedly cultic (not to mention terrifying) bearing as a manifestation of godhead in its most archaic form. It is precisely this bearing that is operative in the concept of a "living dread" whose dwelling presence resides in a specific locale, a site of worship. As the Semichorus makes clear in its celebration of the overwhelming of the Philistines, that site is *Silo,* the "bright Sanctuary" of Milton's deity. In order to understand the full impact of ascribing to the God of dread a local habitation and a name, we must attend more closely to the act of situating the God of *Samson Agonistes* within the confines of Shilo.

The reference to Shilo is significant because it provides a local habitation for "our living Dread." Deity is, as it were, brought down and localized both chronologically and topographically within a specific cultic residence, one in fact that was ascribed to God during the period of Judges and beyond. As one of the three premonarchic sanctuaries between the time of Joshua and the time of Solomon, Shilo is associated with the early history of the ark of the covenant.[30] As the events underlying such a history make clear, this was a violent and tumultuous period, one in which the ark was seen to be imbued with a power at once awesome and destructive, on occasion even unpredictable and unstable. It was a time fully in keeping with a view of deity as the manifestation of the most archaic forces. As such, it not only was seen to reside within its cultic center but also was capable of being transported from one place to the next for the purposes of unleashing its tremendous and devastating energies upon the enemy. If *Samson Agonistes* moves "toward" anything, it certainly moves toward this most primitive conception of godhead.

The import of such a notion of deity becomes significant in the context of 1 Samuel, chapters iv–v. A passage that was commonly associated in the Renaissance with the Samson narrative in Judges, 1 Samuel, chapters iv–v, represents a crucial subtext for understanding both the destruction of the temple of Dagon and the articulation of deity as a source of ultimate dread in *Samson Agonistes.*[31] According to the narrative in question, the Israelites, in battle with the Philistines, attempt to overcome the enemy through re-

course to the ultimate weapon: the ark of the covenant at Shilo. Their stratagem is founded upon the belief that the ark of the covenant is the portable
weapon of utmost power through which God overwhelms his enemies (compare Josh. vi, 6–21; 2 Sam. xi, 11; Ps. lxviii).[32] "When the ark of the covenant
of the Lord came into the camp, all Israel shouted with a great shout, so
that the earth rang again." Hearing the noise of the shout, "the Philistines
were afraid, for they said, God is come into the camp" (1 Sam. iv, 3–7).
The Israelites, however, are in for an unpleasant surprise. Because of the
corruptions arising from the sons of Eli as priestly stewards of the ark at
Shilo, the stratagem unfortunately proves ineffective. Israel is smitten, the
sons of Eli slain, and the ark of God taken captive (10–11). The narrative
thereby ironically reverses expectations as a prelude to the eventual destruction of the Philistines in the aftermath of the conflict. Far from calling
into question the dreadful power of the ark, the narrative serves only to
heighten that sense of power, for it establishes the fact that the power to be
unleashed from the ark will occur at moments that are least expected and
on occasions least anticipated. In this case, the circumstances are appropriate when the power of the Philistines is at its height.

Assuming that they have gained complete power over the Israelites
and their God, the Philistines take the ark and install it in the temple of
Dagon in Ashdod, directly opposite the idol itself as a potent sign that their
god has prevailed over the God of Israel. It is here that Hebrew Scriptures
recount a Dagonalia all its own as a counterpart to the Dagonalia that occurs
in the Book of Judges. What occurs is a series of events through which the
god of the Philistines is overthrown by the power that resides in the ark.
The Philistines come to learn of this power through a process of realization
that culminates in the destruction not only of their idol but of themselves.
Having placed the ark of the covenant next to the idol of Dagon the first
night, they learn to their astonishment the following morning that their god
has been overthrown: "And when they of Ashdod arose early on the morrow,
behold, Dagon *was* fallen upon his face to the earth before the ark of the
Lord." Refusing to acknowledge the force of this lesson the first time, they
must be taught it a second time. Thus, they repeat the offense by setting the
idol of Dagon in his place again and placing the ark of the covenant next to
it. The same thing happens a second time, except with more force. For when
the Philistines "arose early on the morrow morning, behold, Dagon *was*
fallen upon his face to the ground before the ark of the Lord; and the head
of Dagon and both the palms of his hands *were* cut off upon the threshold;
only *the stump of* Dagon was left to him" (1 Sam. v, 3–4).[33]

So frightful is this event to the Philistines that, according to the narrative, in later years no individual, not even the priests of Dagon, dares to

tread upon the threshold of the place where this event has occurred. The destructive force of the ark is not limited simply to the confines of Dagon's temple, however, for the hand of the Lord reaches forth to destroy both the people of Ashdod and those who occupy the surrounding coasts as well (1 Sam. v, 5–6). The only recourse for those who remain is to attempt to return the ark to its rightful place, for the Philistines realize that they have something entirely uncontrollable and terrifying in their midst, something that has the potential to destroy all who would attempt to violate the forces of deity that reside in the ark of the covenant and subvert those forces by taking the ark captive.[34]

The circumstances surrounding 1 Samuel, chapters iv–v, engaged Milton as early as the poem *On the Morning of Christs Nativity*, which alludes to Dagon as "that twise batter'd god of *Palestine*" (199), an idea that is later reintroduced into the account of Dagon in *Paradise Lost:*

> Next came one
> Who mourn'd in earnest, when the Captive Ark,
> Maim'd his brute Image, head and hands lopt off
> In his own Temple, on the grunsel edge,
> Where he fell flat, and sham'd his Worshipers:
> *Dagon* his Name, Sea Monster, upward Man
> And downward Fish.

Along with his temple, this god, the poet observes, was "dreaded through the Coast / Of *Palestine*, in *Gath* and *Ascalon* / And *Acaron* and *Gaza's* frontier bounds" (457–66).[35] The epic account is apposite in its focus upon the overcoming of that "brute Image," the very idolatrous presence of Dagon, by the ark of the covenant made captive but not deprived of its power by the enemy. Confronted by the true God dwelling within the ark, the false god falls discomfited, its cult undermined and its worshipers shamed both within its own unhallowed confines and beyond to the outlying territories. As much as Dagon is "dreaded" throughout these territories, the true dread, that Dread of Dreads resident within the ark, deprives the twice-battered god of its dreadful pretensions. Such is the Dagonalia that Milton envisions in *Paradise Lost*.

From the perspective that we are exploring, the biblical narrative and its rearticulation in Milton's epic are particularly important because they provide a crucial context for understanding the full implications of the theology of dread delineated in *Samson Agonistes*. In the Semichorus's celebration of "our living Dread who dwells / In *Silo* his bright Sanctuary," we encounter the terrifying force of a deity whose residence in the ark of the covenant, momentarily displaced from its sanctified setting and taken captive by the enemy, becomes the occasion for destroying all who would violate and attempt to subvert the sanctity with which it is imbued. Although the events surrounding the Israelite-Philistine wars and the installation of the ark in the temple of Dagon postdate the Judges narrative, the action of Milton's drama looks forward to these events in its reference to the localized site of a deity who dwells as an awesome presence within the confines of Shilo, that most ancient of sanctuaries. Once those confines are violated and the ark removed to an unhallowed site, God's dreadfulness is unleashed in its full fury. Those who stand in its way are destroyed utterly. The god that the unhallowed worship is correspondingly destroyed. All that remains is his "stump."

It is the undoing of Dagon within the confines of his place of worship that renders the narrative in 1 Samuel so germane to an understanding of our own exploration of the cultic dimensions of dread in *Samson Agonistes*. For it is the dread which permeates God's own dwelling presence in the ark of the covenant that underscores this most archaic notion of deity. To view the Judges account of Samson from the perspective of 1 Samuel is to be made aware of the extent to which dread as a cultic phenomenon depersonalizes any concept of God in Milton's drama. What emerges is an emphasis upon "place" as the site of worship and "thing" as the vehicle through which worship is enacted. God is not only depersonalized but localized as the manifestation of the overwhelming power that resides in singular objects. Himself the vehicle of such power, the Miltonic Samson within the temple of Dagon is the means by which the *mysterium* unleashes all the forces of destruction upon the idol and its worshipers.

The manner in which this event is conceived invites us to reassess the notion of deity that emerges in *Samson Agonistes*. No longer is it possible to look upon the God of Milton's drama as the culmination of a movement or progressive revelation toward a more rational conception of the nature of deity. Any attempt to suggest that Milton's God may be understood through what Otto calls the enlightened categories of spirit, reason, purpose, and goodwill is undermined by what actually transpires. The theology of dread that distinguishes the drama is one in which deity is portrayed in its most archaic and terrifying form. Localized in ancient shrines and manifested in the unleashing of devastating powers, the *mysterium* that underlies the archaic sense of godhead in *Samson Agonistes* is one fully befitting a drama that culminates in mass destruction. If Samson is among those destroyed by the very forces he has unleashed, he nonetheless triumphantly fulfills his role as the true avatar of "our living Dread who dwells / In *Silo* his bright Sanctuary."

University of Illinois, Chicago

NOTES

I am deeply indebted to Albert C. Labriola and Jason Rosenblatt for their close and astute reading of my paper and for their suggestions. A shortened version of this paper was delivered before the Fifth International Milton Symposium, University of Wales, Bangor, in July, 1995. I acknowledge here the observations and comments of those in attendance.

1. Mary Ann Radzinowicz, *Toward "Samson Agonistes": The Growth of Milton's Mind* (Princeton, 1978), pp. 267, 271, 283–84, 346, 349.

2. David Loewenstein, *Milton and the Drama of History: Historical Vision, Iconoclasm, and the Literary Imagination* (Cambridge, 1990), pp. 133, 130–31, 136, 145.

3. Michael Lieb, *Milton and the Culture of Violence* (Ithaca, 1994), pp. 226–63.

4. One must account for the fact, of course, that this is the view of God reflected in the outlook of the Semichorus, which functions as one character in a drama comprised of several characters, each no doubt with his own "theology." As I attempt to demonstrate, however, the theology implicit in the view expressed by the Semichorus is so fundamental to the outlook that the drama as a whole embraces that the concept of God as Dread is inescapable in any assessment of the nature of deity in *Samson Agonistes*. Compare John Shawcross's treatment of God in "Misreading Milton" in this volume.

5. References to Milton's poetry in my text are to *The Complete Poetry of John Milton*, 2nd rev. ed., ed. John T. Shawcross (Garden City, 1971). References to Milton's prose by volume and page number in my text are to *The Complete Prose Works of John Milton*, 8 vols., ed. Don M. Wolfe et al. (New Haven, 1953–82), hereafter designated YP. Corresponding references to the original Latin (and on occasion to the English translations) are to *The Works of John Milton*, ed. Frank Allen Patterson et al. (New York, 1931–38), hereafter designated CM.

6. R. H. Pfeiffer, "The Fear of God," *Israel Exploration Journal* V (1955): 41–48. In his study of the subject, Pfeiffer explores the cultural contexts of fear in the ancient world. Citing Statius's observation in the *Thebaid* (III, 661) that "fear first on earth created gods" ("Primus in orbe deos fecit timor"), he notes that Hammurabi in his Code (I, 31) officially designates himself "fearer of the gods."

For biblical Hebrew, one need only resort to the standard concordances, such as that of Mandelkern, *Veteris Testamenti Concordantiae Hebraicae atque Chaldaicae*, 3 vols., comp. Solomon Mandelkern (Tel Aviv, 1971), s.v., and to the standard lexicons, such as *The New Brown-Driver-Briggs-Gesenius Hebrew and English Lexicon, with an Appendix Containing the Biblical Aramaic, Based on the Lexicon of William Gesenius* (Peabody, Mass., 1979), s.v. (hereafter referred to as *BDB*), to discover these terms and to trace the complexity of their significations. I found some eighteen different terms for fear (each term with its own root) extending throughout Hebrew Scriptures. These are confirmed by the list of words under the heading "Fear" in William Wilson, *Old Testament Word Studies* (Grand Rapids, 1978), pp. 159–60. See the discussion of *yare* in *Theological Dictionary of the Old Testament*, 6 vols., ed. Johannes Botterweck and Helmer Ringren (Grand Rapids, Mich., 1978–90), vol. VI, pp. 290–315. The term *pachad* also assumes a sexual bearing, as in Job's celebration of the behemoth: "sinews of his stones [*pachdo*: thigh, testicle] are wrapped together" (xl, 17). See *BDB*, s.v. From the Miltonic perspective, this dimension is particularly interesting, given the emphasis upon sexuality in *Samson Agonistes*. Thus, Samson laments the loss of his own virility and his having been shorn by Dalila "like a tame Weather" (537–38), that is, a castrated male sheep. In regaining his own ability to become a figure of dread, Samson is in a sense regaining his *pachad*, the power of his testicles.

7. See in particular the discussion of contrary views (along with relevant bibliography) by Emile Puech under the heading "fear of Isaac" in *The Anchor Bible Dictionary*, 6 vols., ed. David Noel Freedman (New York, 1992), vol. II, pp. 779–80. Also relevant is B. W. Anderson,

"fear of Isaac," *The Interpreter's Dictionary of the Bible*, 4 vols., gen. ed. George Arthur But-
trick (New York: Abingdon Press, 1962), vol. II, p. 260.

    8. I have explored this idea at length in my *Poetics of the Holy: A Reading of "Paradise
Lost"* (Chapel Hill, N.C., 1981). See Rudolf Otto, *The Idea of the Holy: An Inquiry Into the
Non-Rational Factor in the Idea of the Divine and Its Relation to the Rational*, trans. John W.
Harvey (London, 1928). This book was first published as *Das Heilige* in 1917.

    9. Otto, *The Idea of the Holy*, pp. 1–11.

    10. In his exploration of this daunting dimension of the *mysterium*, Otto, *The Idea of the
Holy*, pp. 12–14, cites the *locus classicus* of the idea as it is revealed in one of the most
inexplicable texts in Hebrew Scriptures, Exodus iv, 24: It came to pass that the Lord met
Moses by the way and "sought to kill him." The unaccountable behavior of God in this instance
is for Otto a prime example of the most frightening dimensions of the *ganz andere*. It is a
dimension that undermines all expectations of deity as that which reinforces human ideas of
morality, rationality, and beneficence.

    11. Ibid., pp. 78–79.

    12. For an interesting discussion of the psychological dimension of dread, see John Fla-
vell, *Two Treatises: The First of Fear, From Isa. 8.V.12, 13, and part of the 14* (London, 1682).
In a similar vein, see Edward Young, *A sermon concerning the wisdom of fearing God* (London,
1693). From an apocalyptic perspective, see the sermon of the Quaker Humphrey Smith, *The
Sounding voyce of the dread of Gods mighty power* (London, 1658). See the entry for "fear" in
Thomas Wilson, *A Christian Dictionary, Opening the signification of the chiefe Words dispersed
generally through Holy Scriptures of the Old and New Testament* (London, 1622), s.v. Among
the texts that Wilson cites are Psalm lxxvi, 11; Isaiah viii, 12, 13; Malachi i, 6; and Genesis xxxi,
42, and xxxii, 9. According to Wilson, fear can be "an instrument of diuine vengeance" upon
those who are wicked (Isa. ii, 1).

    13. References are to John Bunyan, *A Treatise of the Fear of God: Shewing What it is,
and how distinguished from that which is not so* (London, 1679), in *The Miscellaneous Works
of John Bunyan*, 11 vols., ed. Richard L. Greaves (Oxford, 1976–86), vol. IX, pp. 5–8. For an
illuminating discussion of the relationships between Milton and Bunyan, see Roland Mushat
Frye, *God, Man, and Satan: Patterns of Christian Thought and Life in "Paradise Lost," "Pilgrim's Progress," and the Great Theologians* (Princeton, 1960).

    14. *A Treatise of the Fear of God*, vol. IX, pp. 9–14. Alluding both to Hebrew Scriptures
and the New Testament, Bunyan cites Nadab and Abihu (Lev. x, 1–3); Eli's sons (1 Sam. ii);
Uzza (1 Chron. xiii, 9–10); and Ananias and Saphira (Acts v).

    15. Although recent discussion has raised questions concerning the Miltonic authorship
of this work, I shall for the sake of argument assume its place in Milton's canon. At this point
it is unclear if the matter of authorship will ever be settled conclusively. Until it is, I continue
to believe the work is Milton's. The debate was set off by William B. Hunter and continued by
several scholars, including John T. Shawcross, Barbara K. Lewalski, Christopher Hill, and
Maurice Kelley. See Hunter's "The Provenance of the *Christian Doctrine*" and the responses
in "Forum: Milton's *Christian Doctrine*," *SEL* XXXII (1992): 129–42 and 163–66; "The Provenance of the *Christian Doctrine*: Addenda from the Bishop of Salisbury," *SEL* XXXII (1993):
191–207; "Animadversions Upon the Remonstrants' Defenses Against Burgess and Hunter,"
SEL XXXIV (1994): 153–203.

    16. The first book of *Christian Doctrine* is concerned with what it calls the *cognitio dei*
("knowledge of God"). See CM XIV, p. 22.

    17. I use the Sumner translation in CM here. The Carey translation in YP misconstrues:
"Jacob swore by what his father feared." This places the phenomenon of fear in the person of
Jacob, but both in the Hebrew and in the Latin of *Christian Doctrine* the construction is that

of the possessive. As I argue, that is precisely the point: fear itself is an entity identified with God.

18. So it is rendered in the *Testamenti Veteris Biblia Sacra siue Libri Canonici Priscae Iudaeorum Ecclesiae a Deo Traditi, Latini Recens ex Hebraeo facti, brevibusque Scholiis illustrati ab Immanuele Tremellio & Francisco Iunio* (London, 1585), an edition Milton frequently used as the basis for the proof-texts in *Christian Doctrine*. The Junius-Tremellius Bible was "the favorite Latin version of seventeenth-century Reformed divines," including Amesius and Wollebius (Maurice Kelley, introduction to *Christian Doctrine*, in YP VI, p. 45n8). For both Genesis xxxi, 42 and 53, the Junius-Tremellius version has *pavor*: "Nisi Deus patris mei Deus Abrahami & pavor Jitzchaki ad fuisset mihi" (42) and *"Deus Abrahami & Dii Nachoris judicent inter nos Dii patris eorum: cui juravit Jahhakob per pavorem patris sui Jitzchaki"* (53). The Vulgate, on the other hand, adopts *timor*. Thus, the *Biblia Sacra Iuxta Vulgatam Versionem*, 2 vols., ed. Bonifatio Fischer et al. (Stuttgart: Wurttembergische Bibelanstalt, 1969) has "nisi Deus patris mei Abraham et Timor Isaac adfuisset mihi (Gen. xxxi, 42) and "Deus Abraham et Deus Nahor iudicit inter nos Deus patris eorum iuravit Jacob per Timorem patris sui Isaac" (Gen. xxxi, 53). In the Vulgate, *timor* assumes a personified presence as "fear" or "dread."

19. See the respective entries on *pavor* and *timor* in *A Latin Dictionary*, ed. Charlton T. Lewis and Charles Short (Oxford, 1975), s.v.

20. William Riley Parker, *Milton: A Biography*, 2 vols. (Oxford, 1968), vol. I, p. 322. My translation from Psalm lxxx is from the *Biblia Hebraica Stuttgartensia* (Stuttgart, 1967). The Authorized Version has "thou that dwellest *between* the cherubims, shine forth." On the italics, Milton points out in his headnote that *"all but what is in a different Character* [that is, italicized], *are the very words of the Text, translated from the Original."* In *John Milton's Complete Poetical Works, Reproduced in Photographic Facsimile*, 4 vols., ed. Harris Francis Fletcher (Urbana, Ill., 1943), vol. I, p. 86.

21. The terrifying nature of that quality, moreover, is even further reinforced as a result of the way in which the final line of the quatrain is structured in Milton's rendering. Whereas God in his dwelling presence is called upon to "shine forth" and "give light," there is no corresponding verb to indicate what he is actually to do with his dread. The assumption, of course, is that what he does with his dread is tantamount to what he does with his light: he disseminates it. In Milton's addition to the original, however, the Psalmist calls upon the dwelling presence in a way that obliges us to supply the missing verb: *"And on our foes thy dread."* The effect is that of intensifying the identification of subject (God in his dwelling presence between the outspread wings of the ark) and object (dread) even further. God *is* the very dread that distinguishes him in his dwellingness. To violate the sanctity of that dwellingness is to be overwhelmed by the dread that is God.

22. See Milton's full discussion of this phenomenon in the first book of *Christian Doctrine* (CM XV, pp. 70–87; YP VI, pp. 331–38). See also *Paradise Lost*: "But hard be hard'n'd, blind be blinded more, / That they may stumble on, and deeper fall" (III, 200–01).

23. Otto, *The Idea of the Holy*, pp. 31–41. Kierkegaard, *The Concept of Dread: A simple psychological deliberation oriented in the direction of the dogmatic problem of original sin* (1844), in *Kierkegaard's The Concept of Dread*, trans. Walter Lowrie (Princeton, 1957), pp. 38–40. The relationship between Milton and Kierkegaard has recently been explored in depth by John S. Tanner, *Anxiety in Eden: A Kierkegaardian Reading of "Paradise Lost"* (New York, 1992).

24. For the Greek conception of being overwhelmed by such an experience of frenzy, see E. R. Dodds's discussion of *ate* in *The Greeks and the Irrational* (Berkeley, Calif., 1963), pp. 4–8. According to Dodds, *"ate* is a state of mind—a temporary clouding or bewildering of the normal consciousness. It is, in fact, a partial and temporary insanity; and, like all insanity,

it is ascribed, not to physiological or psychological causes, but to an external 'daemonic' agency" (p. 5).

25. As discussed below, Milton accepted the putative derivation of the name Dagon from *dag* (fish). If such is the case, one might note the etymological association between *dag* as "fish" and *daag* (a form of *dag*) as both "fish" and "dread" (compare Isa. lvii, 11). The *BDB*, s.v., confirms this association. Whether Milton was aware of it remains to be seen. If so, his Samson as the embodiment of divine dread overwhelms Dagon as the embodiment of profane dread in a conflict between divine and profane forms of dread.

26. In "Spectacle and Evidence in *Samson Agonistes*," *Critical Inquiry* XV (1989): 567, Stanley Fish argues on behalf of the complete indeterminacy of this moment. Although I agree with this outlook, I take issue with the conclusion that Fish ventures: Samson "may be speculating on the shape of Hebrew history or wondering whether anyone will ever pick up his best robe from the laundry; that is, the matter he revolves in his mind (if he is revolving one at all) may be great or it may be trivial." This, I suggest, is hardly the case. Although it is a profoundly mysterious moment, it is clearly not one that lends itself to trivialization.

27. Joseph Wittreich, *Interpreting "Samson Agonistes"* (Princeton, 1986), pp. 111–12. Wittreich associates Judges, chapter xvi, with John, chapter xi, that is, the temple holocaust with the prophecy of Caiaphas. Despite the liturgical basis of the association that Wittreich offers, I am not convinced that the two texts can be profitably paired. The other scriptural references that Wittreich cites (2 Cor. viii, 17, and Acts xii, 10) likewise do not appear to illuminate the use of the phrase "*Of his own accord.*" Fish, "Spectacle and Evidence," is generally in agreement with such a reading and cites it with approval. Asserting that he will act "of his own accord," Samson, according to Fish, behaves in a manner "for which he has no final warrant except what he himself at the moment thinks best to do" (579–80*n18*).

28. In addition to the texts discussed here, see Jeremiah li, 13, Isaiah xlv, 23, and Amos vi, 8. God also swears by his holiness (Ps. lxxxix, 35), by his name (Jer. xliv, 26); and by his right hand (Isa. lxii, 8). On oath-taking, compare God's declaration in *Paradise Lost*: "your Head I him appoint; / And by my Self have sworn to him shall bow / All knees in Heav'n" (V, 606–08). Milton was fond of the phrase. It appears several times in his prose works. Of particular interest is its use in *A Treatise of Civil Power*, where it is applied to Saint Paul: "None more cautious of giving scandal then St. *Paul*. Yet while he made himself *servant to all*, that he *might gain the more*, he made himself so of his own accord, was not made so by outward force, testifying at the same time that he *was free from all men*, 1 *Cor.* 9.19" (YP VII, p. 267). For Milton, Paul represents a prime example of the inspired prophet-servant who acts of his own volition.

29. Although Jacob does not adopt the *biy nishbati* locution, he makes a point not only of invoking God as the Dread of Isaac (*pachad yitschaq*) but of swearing by that Dread as well (Gen. xxxi, 53).

30. The other two premonarchic sanctuaries are Gilgal and Shechem. For a discussion of Shilo, see Baruch Halpern, "Shiloh," in *The Anchor Bible Dictionary*, vol. V, pp. 1213–15; and N. K. Gottwold, "Shiloh," in *The Interpreter's Dictionary of the Bible*, vol. IV, pp. 328–30.

31. In the Renaissance, the pairing of the Samson narrative in Judges and the fall of Dagon in 1 Samuel was commonplace. The second narrative was looked upon as a commentary on the first. See, in this respect, Sir Walter Raleigh, *The History of the World, in Five Books* (London, 1617), book II, chapter 15, sections I–II; and Matthew Poole, *Annotations upon the Holy Bible*, 2 vols. (London, 1683), vol. I, sig. Nnnn2ᵛ–Nnnn2ʳ.

32. See my chapter on holy war in *Poetics of the Holy*, pp. 246–312.

33. Although this is the translation that appears in the Authorized Version, it should be noted that the phrase "the stump of Dagon" is not in the Hebrew. Rather, the Hebrew has

"roc dagon nishar alav" ("only dagon was left to him"). It is a very vexed phrase that has been variously translated. The LXX and the Vulgate have their own variant readings. See *BDB*, p. 186. Exegetes during Milton's own time were aware of the issue. See, for example, Poole, *Annotations upon the Holy Bible*, vol. 1, I, sigs. Nnnn2ᵛ–Nnnn2ʳ. According to Poole, "roc dagon" refers to "that part of it [the idol] from which it was called *Dagon*, to wit, the Fishy part, for *Dag* in *Hebrew* signifies *a Fish.*" Interestingly, Poole also has a marginal gloss for "stump" as "the filthy part," but this may actually be "the fishy part."

34. Even after it is returned to the Israelites, moreover, it wreaks havoc. See 1 Samuel, chapter vi.

35. Milton understood "Dagon" as a bipartite figure "upward Man / And downward Fish," in part because of the prevailing etymology of the term *Dagon* as derived from *dag* (fish). One should be aware, however, that the precise etymology of the term is still very much debated. For discussion, see the entries on Dagon in Lowell K. Handy, *The Anchor Bible Dictionary*, vol. II, pp. 1–3; J. Gray, in *The Interpreter's Dictionary of the Bible*, vol. I, p. 756; and H. Ringrenn, *Theological Dictionary of the Old Testament*, vol. III, pp. 139–42. Among the many treatments of Dagon in the Renaissance, see John Selden, *De Dis Syris Syntagmata* (London, 1629), pp. 262–80; and Poole, *Annotations*. According to Poole, "this Idol of *Dagon* had its upper parts in human shape, and its lower parts in the form of a *Fish;* for such was the Form of divers of the *Heathen* gods, and particularly of a god of the Phoenicians (under which Name the *Philistines* are comprehended)" (I, sig. Nnnn2ᵛ–Nnnn2ʳ).

"THEN STOOD UP PHINEHAS": MILTON'S ANTINOMIANISM, AND SAMSON'S

Norman T. Burns

I N THE MIDST of the Irish campaign Cromwell wrote his friend Lord Philip Wharton in an effort to persuade him to resume an active role in the parliamentary cause, a role he had given up because of his scrupulous objections to the purging of the Parliament and to the judgment and execution of the king almost a year earlier. Cromwell appears to concede the illegality of the proceedings against the king when he appeals to the example of Phinehas, the son of Eleazar and grandson of Aaron celebrated in Numbers, chapter xxv, for taking it upon himself to rid the tribe of the uncleanness that had brought the plague upon them. Phinehas took a spear and murdered Zimri, son of an Israelite prince, and Cozbi, daughter of a Midianite prince, as the two were copulating in Zimri's tent. The Lord thereupon told Moses that because of Phinehas's deed he had lifted the plague. Psalm cvi helped establish Phinehas as the type of zeal: "Then stood up Phinehas, and executed judgment: and so the plague was stayed. / And that was counted unto him for righteousness unto all generations for evermore" (30–31). Cromwell suggests that his own actions, though also undertaken without the guidance of positive law, have been similarly blessed by the divine endorsement evident in the successes of the Commonwealth, those "signal outward acts" in which one can read the judgment of Providence, and in the divine approval that he feels in his heart. He asks Wharton to accept God's "glorious actings" without scrupling the means used by God's agents:

Be not offended at the manner; perhaps no other way was left. What if God accepted the zeal, as He did that of Phineas, whose reason might have called for a jury? What if the Lord have witnessed his approbation and acceptance of this also, not only by signal outward acts, but to the heart also?

Many of his countrymen, then and in subsequent generations, deplored Cromwell's disregard for law and denounced his faction as fanatics, but Cromwell was here content "to stand approv'd in sight of God" and to read events as God's providences that bear "witness gloriously" to God's approval of his deeds.[1]

27

As we shall see, it was common enough in the period to use, as Cromwell did, the example of a biblical lawbreaker as a rhetorical aid in defense of lawbreaking by the godly. Only a few, and Milton was one of them, tried to think through a sufficiently developed theory of the believer's freedom from the moral law to justly earn the name of "antinomian." Early in his career, Milton found attractive the antinomianism implicit in the Phinehas and Abraham stories and wrote brief plans for plays that emphasized the antinomianism of those heroes. Later, in *Christian Doctrine,* he worked out the theological grounds for antinomianism. Committed to this doctrine, Milton reconceived the character of Samson found in the Book of Judges and, in *Samson Agonistes,* presented Samson in a new light, as an antinomian hero of faith, the only one, I think, in English literature.

I

Phinehas was but one of the saintly lawbreakers whose stories were ready at hand to justify illegal acts done in what could be claimed to be God's cause. Blair Worden finds "an antinomian streak in the saints . . . even among those of them who professed to be horrified by antinomianism." As part of the preparations for the effort to destroy Strafford, the king's powerful servant, Stephen Marshall, in his famous sermon, "Meroz Cursed," reminded the House of Commons that Jael was "blessed above women" for driving a tent spike through the head of her sleeping guest Sisera, the Canaanite commander. While Strafford was successfully defending himself in the House of Lords against charges of treason, in a sermon before the House of Commons Samuel Fairclough urged speedy execution of justice, recalling how God had blessed Phinehas and credited his zeal as righteousness; a few days later a bill of attainder was introduced in the Commons that made it possible to execute Strafford without having to prove any particular crime. Three years later, as a suitable prelude to the attainting of Archbishop Laud, the House of Lords heard Edmund Staunton take as his text "Then stood up Phinehas," denounce unfounded pity, and praise Phinehas's zeal that could not be stayed by legal considerations. Bishop Gilbert Burnet notes with horror how Cromwell's intimates justified their hypocritical behavior in Parliament by the biblical precedents of David (who ate the sacred showbread to nourish him in his flight from Saul), and Ehud (who guilefully murdered the foreign tyrant Eglon), Jael, and Samson.[2]

The lawbreaking, the violence, and the treachery could only be acceptable if one understood the motive to be an immediate inspiration from God. In a preface to his epic treatment of the Judith story, du Bartas nervously separated himself from any seditious spirits who from "private inspirations" conspire against the lives of princes while justifying their actions by the example of Old Testament heroes like Judith, Ehud, and Jael. Accordingly, in the poem that followed, du Bartas invented a scene that supplied Judith with a kind of divine inspiration. As Judith debated with herself whether it would be right to murder Holofernes, the question is decided when a wind blows the pages of her "Scripture" and stops at the account of Jael's murder of Sisera, a wind that Judith understands as divine direction.³ From the Middle Ages on, the antinomianism implicit in the lawbreaking of Old Testament heroes was usually tamed by asserting that they acted on divine commands and that God no longer communicated such commands directly to individuals. For orthodox believers the inspiration of the Holy Spirit in the present day was never immediate to the individual, but only mediated through the institution of God's church. George Herbert thought that the godly were justly not exempt from social control: if Abraham had lived in England and had killed Isaac, the magistrate might justly hang him unless he could make it evident to others as well as himself that he had done it at God's immediate command, for "otherwise any Malefactor may pretend motions."⁴

Hypocritical behavior was commonly charged against Puritans, notably in the characterizations of Malvolio, Jonson's Tribulation Wholesome and Zeal-of-the-Land Busy, and Jack in Swift's *Tale of a Tub*, but Samuel Butler believed he saw the antinomian principles that were the foundation of the hypocrisy. Ralpho's attempt to persuade Hudibras that only the unilluminated consider oaths to be binding on the Saints suggests how ready conservatives like Butler were to see antinomian principles not just in the discredited Ranters (with whom we have come to associate high-flying antinomianism), but also in the Independents and Presbyterians:

> But they are weak and little know
> What Free-born *Consciences* may do.
> 'Tis the *temptation* of the Devill,
> That makes all humane actions evill:
> For *Saints* may do the same things by
> The *Spirit*, in *sincerity*,
> Which other men are tempted to,
> And at the Devils instance do;
> And yet the Actions be Contrary,
> Just as the *Saints* and *Wicked* vary.⁵

We cannot dismiss the charges of Burnet and Butler as the calumnies an utterly defeated party must suffer. An examination of Milton's doctrine of Christian liberty and of his enduring interest in Phinehas, Abraham, and Jael will reveal a Milton who is a kind of antinomian, one who believes in doing the will of God even when that will is not revealed by the Holy Scripture or reason, not supported by the law of nature or of nations, and when the deed of faith does not appear to be good in the eyes of men. This belief found expression in *Samson Agonistes*, which Milton carefully crafted to show the operations of faith in the life of a hero moving toward true liberation.

II

Milton's antinomianism has nothing to do with that of John Eaton, Tobias Crisp, or John Saltmarsh who, in the early years of the Long Parliament, argued that believers are not bound by the moral law because God gives his saving grace unconditionally and does not see sin in his elect, who shall persevere in his favor to the end. Milton expressly and repeatedly asserts his belief in conditional election and denies the doctrine of perseverance (YP VI, pp. 157, 459, 505–14). Nor is his antinomianism like that of the Ranter Laurence Clarkson, who considered sin a merely human construction. Nonetheless, Milton may be called "antinomian" for his well-known assertion in *Christian Doctrine* that Christ abrogated the *whole* Mosaic law, the moral parts as well as the ceremonial and judicial (YP VI, pp. 525–41). It has not been sufficiently recognized that Milton is here breaking with established Christian tradition. That Christ left the moral law, the Ten Commandments, binding upon Christians is expressly asserted by Luther's Small Catechism, the Council of Trent, the Thirty-nine Articles of the Church of England, the Westminster Confession (which was accepted by the Congregational churches), as well as by Milton's model, Wollebius. It is true, of course, that Milton hastens to say that the law "is now inscribed on believers' hearts by the spirit" (YP VI, p. 532) and thus separates himself from Ranter antinomianism, but I believe A. S. P. Woodhouse is wrong to think that Milton hereby separates himself from antinomianism entirely by leaving reason and natural law in authority.[6]

Milton does not say that the Decalogue itself is, under the Gospel dispensation, now inscribed in the believer's heart; indeed, he says that he does not "consider the decalogue a faultless moral code" (YP VI, p. 711). Rather, he says that it is the *substance* of the Law, the "love of God and of our neighbor which is born of faith, through the spirit," that is preserved in the hearts of believers through the agency of the Holy Spirit (YP VI, p. 531). Whereas Luther in his influential *Small Catechism* starts with an exposition of the Decalogue,[7] and Milton's model Wollebius uses an exposition of the Decalogue to structure his entire book on the service of God, Milton rejects that structure in favor of a view that makes faith, not law, that which under the gospel determines the goodness of a work:

If anyone should, then, under the gospel, keep the commandments of the whole Mosaic law with absolute scrupulousness, but have no faith, it would do him no good. So good works must obviously be defined with reference to faith, not to the commandments. Thus we ought to consider the form of good works to be conformity not with the written but with the unwritten law, that is, with the law of the Spirit which the Father has given us to lead us into truth. For the works of the faithful are the works of the Holy Spirit itself. These never run contrary to the love of God and of our neighbor, which is the sum of the law. They may, however, sometimes deviate from the letter even of gospel precepts . . . , in pursuance of their over-riding motive, which is charity. (YP VI, p. 640)

This reduction of the moral law to its substance yields a wide latitude in behavior, wider even than the law of nature or right reason can justify. This view allows Milton to prefer the spirit to the letter of the law: "So we, freed from the works of the law, follow not the letter but the spirit, not the works of the law but the works of faith" (YP VI, p. 536). Although Milton believes that both Jew and Gentile may be saved by belief in God without knowledge of Christ (p. 475), this moral liberty is greater than and radically different from any freedom available to the just nonbeliever who has only reason and the law of nature for guidance.

III

In his chapter on justification in *Christian Doctrine*, Milton attempts to reconcile the apparent discrepancy between Paul's doctrine that man is justified by faith without the works of the law, and James's doctrine that man is justified by his works and not by faith only. To effect this reconciliation, Milton makes a sharp distinction between the works of the law and works of faith, arguing that it is only the works of the law that cannot justify while faith must be expressed in works:

Faith has its own works, which may be different from the works of the law. We are justified, then, by faith, but a living faith, not a dead one, and the only living faith is a faith which acts. . . . So we are justified by faith without the works of the law, but not without the works of faith; for a true and living faith cannot exist without works, though these may be different from the works of the written law. (YP VI, p. 490)

Milton here offers as examples of the works of faith the deeds of Abraham and of Rahab, the Canaanite harlot who protected Joshua's spies just before the assault on Jericho. In both cases Milton stresses the illegality of their actions: "The one offered his son as a sacrifice, the other harbored spies" (YP VI, p. 490). Abraham and Rahab were named in Hebrews, chapter xi, as heroes of faith, and James (ii, 21, 25) gave them as examples of a living faith, but Milton added a faithful hero of his own—Phinehas, noting that

Psalm cvi, 31, imputes his bloody deed to him as righteousness and that it uses the very words in which Romans iv, 9, credited Abraham's faith as righteousness. Here again Milton insists on the illegality of this work of faith: "It will be difficult for anyone to deny that Phinehas was justified in the sight of God rather than in the sight of man, or that his act . . . was a work of faith and not of the law. It follows that Phinehas was not justified by faith alone but by the works of faith as well" (YP VI, pp. 490–91).

The idea that the works of faith are not bound by law had been present in Milton's mind long before he wrote *Christian Doctrine*.[8] About 1641, Milton leafed through his Bible noting those stories that might make material for drama. In the manuscript now preserved at Trinity College, Cambridge, he listed those subjects, elaborating some of them to suggest how the ideas might be developed. Sometimes scholars interested in *Samson Agonistes* study the notes he made on subjects drawn from Samson's life, but the notes that most illuminate his mature play are not about the Samson figure at all. One of his more extensive sketches is the story of the zeal of Phinehas. Milton's treatment takes up the story after the murders and emphasizes the illegality of Phinehas's action "in the sight of man," an illegality that is no more than implicit in the biblical text. Except for Jehovah's approval of Phinehas's deed, all of the drama imagined by Milton is extrabiblical.

Moabitides or Phineas
the Epitasis whereof may lie in the contention first between ye father of Zimri & Eleazer whether he to have slain his son without law. next ye Embassadors of ye Moabite[s] expostulating about Cosby a stranger & a noble woman slain by Phineas. it may be argud about reformation & punishment illegal & as it were by tumult after all arguments drivn home then the word of the lord may be brought acquitting & approving phineas. (YP VIII, p. 560)

It is notable that Milton's plan suggests no argument to be made on *behalf* of Phinehas's deed. It appears that the Moabite ambassadors were to argue that the Israelites owed hospitality and protection to a stranger and noblewoman. Zimri's father was to argue that Phinehas's precipitate judgment did not give Zimri a chance to reform and that, since it had no basis in law, the killing substituted force for law, tumult for judicial procedure. These are powerful arguments against Phinehas; Cromwell would grant that Phinehas's "reason might have called for a jury." Despite his taste for debate, however, Milton seems to have intended these arguments to stand unrefuted for most of the play ("after all arguments drivn home") so that the reversal of the end might be the more surprising and doctrinal. God may acquit where human understanding condemns.

At about the same time that he sketched the Phinehas drama, Milton made notes for a drama about Abraham, the father of the faithful, that also stressed that the work of faith cannot be confined in the categories of the lawful and reasonable. The author of the Epistle to the Hebrews was aware that Abraham's confidence in the promises of God had to be stronger than his urge to follow reason; when the author gave Abraham the most prominent place in his list of the heroes of faith, he emphasized that Abraham was willing to kill Isaac even though he had rejoiced in the promise that through Isaac he would father an innumerable nation: "By faith Abraham, when he was tried, offered up Isaac: and he that had received the promises offered up his only begotten son, of whom it was said, That in Isaac shall thy seed be called: accounting that God was able to raise him up, even from the dead; from whence also he received him in a figure" (Heb. xi, 17–19). To capture in his drama this sense that the divine command could not be rationally comprehended, Milton planned to keep Abraham and the sacrificial scene offstage while he focused on the responses of the people in Abraham's household to reports about what Abraham was doing at the scene of sacrifice. Thus Milton emphasized the gap between common humanity and the God-directed man who was to be the great exemplar of faith:

Abram from Morea, or Isack redeemd. the oiconomie may be thus the fift or sixt day after Abrahams departure, Eleazer Abrams steward first alone and then with the chorus discours of Abrahams strange voiage thire mistresse sorrow and *per*plexity accompanied with frighfull dreams, and tell the manner of his rising by night taking his servants and his son with him next may come forth Sarah her self, after the Chorus or Ismael or Agar next some shepheard or companie of merchants passing through the mount in the time that Abram was in the mid work relate to Sarah what they saw hence lamentations, fears, wonders, the matter in the mean while divulgd Aner or Eshcol, or mamre Abrams confederats come to the hous of Abram to be more certaine, or to bring news, in the mean while discoursing as the world would of such an action divers ways, bewayling the fate of so noble a man faln from his reputation, either through divin justice, or *super*stition, or coveting to doe some notable act through zeal. at length a servant sent from Abram relates the truth, and last he himselfe comes in with a great Train of Melchizedec whose shepheards beeing secret eye witnesses of all passages had related to thir master, and he conducted his freind Abraham home with joy. (YP VIII, pp. 557–58)

As in the sketch for the Phinehas drama, the theme is that the faithful hero is "justified in the sight of God rather than in the sight of man" because "faith has its own works, which may be different from the works of the law." Again the hero's actions are discussed in his absence by ordinary humanity. Even Sarah is sorrowful and perplexed, and Abraham's allies bewail his fall from his noble reputation, speculating (like Job's counselors) whether

Abraham is being punished by God or whether he is motivated by superstition or misguided zeal. Again Milton has set the ending of the drama in stark contrast to the rest of the play, the heroic Abraham entering as a triumphant figure, belying all concerns that he has somehow fallen from greatness. And the Abraham play was to be as free a treatment of its biblical source as was the Phinehas play, Milton's invention in both sketches being mainly devoted to contrasting the heroic acts of faith with the ordinary understandings of men. The Phinehas and Abraham sketches thus show, from an early stage in Milton's career, his commitment to this radical version of the idea that all believers, whether Jew, Gentile, or Christian, are free to act as mature Sons of God, guided by the Holy Spirit. Abraham and Phinehas exemplify the Christian liberty that, in *Christian Doctrine*, Milton was to say means that "Christ our liberator frees us from the slavery of sin and thus from the rule of the law and of men, as if we were emancipated slaves. He does this so that, being made sons instead of servants and grown men instead of boys, we may serve God in charity through the guidance of the Spirit of Truth" (YP VI, p. 537).

IV

In some formal respects *Samson Agonistes* resembles these Abraham and Phinehas scenarios. *Samson Agonistes* also presents a hero of faith in a classical drama that meets strict standards for unity in time and place. In all three pieces Milton freely invents extrabiblical incidents and characters that emphasize how ordinary moral categories cannot comprehend the behavior of liberated believers who trust in God. Since the Phinehas and Abraham ideas are limited to mere sketches, they more narrowly focus on the concern to celebrate Christian liberty, but *Samson Agonistes* is also shaped in a way that illuminates the antinomian freedom of the hero of faith.

We may examine two places in the play that show a faithful action taken at the urging of the Spirit despite the fact that it violates commonly understood law: Jael's murder of Sisera, cited by Dalila as justification for her own betrayal of her husband, and, more important, Samson's decision to perform in the temple of Dagon despite his testimony in favor of the law that forbids him to do it.

When in her final speech Dalila has abandoned her attempt to win back Samson, she declares that she is proud of having betrayed him. Conceding that she will be defamed among the Israelites, Dalila takes comfort in the thought that she will be honored among the Philistines: "Not less renown'd than in Mount *Ephraim*, / *Jael*, who with inhospitable guile / Smote *Sisera* sleeping through the Temples nail'd" (988–90). It is characteristic of Milton to give strong arguments to his unsympathetic characters, and here the ugly violence, treachery, and inhospitality of Jael's action are insisted upon in Dalila's marvelously succinct indictment. In the biblical account (Judg. iv, 17–22), when Sisera's army is destroyed he flees to the tent of Jael, whose husband is a neutral. Jael goes out to meet him and, unasked, offers him refuge. She gives him a place to sleep; when he asks for water she gives him milk, and she agrees to tell inquirers that there is no man in the tent. Then, when Sisera falls asleep, she drives home the tent spike. Dalila's attempt to sweeten her reputation at the expense of Jael's is allowed to stand unrefuted in the play and thus seems open to interpretation, but the passage has received scant attention from critics. Though William Empson thinks Dalila's self-justification is "one of the noblest speeches in Milton" and her reference to Jael "a telling stroke," no one has followed his vigorous interpretive lead, not even those whose concern to distance Milton from Samson's violence would appear to have an interest in reading this passage as a repudiation of Jael's violence.[9]

Empson, however, assessed the moral relationships in Dalila's speech without sufficient regard for how Milton (and his Christian culture) unhesitatingly supported violence when it served the cause of God or his people, reserving contempt only for tyrants and self-aggrandizing conquerors and their aggressive wars. Those who think that Samson in his violence culpably fails to discern moral differences among the Philistines, might consider how sweeping is the usual biblical condemnation of the enemies of God and his people.[10] One passage may stand for many: in lines that have shocked not a few, from captivity in Babylon the psalmist sings:

O daughter of Babylon, who art to be destroyed; happy shall he be, that rewardeth thee as thou hast served us.
Happy shall he be, that taketh and dasheth thy little ones against the stones. (Ps. cxxxvii, 8–9)

When in *Christian Doctrine* Milton listed proof-texts to support his belief that "we are not forbidden to take or wish to take vengeance upon the enemies of the church," he included these verses from Psalm cxxxvii among them, apparently content to count children among the enemies of God (YP VI, p. 755). Since he believed it a religious duty to hate the enemies of God (p. 743), Milton could let Dalila compare herself to Jael without contradiction because her error was evident to all: this servant of Dagon and his priests could not compare to the faithful Jael, who destroyed an enemy of Jehovah and his people with the means that were at hand. In *Christian Doctrine* Milton excused the deceitfulness of those who lied to the enemies of God, among them Rahab, Ehud, and Jael, "who enticed Sisera to his death when he sought refuge with her . . . though he was God's enemy rather than hers" (p. 764). Joan Bennett astutely observes that Dalila is to be judged not only by her faults, which she shares with her opponents, but as Milton thought the royalists in the late war were to be judged, by "the grand sin of thir Cause."[11]

Even the force of Dalila's indictment, the "inhospitable guile," more likely pleased than shamed the godly audience. The "antinomian streak in the saints" that Blair Worden speaks of often showed itself in the unequivocal delight the pious took in the means that heroes used. In the Judges narrative, Deborah's song of triumph declares that Jael is blessed above women and recites the details of the killing, emphasizing the deceit ("He asked for water, and she gave him milk; she brought forth butter in a lordly dish") and adding to the pleasure by imagining Sisera's mother wondering about his delayed return and being assured by her ladies that he has conquered and is slowed only by having to take spoil (v, 24–31). It might be well to have Deborah's spirit in mind as we assess the moral meaning of Manoa's feeling himself compensated for the death of his son by the thought that Samson has left his enemies "years of mourning, / And lamentation" (1712–13) or of the Chorus's delight in thinking of Samson as "an ev'ning Dragon" got loose among the "tame villatic Fowl" (1692, 1695). To think of the Philistines as tame and helpless against a predator may seem strange for this militant, aggressive people, but it pleases the Chorus to think of the mighty being victimized in this way, just as it pleased Deborah to think the mighty Sisera a helpless victim of deceit and to picture his vulnerable mother waiting for him confidently before she will be cast down.[12] John Bunyan was so little embarrassed by Jael's methods that he had Christian view Jael's hammer and nail in the House Beautiful, and an establishment figure like Bishop Joseph Hall shows Jael struggling to overcome her "idle fancies of civility" (her scruples about betraying Sisera's trust) and implicates God in the details of the murder: "He that put this instinct into her heart, did put also strength into her hand; Hee that guided *Sisera* to her Tent, guided the naile thorow his temples." Hall regretted that, in the nature of the murder, Sisera could not know the humiliation that would have crowned his infelicity, that "the great terror of Israel [lies] at the foote of a woman."[13]

Neither Milton nor his contemporaries were likely to confuse Dalila's "motions" with the leadings of the Spirit of Truth. Butler's lines, if we can see past their mocking irony, may help us to see how an antinomian could think it obvious that the deed of Jael was preferable to the deed of Dalila:

> For *Saints* may do the same things by
> The *Spirit,* in *sincerity,*

Which other men are tempted to,
And at the Devils instance do;
And yet the Actions be contrary,
Just as the *Saints* and *Wicked* vary.

V

As told in Judges, the story of Samson did not have the clear antinomian implications of the Phinehas, Jael, Ehud, Judith, and Rahab stories. While Bishop Burnet named Samson as one of the biblical heroes the Cromwellians used to justify their crimes, it is not apparent how what antinomianism there may be in the Judges narrative could have been useful to them. Certainly Samson is a lawbreaker, but his exogamous liaison and marriage, even his feats of revenge and slaughter, do not have the political resonance of the biblical tyrannicides. If a hero of faith is a person who follows "the evidence of things not seen" (Hebrews xi, 1), the Samson of Judges is not notably heroic in that sense: unlike Abraham, he does not allow God to find his way for him. If Milton wanted to present an antinomian hero of faith in a play about Samson, he would have to supplement the scriptural record. In the episode with the Public Officer Milton created an antinomian Samson who is, like Phinehas, zealous to honor the name of God, yet ready, like Abraham, to follow divine leadings, even to the extent of violating a law intended to preserve God's honor.

Milton's interest in the antinomianism of heroes of faith causes him to devote seventy-one lines (1319–89) to Samson's scruples about participating in the feast of Dagon. There is no biblical precedent for Samson's concerns, and if the problem of the Hebrew law against attending idolatrous religious rites had never been brought up, it would scarcely have been missed. The plot demands only that Samson follow the officer to the temple, a movement that could easily be economically accomplished if a rush to the catastrophe were Milton's aim. John Steadman points out that the scene contains the drama's point of highest tension, but it was not essential to introduce the law against idolatry: without it a bellicose hero could nonetheless have wanted to resist the imperious commands of his captors, causing the tension, and the tension could still have been released by divine direction.[14] But *Samson Agonistes* is a play more concerned with states of mind than with the rush of events, and here Milton, very economically for his purpose, takes care to reveal the antinomian component of the heroic, faithful act just as he had in the dramatic sketches about Abraham and Phinehas. He shows us a Samson whose "trust . . . in the living God" (1140) is so restored that he is willing to follow an inner impulse even though it involves breaking a holy law.

The moral authority of the law against idolatry, so forcefully acknowledged by Samson, is set aside when he feels "Some rousing motions" (1382). Samson does no more than hint at the nature or content of those motions because, like Jesus in the companion poem *Paradise Regained* (I, 290–93), he knows nothing of the meaning of these impulses and responds only to their strength. The motions are not explicit divine instructions such as Noah or Abraham got when God spoke directly to them, but we can discern something of the nature of the motions by noting how powerful is their effect in this scene and later in the temple.

Critics have not sufficiently appreciated the validity of Samson's view that he is forbidden to attend idolatrous rites. The importance of the prohibition of idolatry can scarcely be overstated. In Exodus it is the first of the commandments given to Moses, the first breach whereof he is commanded to punish by having the Levites kill three thousand idolatrous Israelites (xxxii, 27–28). God reminds the Israelites that his very name is "Jealous" and commands them to destroy the altars and break the images of the gods of the surrounding heathens (Exod. xx, 2–5; xxxiv, 13–14). Though Samson in the Judges narrative shows no concern about idolatry, Milton adds to Samson's character two traits that are never far from Samson's consciousness: shame for having encouraged idolatry by his failure, and zeal to sanctify the divine name.[15] When Manoa remarks that worse than Samson's enslavement and blinding is the fact that his fall will be the occasion for a feast celebrating the victory of Dagon over God, Samson agrees that his having brought dishonor to God is his "chief affliction, shame and sorrow" (433–57). Samson understands that displeasing his jealous God for fear of Philistine threats would be a sin that would "never, unrepented, find forgiveness" (1376). Samson uncompromisingly describes the blasphemous situation that would result if he were to go and entertain the idolaters with his strength, now returning by the grace of God:

> prostituting holy things to Idols;
> A *Nazarite* in place abominable
> Vaunting my strength in honor to thir Dagon?
> Besides, how vile, contemptible, ridiculous,
> What act more execrably unclean, profane?　　　(1358–62)

In an impressive show of his reasoning ability Samson rejects the excuses for going that the Chorus offers. Yet suddenly and without apparent reason he responds to "some rousing motions in me which dispose / To something extraordinary my thoughts" (1382–83) and decides to ignore the law to whose force and applicability he has just testified at length. We have seen how central to being "an *Ebrew*" (1319) is the prohibition of attendance at idolatrous rites. The rigor and validity of this law establish the identity of Samson and his people: he is one of those who worship only "the Holy One / Of *Israel*" (1427–28). The "rousing motions" must indeed be powerful if they can move Samson to break such a fundamental law.[16] Before we examine all the circumstances in the play that show the power of the motions, however, we can learn something about the nature of the motions if we first examine the implications of their being "sudden."

It is a fundamental habit of our thought to believe that in the created world all things, all thoughts, have antecedents, and that we can know the nature of something if we see how it relates to its antecedents and their natures; all thought is part of a process of thought; even inspiration is said to come to the prepared mind. So it is commonly assumed that the decision to go with the officer must be the culmination of a process of thought, that the motions have an antecedent or cause, and that the motions, whatever they are, can be understood if we perceive their antecedents. There has therefore been much critical discussion that relates Samson's decision to go to the temple to his alleged habit of confusing his sexual urges with divine commands, to his recent thought that God may grant dispensations from his laws, and to his desire to destroy his enemies. All these positions are bulwarks against the idea that the "rousing motions" have *no* antecedents, which is to say that they are beyond common understanding, that they come from the unconditioned, from God. Yet that idea has not proved hard to accept in *Paradise Regained* where, as far as I know, no one has inquired after the antecedent or cause of the "strong motion" (I, 290) that leads Jesus into the desert: it is strong, it carries no information, the faithful man cooperates with it, and it is generally accepted that it simply comes from the Father. Critics treat Samson's motions very differently.

The explanation that most simply brings Samson's decision within the naturalistic sphere of understanding is the association of these "rousing motions" with the "intimate impulse" that Samson took to be divine justification for his first exogamous marriage and, by extension, for his second (221–32). Critics who discuss the earlier motions and impulses sometimes suspect that Samson mistook his sexual urge for divine direction, for it is easy to assent to T. S. Eliot's dry observation that "the most imperative of instincts may be strong enough to simulate to perfection the voice of the Holy Spirit."[17] But even if we believe that it was a self-deluded Samson who confused his sexual drive with divine impulsion, we should not let this opinion direct us to see similar self-deception in his final "rousing motions."[18] If Samson rationalized his illegal marriages by alleging divine guidance, it was because he desired these Philistine women, but he has no desire to go to Dagon's feast. From the time Manoa first announces that there will be a feast to celebrate Dagon's victory over Samson and his God, Samson sees the feast as an occasion that will feature his shameful role in the dishonoring of God and the glorifying of Dagon (433–58). When the Philistines command him there to exhibit his strength, he has a lively image of how he will be expected to perform among the jugglers and mummers (1323–25) and declares that playing before Dagon would be for him "the worst of all indignities" (1340–41). Thus, however we may read the earlier "intimate impulse," the "rousing motions" cannot be read as merely another name for the desires of the natural man.

It is sometimes proposed that Samson's motions should be seen as the consequence of his just having thought, or remembered, that God may grant a dispensation to allow attendance at idolatrous rites "for some important cause" (1377–79), for if the motions follow from a previous thought they are not so disturbingly "sudden"; but this idea of a dispensation does not reveal the nature of the motions, but merely poses the question differently.[19] If to qualify for a dispensation one has to have an "important cause," are we to believe that these motions have brought knowledge of a sufficiently "important cause" to excuse Samson from obeying this most solemn of the laws of a jealous God? What cause or "great act" (1389) might Samson be thinking about? Does this knowledge of a "cause" have an antecedent? What might be the content of his extraordinary thoughts (1383)? Samson gives no answers to these questions and so reveals nothing about the motions.

What does Samson anticipate when he decides to follow the officer to the temple? A common view, explicitly stated or implied, is that the motions assure him that he will have the opportunity to satisfy his desire to destroy his enemies. Wittreich surmises that Samson has some program to execute his revenge, Samuel believes he goes knowing "he can deal death," Burton J. Weber thinks that through the "rousing motions" God tells Samson he is to go on a military mission, and William Kerrigan says "Samson knows what to do in the theater. He leaves the stage with the scheme in mind"; but none of these readings satisfactorily explains what plan a blind man could have to hurt his enemies. When he challenged Harapha to single combat, bold as that was, Samson was careful to specify that it be fought in a narrow place to reduce the giant's advantage of vision (1116–18), but what could be planned in an arena?[20]

No matter, for Milton declines to portray a Samson who has anything specific on his mind. After the catastrophe the Hebrew Messenger gives a succinct account of the seating arrangements of the temple (1605–10); Milton could easily have supplied Samson with this information (in a passing remark from Manoa, perhaps, or the Public Officer) if he wanted us to think Samson was breaking the law to achieve the greater good of destroying the oppressors of his people, but going by "the evidence of things *seen*" does not make a hero of faith any more than Abraham would if he had known all along that there would be a ram caught in a thicket on Mount Moriah. The play does not even hint that Samson knows anything of the opportunity that the pillars will present. Neither does Milton show a Samson who has by God's gift attained such an enlightened understanding that he sees rationally that the law should not constrain him from going to the temple. Joan Bennett thinks that the Holy Spirit rectifies the reason of believers, who are left free of positive law whenever it proves inadequate to the needs of a situation, but the question must be asked: is there something rationally faulty with refusing to attend idolatrous rites? On the contrary, when we last see Samson reasoning it is to uphold, with the utmost vigor and confidence, the validity of the law prohibiting his presence at Dagon's festival. The decision to behave contrary to this reasoning is sudden and, above all, the rational basis for the reversal, if any, is not presented. It is therefore difficult to see the "rousing motions" as supplementing Samson's reasoning powers that have until now been ranged against this decision to "go along." To be sure, Samson has a presentiment that his decision will lead to his doing "some great act," but there is no specific content to the feeling, and alternatively the decision might lead to his death (1388–89).[21]

Amid such uncertainties, Samson is no more anxious about his immediate future than is the Jesus of *Paradise Regained,* for both are led by a strong motion into a perilous situation for an unknown purpose; Samson might have said what Jesus said, "perhaps I need not know; / For what concerns my knowledge God reveals" (*PR* I, 292–93).

Samson's motions are so strong that he surrenders to them his own views and instincts. Breaking a holy law is just the beginning of this test of his faithfulness to divine direction, his confidence in God. He gives solemn assurances to his countrymen that he will do nothing "that may dishonor / Our Law, or stain my vow of *Nazarite*" or "unworthy / Our God, our law, my Nation, or myself" (1385–86, 1424–25). These promises are usually taken at face value by critics who use them as evidence that a regenerate Samson will sin no more, but the promises are not impressive in the light of the ensuing events at the temple. It has scarcely been noticed that Samson's athletic performance at the Dagonalia contradicts his commitment to do nothing unworthy or dishonorable there.[22] The Philistine crowd greets his very appearance with "a shout / [That] rifted the Air clamoring thir god with praise" (1620–21), for he has donned state livery (1615–16), thereby falling in with the state's plan to "magnify" Dagon by crediting him with having made the people's "dreadful enemy thir thrall" (1622). Samson seems an enthusiastic collaborator. Set to athletic tasks designed to show what a for-

midable power Dagon has bent to his service, Samson could not have made
a better spectacle: "To heave, pull, draw, or break, he still perform'd / All
with incredible, stupendious force" (1626–27). Samson's evident submission
to Dagon and the regime belies the assurances he gave the Chorus and
mocks the optimistic prayer they sent with him:

> Go, and the Holy One
> Of *Israel* be thy guide
> To what may serve his glory best, and spread his name
> Great among the Heathen round.   (1427–30)

Samson's performance before he comes to the pillars is condemned out of
his own mouth: "What act more execrably unclean, profane?" (1362). Samson's worst fears are realized: Dagon *is* magnified and God *is* disglorified,
and the shame of it falls on Samson and his father's house.

But Samson is beyond concerns about personal disgrace or unclean and
profane acts. He has broken a holy law that helps define his identity, being
moved to attend an idolatrous feast where he expects personal humiliation
and possible death at the hands of a fanatic mob (1413–22).[23] Perhaps hard-
est of all for a courageous and active hero, cooperation with the motions
requires that he show restraint without knowing how restraint will benefit
him or God; though determined to do nothing more that will dishonor God,
he causes the Philistine crowd to praise Dagon; he performs as his captors
direct and moves through this shameful exhibition without any rational plan
apparent, sustained only by his confidence in his "rousing motions" while
he plays the fool in the triumph of his enemies.[24] His newfound antinomianism, call it his faith or his proleptic Christian liberty, frees him to suffer
indignity and risk blasphemy while he awaits the presaged "remarkable"
moment in his life (1387–88), sure that he will know it when it presents
itself: "For what concerns my knowledge God reveals."

Samson's decision to join the festivities of Dagon was an act of faith
greater than Phinehas's, who had to suffer no humiliation as prelude to his
action to protect God's honor. And it was greater than Jael's, Ehud's, or
Judith's (or Cromwell's), who could see that their lawbreaking would destroy tyrants, whereas Samson did not know what opportunity he would
have for redemption when he followed a powerful and holy impulse that
involved him in dishonoring God and himself for the pleasure of his enemies. Abraham earned his preeminent place in Hebrews, chapter xi, by
obeying without knowing—when God called him to leave his native land
Abraham "went out, not knowing whither he went" (8); in Samson Milton

created a hero like the father of the faithful, a man ready to follow commands that he believes to be divine without knowing whither he is going.

State University of New York at Binghamton

NOTES

1. The letter is dated from Cork on 1 January 1650: *The Writings and Speeches of Oliver Cromwell*, ed. W. C. Abbott, 4 vols. (Cambridge, Mass., 1937–47), vol. II, pp. 189–90. *Paradise Lost* VI, 36, and *Samson Agonistes*, 1751–52, in *John Milton: Complete Poems and Major Prose*, ed. Merritt Y. Hughes (New York, 1957). All further references to Milton's poetry are to this edition, and the line numbers will be cited in the text.

2. Blair Worden, "Milton, *Samson Agonistes*, and the Restoration," in *Culture and Society in the Stuart Restoration: Literature, Drama, History*, ed. Gerald MacLean (Cambridge, 1995), p. 132; *In God's Name*, ed. John Chandos (London, 1971), pp. 369, 374, 414; Christopher Hill, *The English Bible and the Seventeenth-Century Revolution* (Allen Lane, 1993), p. 91; Gilbert Burnet, *History of His Own Time*, 2 vols., ed. Osmund Airey (Oxford, 1897–1900), vol. I, p. 77. Thomas Edwards complains in *Gangraena* [London, 1646; rpt. Exeter, 1977], pt. 3, p. 170) that a sectarian book "highly magnified . . . the brasen-faced audacious old woman" Katherine Chidley by praising her as a Jael (apparently Edwards was Sisera).

3. Guillaume de Saluste du Bartas, *His Diuine Weekes, and Workes with a Compleate Collectiō of All the Other Most Delight-full Workes*, trans. Josvah Sylvester ([London], 1621), pp. 683, 719–20. Judith had read about Ehud but, feeling that she could not perform such a masculine deed, needed the revelation of Jael's deed to authorize her to act.

4. See Roland H. Bainton, "The Immoralities of the Patriarchs according to the Exegesis of the Late Middle Ages and of the Reformation," *HTR* XXIII (1930): 39–40 on antinomianism of Old Testament heroes. "Briefe Notes on Valdesso's *Considerations*," in *The Works of George Herbert*, ed. F. E. Hutchinson (Oxford, 1941), p. 316. Richard Hooker thought private inspirations insufficient unless God supported such claims by miracle or by inspiring the claimant with invincible arguments to prove them: *Of the Laws of Ecclesiastical Polity*, 2 vols. (London, 1964), vol. II, p. 37 (book 5, sect. X). In *Christian Doctrine* Milton shows no interest in how one can demonstrate that a particular command is divine; he says only that "God's command . . . is absolutely binding" and that Abraham was doing no more than his duty when he went to sacrifice his son: *Complete Prose Works of John Milton*, 8 vols, ed. Don M. Wolfe et al. (New Haven, 1953–82), vol. VI, p. 643. All references to Milton's prose are to this edition, cited parenthetically in the text as YP.

5. Samuel Butler, *Hudibras*, ed. John Wilders (Oxford, 1967), p. 133 (Second Part, Canto II, 231–40). Worden, "Milton, *Samson Agonistes*," pp. 132–33, shows how Edmund Ludlow, though deeply troubled by the wild behavior of some who claimed divine direction, hesitated to condemn them.

6. R. T. Kendall, *Calvin and English Calvinism to 1649* (Oxford, 1979), pp. 185–87; Laurence Clarkson, *The Lost Sheep Found* (London, 1660; rpt. Exeter, 1974), p. 27; *Creeds of the Churches*, ed. John H. Leith (Garden City, N.Y., 1963), pp. 115, 414, 269, 214; Johannes Wollebius, *Compendium Theologiae Christianae*, in *Reformed Dogmatics*, ed. and trans. John Beardslee III (New York, 1965), p. 76; *Puritanism and Liberty*, ed. A. S. P. Woodhouse, 2nd

ed. (Chicago, 1951), Introduction p. [65]n. Woodhouse thinks that Luther as well as Milton believed that Christ abrogated the whole Mosaic law (p. [65]), but in the passage Woodhouse cites (p. 224) from *Commentary upon Galatians,* Luther says only that Christ has delivered us from the curse of the Moral Law, from its power to accuse us and overwhelm us with guilt. As we shall see, Milton goes much further, denying that we are bound to obey the Law in every circumstance.

7. *Creeds of the Churches,* pp. 113–15. Luther concludes by leaving the obligatory force of the commandments very much in place: "God threatens to punish all who transgress these commandments. We should therefore fear his wrath and not disobey these commandments" (p. 115).

8. It will be clear by now that I accept the traditional attribution of *Christian Doctrine* to Milton. Those engaged in the debate about attribution may wish to compare the treatments of Phinehas and Abraham in the passages just cited from the treatise with the treatments of both heroes in the dramatic sketches I am about to discuss. They might agree with me that the emphasis on the antinomianism of these heroes in both *Christian Doctrine* and a manuscript notebook universally acknowledged to be Milton's encourages the view that the treatise is also Milton's.

9. Mary Ann Radzinowicz did not comment on the lines about Jael in *Toward "Samson Agonistes"* (Princeton, 1978), but in a later essay, "The Distinctive Tragedy of *Samson Agonistes,*" in *Milton Studies* XVII, ed. Richard S. Ide and Joseph Wittreich (Pittsburgh, 1983), p. 273, she appears to think that the play shows Jael's deed to be repugnant because neither the Chorus nor Samson speaks in favor of Jael and because (1112–13) Samson scorns Philistine ambushes. William Empson, *Milton's God,* rev. ed. (London, 1965), p. 221. John Carey, *Milton* (London, 1969), p. 143, without referring to Empson, seems to think that Dalila makes telling use of Jael. There is no mention of Jael in Irene Samuel, "*Samson Agonistes* as Tragedy," in *Calm of Mind,* ed. Joseph Anthony Wittreich Jr. (Cleveland, 1971), pp. 235–57; in Helen Damico, "Duality in Dramatic Vision: A Structural Analysis of *Samson Agonistes,*" in *Milton Studies* XII, ed. James D. Simmonds (Pittsburgh, 1978), pp. 91–116; or in Joseph Wittreich, *Interpreting "Samson Agonistes"* (Princeton, 1986).

10. See Samuel, "*Samson Agonistes* as Tragedy," 251–52; Wittreich, *Interpreting,* p. 312; and Stanley Fish, "Question and Answer in *Samson Agonistes,*" *Critical Quarterly* XI (1969): 258–59.

11. For discussion of God's hate and violence, see in this volume Michael Lieb, " 'Our Living Dread': The God of *Samson Agonistes,*" and especially his " 'Hate in Heav'n': Milton and the *Odium Dei,*" *ELH* LIII (1986): 519–39; also David Loewenstein, *Milton and the Drama of History* (Cambridge, 1990), esp. pp. 145–46, and Lieb, *Milton and the Culture of Violence* (Ithaca, 1994). Joan Bennett, *Reviving Liberty: Radical Christian Humanism in Milton's Great Poems* (Cambridge, Mass., 1989), p. 141; YP III, p. 532.

12. Despite Edward Tayler's argument in "Milton's Firedrake," *MQ* VI (1972): 7–10, that the dragon is not a serpent but a fiery phenomenon in the sky, I believe that the syntax makes the dragon the "assailant" of the fowl and that a serpent makes a better assailant than a portentous light in the heavens. My larger point is not affected whether one believes the predator is serpent or eagle.

13. John Bunyan, *The Pilgrim's Progress,* 2nd ed., ed. James B. Wharey (Oxford, 1960), p. 54; [Joseph Hall], *Contemplations vpon the Principall Passages of the Holy Storie* (London, 1625), p. 977. As for Jael's "idle fancies of civility," Milton declares that "we are not forbidden to tell lies, as often as need be, to those who have not earned the name of neighbor" (YP VI, p. 762) and uses the Jael story to support the idea (p. 764).

14. John Steadman, "Milton's '*Summa* Epitasis': The End of the Middle of *Samson Agonistes*," *MLR* LXIX (1974): 731–32.

15. In *Christian Doctrine* (YP VI, p. 697), Milton names Phinehas as an example of zeal, the "eager desire to sanctify the divine name, together with a feeling of indignation against things which tend to the violation or contempt of religion." He does not name Samson, who shows no particular zeal in Judges.

16. Wittreich, *Interpreting*, p. 69, thinks this lawbreaking is meant to show that Samson is not a proper judge; Damico, "Duality," pp. 105, 107, considers the lawbreaking to be a demonstration that the motions are not divine in origin and that the destruction of the temple is willed by Samson, not God. I hope that my essay will go some way toward showing how hopelessly "carnal" such views of the play are.

17. T. S. Eliot, "Thoughts after Lambeth," in *Selected Essays: 1917–32* (New York, 1932), p. 320; I owe this reference to Alan Rudrum, *A Critical Commentary on Milton's "Samson Agonistes"* (London, 1969), p. 27. The critics I have in mind are Fish, "Question and Answer," 242–43, who thinks the question of Samson's marriage motivation is unresolved in the play and considers "wayward passion" to be one possibility; John T. Shawcross, "The Genesis of *Paradise Regained* and *Samson Agonistes*: The Wisdom of Their Joint Publication," in *Milton Studies* XVII, ed. Richard S. Ide and Joseph Wittreich (Pittsburgh, 1983), p. 243; Damico, "Duality," p. 106; and Albert C. Labriola, "Divine Urgency as a Motive for Conduct in *Samson Agonistes*," *PQ* L (1971): 100–03, who argues that the marriages were divinely urged in that God hardened Samson's heart after he lusted for the alien women.

18. Samuel, "*Samson Agonistes* as Tragedy," pp. 249–50; Damico, "Duality," p. 107. My discussion owes much to Labriola's insight ("Divine Urgency," 106–07) that the "rousing motions" cannot be thought to be like the impulse to marry sexually attractive women because, since the feast of Dagon is repulsive to Samson, going there is not a natural instinct that can be mistaken for a divine command.

19. Merritt Y. Hughes's note on the lines is not useful. It refers us to *Christian Doctrine* (YP VI, p. 694) where Milton says there can be such a dispensation if it is necessary for the performance of some civil duty, but Samson has made it clear (1363–67) that he has no duty in the temple. Christopher Grose, " 'His Uncontrollable Intent': Discovery as Action in *Samson Agonistes*," in *Milton Studies* VII, ed. Albert C. Labriola and Michael Lieb (Pittsburgh, 1975), pp. 62–63, believes these lines about dispensations reveal the content of the "presage in the mind" and the "rousing motions" that Samson speaks of later.

20. Wittreich, *Interpreting*, p. 359; Samuel, "*Samson Agonistes* as Tragedy," p. 246; Weber, "The Worldly End of Samson," in *Milton Studies* XXVI, ed. James D. Simmonds (Pittsburgh, 1990), pp. 292–93; Kerrigan, "The Irrational Coherence of *Samson Agonistes*," in *Milton Studies* XXII, ed. James D. Simmonds (Pittsburgh, 1986), p. 223. Both Weber and Kerrigan think God put a scheme into Samson's mind, but they are not clear about how God accomplished this and, more important, how we know he did so.

21. Radzinowicz, *Toward "Samson Agonistes,"* p. 349, asserts "the reasonableness of Samson's 'rouzing motions' " and that Samson comes to a rational conception of God. Joan Bennett's more extended discussion, *Reviving Liberty* (Cambridge, Mass., 1989), pp. 137, 107, argues that the motions are rational in that "Milton's God inspires rational creatures with reason." Bennett's Christian humanist analysis of how believers use their rectified reason to deal with difficult moral problems is often cogent, but does not adequately handle such nonrational inspirations as Samson's motions surely are.

22. Labriola, "Divine Urgency," 107, and Bennett, *Reviving Liberty*, pp. 136–37, think Samson humbles himself in the temple; Damico, "Duality," p. 109, thinks he merely disgraces

himself; Hugh MacCallum, "*Samson Agonistes:* The Deliverer as Judge," in *Milton Studies* XXIII, ed. James D. Simmonds (Pittsburgh, 1987), p. 283, sees that he endures humiliation, but supposes that he is thereby trying to catch the Philistines off guard. Only Mason Tung, "Samson Impatiens: A Reinterpretation of *Samson Agonistes*," *TSLL* IX (1967): 490–91, emphasizes that Samson's public display disglorifies God and reads it as God's test of his patience and obedience.

23. Balachandra Rajan, *The Lofty Rhyme: A Study of Milton's Major Poetry* (Coral Gables, 1970), p. 142.

24. Barbara Lewalski, "Milton's *Samson* and the 'New Acquist of True [Political] Experience'," in *Milton Studies* XXIV, ed. James D. Simmonds (Pittsburgh, 1988), p. 244, is one of a number of critics who sees Samson as without a plan when he leaves for the temple, but in a posture "of openness to further illumination"; others are Anthony Low, *The Blaze of Noon* (New York, 1974), p. 80, and N. H. Keeble, *The Literary Culture of Nonconformity in Later Seventeenth-Century England* (Leicester, 1987), pp. 195–96. Rajan, *The Lofty Rhyme*, pp. 141–45, Tung, "Samson Impatiens," 490–92, and Hugh M. Richmond, *The Christian Revolutionary: John Milton* (Berkeley, 1974), pp. 185–90, all take a position like this and develop from it their own views of Samson's final state of mind. David Loewenstein's essay in this volume, "The Revenge of the Saint: Radical Religion and Politics in *Samson Agonistes*," shows how the saints expected God's providence to be mysterious and knew they had to act amid uncertainties. Stanley Fish's stimulating "Spectacle and Evidence in *Samson Agonistes*," *Critical Inquiry* XV (1989): 556–86, gives a reading of Samson's final state of mind with which I have much sympathy (especially his use of Abraham on p. 579), though I see Samson as more God-directed than does Fish and thus not so radically alone.

JUST MEASURES? VERSIFICATION IN
SAMSON AGONISTES

Janel Mueller

Tragedy, as it was antiently compos'd, hath been ever held the gravest, moralest, and most profitable of all other Poems: therefore said by *Aristotle* to be of power by raising pity and fear, or terror, to purge the mind of those and such like passions, that is to temper and reduce them to just measure.

John Milton, preface to *Samson Agonistes* (1671)[1]

N O L E S S T H A N in its thematics and character portrayals, *Samson Agonistes* (arguably the last product of Milton's arduous career of poetic experimentation) has proven a contested object among would-be analysts of its prosody. Some significant recent advances, however, have been made in understanding how historical rules for composing in a particular verse form might be conjoined with contemporary developments in metrical theory and its formalizations for representing the set of specific licenses and constraints that individuate a poet's practice, line after line, in a given work. In this essay I will undertake to show that a comprehensive and self-consistent description can be made of the verse design that governs Milton's composition in *Samson Agonistes* (including the limits of this design in deviations and unmetricality); I will proceed thereafter to argue for a no less comprehensive and self-consistent expressivity in Milton's prosodic effects. I hope to make a case that Milton's verse design encodes crucial and crucially overlooked pointers for interpreting *Samson Agonistes,* both through what it offers by way of stable connotations and through what it signals as irresolvable sites of indeterminacy or of outright violation within the drama's shifting sequence of local contexts.

1

In *Milton's Prosody* Robert Bridges reached the conclusion that, despite its subtitle, "A Dramatic Poem," *Samson Agonistes* lacked a consistent verse design: the whole was an intermixture of what he called "rising" and "falling" (or iambic and trochaic) line rhythms. Bridges considered that the drama's variable line lengths posed special complications for metrical analysis.

While he reviewed other features of the verse—Milton's practices regarding so-called reversed feet and elided syllables—as intelligible extensions of the principles followed in *Paradise Lost* and *Paradise Regained,* Bridges was unable to find adequate precedent in those poems for what he wanted to establish as a species of blank (although intermittently rhymed) verse in *Samson Agonistes.*[2] S. Ernest Sprott sought to challenge what had become Bridges's influential claim that *Samson Agonistes* exhibited at most only local system and regularity. Sprott's ascription of a single, comprehensive verse design to the drama depended, however, on a far too lax provision. He argued that *Samson Agonistes* could be regarded as basically iambic pentameter verse if further allowance were made for free substitution within the iambic design of what he termed "monosyllabic feet"—that is, feet consisting of one stressed syllable only.[3] It is obvious how potent a resource "monosyllabic feet" would be in any two-valued system, iambic or trochaic, but it is equally obvious that the free substitution of monosyllabic feet in any such system would be its destruction. To allow an alternating pattern to be broken off and replaced at any point by a single-valued element is tantamount to saying that anything goes. Thus Sprott's proposed solution only aggravated the problem with which Bridges had wrestled—the impression that *Samson Agonistes* lacked inclusive and consistent metrical form. It was this sense of insoluable difficulty that James Holly Hanford impressed upon generations of students: "The variations from the iambic pattern are so great that one is inclined to abandon the attempt to recognize a theoretical conformity to this English pattern and consider them frankly as a reproduction of Greek and Roman rhythms."[4]

F. T. Prince gave a direct answer to Hanford's call for a different paradigm, although not by way of Greek and Roman rhythms. Prince argued that Milton's verse designs owed much in their earlier phases to Renaissance Italian composers of *canzone,* lyrics employing variable line lengths and rhyme schemes, and in the later phases of the heroic poems to the Italian epic form known as *versi sciolti.* The basic unit of *versi sciolti* is an unrhymed eleven-syllable line (*hendacasillabo*) in a dominant iambic or rising rhythm that requires a strong lexical stress in the tenth position of the line and another in either the fourth or the sixth position. Prince argued further that the "verbal devices" specifically endorsed by Torquato Tasso in his *Discorsi del Poema Eroico* were adopted by Milton as a three-point "prosodic system" to be applied in the English of his own epic verse. As formulated by Prince these points include (1) "the clogging of the verse by means of accumulated consonants"; (2) "the conjunction of open vowels, which may be . . . either (a) elided, or (b) unelided"; (3) "the use of double consonants in the penultimate syllables [that is, the stressed tenth position] of the line." The particular significance of Prince's emphasis on Italian influences in Miltonic versification appears large if *Samson Agonistes* is taken to be Milton's last poem, for Prince's study projects an evolutionary, cumulative dynamic that could disclose in this "dramatic Poem" a climactic synthesizing of the compositional models of the *canzone* and *versi sciolti* in Renaissance Italian theory and practice.[5]

Prince's revisionary approach to the analysis of constitutive formal features in Milton's poetry had a deservedly large impact in several areas of study. The broadest of these was, simply, the serious pursuit of the interpretive significance of those repeated references where Milton uniquely ranks Italian poets and theorists together with classical counterparts, whether in *Of Education* invoking "that sublime art which in *Aristotles poetics*, in *Horace*, and the *Italian* commentaries of *Castelvetro, Tasso, Mazzoni*, and others, teaches what the laws are of a true *Epic* poem, what of a *Dramatic*, what of a *Lyric*, what decorum is, which is the grand masterpiece to observe" or in the preface to *Samson Agonistes* declaring, by comparison with current English playwrights, that "in the modelling . . . of this Poem, with good reason, the Antients and *Italians* are rather follow'd, as of much more authority and fame."[6] In my judgment, however, the greatest impetus to reconsideration and further analysis has stemmed from the emphasis Prince laid on two features that Milton ostensibly adapted from Tasso and made very prominent in his own later poetry: sequential "open vowels" (that is, vowels with no intervening consonantal sounds) and clusters of "double" or "accumulated consonants" (that is, consonants with no intervening vowel sounds).

If multiple contiguous vowels and multiple contiguous consonants are considered in the abstract as a pair of basic prosodic elements, it is obvious that they stand to one another in the alternating or contrast relation on which the creation of all rhythmic patterning in poetry depends. Yet within Milton's verse composition the specific roles and effects of these two elements maintain no such complementary pairing. Multiple contiguous consonants affect the tempo of an already signaled rhythmic pattern, "clogging" the verse, as Prince aptly says, and producing an evocatively muscular, strenuous texture in numerous lines of *Samson Agonistes*. Later I will discuss what I take to be some chief interpretive implications of the frequent occurrences of multiple contiguous consonants in the drama; here I will merely illustrate the phenomenon (boldface indicates consonant clusters):

> Bound with two cords; but cords to me were threds (261)
> Then thine, while I preserv'd these locks unshorn (1143)
> Thir once great dread, captive, and blind before them (1474)

Although multiple contiguous consonants make for difficulty in pronouncing the verse lines, they do leave the sense of metrical pattern intact. Multiple contiguous vowels, however, work their effects at a much more fundamental level of poetic form—that of the rhythm itself—by constantly raising the possibility of elision. The optional variation presented by elision—whether to collapse two syllables into the sound value of one or to leave them as two—can profoundly destabilize any sense of metrical pattern that has not been clearly established at other sites in the line or by other lines whose rhythm has been rendered unambiguous by eliminating possibilities for elision within them. A few examples will illustrate the metrical uncertainty that multiple elidable vowels (indicated in boldface) can produce:

At my affliction, and perhaps to insult (113) [p'rhaps? or: t'insult?]
From forth this loathsom prison-house to abide (922) [pris'n? or: t'abide?]
Conceiv'd, agreeable to a Fathers love (1506) [agree'ble? or: to'a?]

In fact, the activation of phonetic conditions that make elision a genuinely available—that is, a pronounceable—option in English is so prominent a feature of Milton's versification in *Samson Agonistes* that it encompasses a range of other local environments where two syllables of a line may become one or remain two. More than any other feature or combination of poetic features it was this amplitude of possibility for elision that brought Bridges to conclude that *Samson Agonistes* had only shifting runs of iambic and trochaic rhythms. Presumably the same amplitude of possibility for elision and its accompanying effects of metrical uncertainty prompted Prince's conclusion that Milton in his English heroic poems was writing in the comparatively permissive meter of *versi sciolti*. This is the point, therefore, to consider the descriptive accuracy and adequacy of Prince's claim. The *hendacasillabo* line unit of *versi sciolti* can be schematized as a sequence of eleven positions, with obligatory strong stresses in the tenth position and in either the fourth or the sixth position. The numbers and letters below the position marks specify the contrasts between s (strong) and w (weak) stresses that are required of the linguistic material filling those positions if the material rhythm of the line is to be perceptible:

verso sciolto   ___ ___ ___ ___ ___ ___ ___ ___ ___ ___ ___
                  3w   4s   5w   6s   9w   10s 11w

Minimal condition: 10s and either 4s and 6s

Lines that register straightforwardly as eleven-syllable units meeting these rhythmic specifications comprise a sizeable group of 253 instances in

Samson Agonistes and, as such, can be taken to support maximally Prince's claim that Milton's compositional model is *versi sciolti*. Examples include:

> By how much from the top of wondrous glory (167)
> Spare that proposal, Father, spare the trouble (487)
> I came, still dreading thy displeasure, *Samson* (733)
> So let her go, God sent her to debase me (999)
> And sense distract, to know well what I utter (1556)

However, it rapidly becomes evident that a far more sizeable group of lines (by my count, 1042 of a total of 1758) both unambiguously contain only ten, not eleven syllables and also typically actualize—that is, make audible—more stress contrasts in iambic rhythm than the minimum of two required for *versi sciolti*. Examples of this group include:

> A little onward lend thy guiding hand (1)
> The work to which I was divinely called (226)
> In feeble hearts propense anough before (455)
> It was the force of Conquest; force with force (1206)
> What noise or shout was that? it tore the Skie (1472)

Lines of this rhythmical type, by far the largest group in *Samson Agonistes*, doubly fail to meet the criteria for *versi sciolti*, for they are on the one hand deficient (lacking a weak eleventh syllable) and on the other excessive (they contain more stressed syllables in s positions than the form requires). As Edward Weismiller has roundly declared, echoing M. Whitely, in his rejection of Prince's case for *versi sciolti* as the underlying rhythmic structure of Miltonic versification, "A theory should fit the facts."[7] Relevant compositional facts go beyond these that I offer as indicative here, and altogether they point to English iambic pentameter as the best candidate for the verse design of *Samson Agonistes* on the grounds of adequacy and accuracy alike. O. B. Hardison, in a significant revision of Prince, argues that, to the extent that Italian *versi sciolti* were adapted and assimilated into English, they were simply one of two principal prototypes for what became a verse form in its own right: English iambic pentameter.[8] Sprott endorsed iambic pentameter as the compositional model for the verse of *Samson Agonistes* in the face of Bridges's and Hanford's sense of merely local, intermittent patternings in rising (iambic) or falling (trochaic) rhythms. Clearly the challenge is to preserve Sprott's central insight into Milton's compositional principles without resorting to the monosyllabic feet that voided his claim to the systematic comprehensiveness that is the sine qua non of any metrical analysis. But how might such a challenge be met?

Linguistically oriented approaches to the study of versification, espe-

cially the work of Paul Kiparsky, show that two interrelated things are required.[9] On the one hand, there must be an abstract representation of the
basic verse form in a so-called verse design. This is a general pattern for the
poetic lines of a given work that specifies how to arrange linguistic material
in a sequence of "weak" and "strong" positions in order to produce a given
metrical rhythm and also provides for certain optional variations in such
features as line length (reckoned by numbers of rhythmical units) and caesu-
ral placement (one or more breaks in the even alternation of the contrasting
positions in the line). On the other hand, the verse design needs to be com-
plemented by a set of so-called correspondence rules to link abstract design
with concrete practice—either of a school of poets or of a given poet. My
focus will be the latter: to stipulate exactly how the syllabic stress values of
the actual English words and phrases in Milton's poetic lines count as satisfying (or as violating) the individuated features of the verse design for *Samson Agonistes*.

It is the job of correspondence rules to denote that a line unit respects
both word and phrase boundaries in the language by virtually never ending
in the middle of one or the other, while also frequently overriding clause
boundaries (in the phenomenon conventionally called enjambment). Correspondence rules additionally encompass what the poet's lines show to be
the work's rhythmical range by specifying how syllables must be positioned
in order to make the pattern of lines perceptible through stress contrasts as
well as the variations that can be allowed without breaking the overall metrical pattern—for example, permissible sites for so-called stress reversal
(here, a trochee for an iamb), for two strongly stressed syllables in succession, and weak intervals of two or more successive syllables that lack strong
stress. It is also the job of such rules to specify the sound conditions under
which the poet opts for elision and treats two syllables in the language as
prosodically one in the verse.

If the verse design and the correspondence rules are correctly formulated for a given work, then the interesting and potentially highly expressive
categories of metrical complexity and unmetricality come into sharp relief.
The metrical analyst will be able to identify what, in a poet of Milton's
stature, will be both the (necessarily small) class of lines that show as unmetrical because they violate the limits of possibilities for matching syllables,
words, and phrases with the pattern of stress contrasts encoded in the verse
design and the (considerably larger) class of lines produced by the exercise
of multiple options for complicating the basic, most neutral realization of
the verse design within the confines of the single line unit. I will be arguing
that unmetrical and metrically complex lines make important contributions
to the rhythmical effects that key interpretive cues in *Samson Agonistes*.

To resume, then, the argument for iambic pentameter as the basic compositional norm of Milton's drama, I propose the following formulation as a first approximation of its verse design:

iambic pentameter ___ ___ | ___ ___ | ___ ___ | ___ ___ | ___ ___ | (___)
                  1w   2s | 3w   4s | 5w   6s | 7w   8s | 9w 10s | (11w)
                  [[PHRASE [WORD]]] . . . [[PHRASE [WORD]]]] [[PHRASE [WORD] . . . [WORD]]]

Parentheses enclose optional elements; this formulation makes basic a sequence of linguistic material that counts as a ten-syllable iambic line but permits one with an eleventh syllable bearing weak stress (a conventionally termed "feminine" ending). Single square brackets signal lexical word boundaries, double square brackets signal phrase boundaries, triple square brackets signal the convergence of a lexical word and phrase boundary, quadruple square brackets signal the convergence of a lexical word boundary with two phrase boundaries—say those of a verb phrase and a prepositional phrase—all notations indicating that this is a verse design, a model for sequences of English words and phrases, and that Milton matches line beginnings and endings to both.

Even this barely begun specification of a verse design for *Samson Agonistes* permits testing against the lines of the work, and their testing against the verse design. In 1758 lines there are only three exceptions to Milton's otherwise unbroken respect for phrase boundaries in his placement of line end breaks: "It would be to ensnare [[an [irreligious] / [[Dishonorer]]]] of Dagon" (860–61) and "And of my Nation [[[[chose] thee]] [from among / [[My [enemies]]]], lov'd thee" (877–78), "Exempt [[from [[many] [[a [care]]]] [and [[[chance]]]] [[to which / [[Eye-sight]]]] exposes daily men abroad" (918–19).[10] On analogy with metrical violation I regard these unique instances as syntactic violations, forms classed as anomalous by the criterion of the verse design that in turn signal anomalies within the drama. In equating irreligion with dishonor to the Philistine god Dagon, lines 860–61 clash sharply with the monotheistic, Hebraic outlook that the drama elsewhere enforces. The more anomalous ending of line 877 in two prepositions ("from among"), weakly stressed functional elements rather than a phrase and lexical word boundary, evokes the strain and tenuousness of Samson's choice of Dalila as his wife. And the most minimal line ending of all, the preposition and relative pronoun "to which," dissolving into the initial stress reversal of "Eye-sight" in the next line, doubly belies the slippery sophistry with which Dalila is plying Samson: that to be sighted is a more dangerous state than to be blind. I offer these examples to suggest the kind of poetic expressiveness that concerns me in the latter part of this essay, and take my rationale for thus proceeding from Milton's own reference to "just measure with a

kind of delight, stirr'd up by reading or seeing . . . passions well imitated"
in the preface to *Samson Agonistes*. Specifically I understand the "just measure" of "passions well imitated" to consist not merely in plot design, character portrayal, and thematic development but to extend profoundly to verse
measures written by Milton under the same demands of emotional and psychological verisimilitude.

My proposed verse design incorporates pairings of stress contrasts as
formal units that correspond to "feet" in traditional prosody. What kind of
entity such a two-valued pair might be and how it might function in prosodic
analysis remain contested issues on which one can only take a position and
give one's reasons for it. I incorporate iambic feet in the abstract formulation
of this verse design to provide a measure by which the mind and ear can
monitor the succession of patterning in a line, which absolutely depends on
being able to track whether the stress contrasts are actualized by its linguistic elements or not. Although his vocabulary differs from mine, Edward
Weismiller pronounces admirably for my purposes on the nature and utility
of a verse design formulated with two-valued units of stress contrasts:

The . . . idea that the English line . . . is *notionally* iambic supposes the existence of
an abstract x/| x/| x/| x/| x/, a 'norm' or 'base' in a kind of continuing counterpoint to
which we hear each successive line. The idea is widely held, and seems harmless;
something of the kind must even be true, since inversion of accent, for example,
would scarcely attract our attention if when we heard it we were not as sharply
aware of what /x is not as of what it is. Note, however, that *being aware* of difference
implies no correction of what we hear; most rhythmic differences we welcome, indeed, and correction is not desired, far less required.[11]

Weismiller's insistence that there be no overriding of the normal pronounciation of words to make them conform to a metrical beat also captures
the principle that the phonological rules for ordinary stress assignment in
words and phrases of English continue to apply in all matchings of linguistic
elements with positions in the verse design. In simply assuming that the
rhythms of *Samson Agonistes* will be perceptible and pronounceable to a
native speaker of English as verified by his or her ability to pick up and read
aloud a text never seen before, I am building on Noam Chomsky's notion,
so central to generative linguistics, of the "linguistic competence" that
marks what anyone who is a native speaker of any language knows about it.
Hence I consider it unnecessary to rehearse the precise technical formulations that have been given for the stress assignment rules of English when
I can legitimately presuppose these to hold for myself and the readers I
envisage.[12] That presupposition underlies my statement of my first pair of
correspondence rules:

Correspondence Rule 1—[WORD] Rule: In a verse line, enclose with word boundary signs [ ] all members of so-called major or lexical categories: nouns, notional verbs and verbals, adjectives, and adverbs derived from adjectives (including, for all these categories, individual enclosure of the members of compounds). Every such [WORD] will bear primary lexical stress on one of its syllables as determined by the rules for stress assignment in English.

Correspondence Rule 2—[[PHRASE]] Rule: In a verse line, divide the linguistic material fully into its noun phrases, verb phrases (including participles and infinitives), adjective phrases (including gerundives and relative constructions), adverbial phrases, and prepositional phrases [[ ]]. A [[PHRASE]] is comprised of a core [WORD] bearing primary phrasal stress plus all other elements which are grouped with the [WORD] in speech, including members of so-called minor or nonlexical categories: definite and indefinite articles, pronouns, prepositions, conjunctions, and nonnotional verbs (copulas, modals, and auxiliaries). Phrase divisions must be well formed—that is, no linguistic material may be overlapped across a [[PHRASE]] division, all of the linguistic material of a sentence in verse must be exhausted by [[PHRASE]] divisions, and the rhythmic contour of a [[PHRASE]] must be determined by the rules for stress assignment, promotion, and demotion in English.

Application of these two correspondence rules to the three examples of verse lines below yields line-internal divisions as indicated. The utility of these divisions for specifying the range of permissible variety in actualizing metrical stress contrasts will emerge later. Here it will suffice to note that the word-end and phrase-end boundaries signaled by]]] or]]]] under application of the second correspondence rule mark possible sites for so-called caesura, or a metrically significant phrase break, which accordingly becomes an optional feature of the verse design.

[[She [[proving] [false]]]] [[the [next]]] [[I [[[took]]] [to [[wife]]]] (227)
[[To [[folly]]]] [[and [shameful] [[deeds]]]] [[which [[ruin]] [[ends]]]] (1043)
[[[Horribly] [loud]]] [[unlike [the [[former] [[shout]]]] (1510)

Correspondence Rules 1 and 2 can be formalized thus in relation to the verse design:

$$_x[[\text{PHRASE} \ldots _y[\text{WORD}]] \ldots]]] [[\text{PHRASE} \ldots [\text{WORD}] \ldots]]]$$

$$\underline{\quad} \ \underline{\quad} \ \underline{\quad} \ \underline{\quad} \ \underline{\quad} \ \underline{\quad} \ (||)_z \ \underline{\quad} \ \underline{\quad} \ \underline{\quad} \ \underline{\quad} \ (\underline{\quad})$$

iambic pentameter [[1w 2s | 3w 4s | 5w 6s | 7w 8s | 9w 10s | (11w)]]

[[PHRASE [WORD]]] ... [[PHRASE [WORD]]]] [[PHRASE [WORD]] ... [WORD]]]]

Values of variables: x = up to 5 [[PHRASE]] units per line
y = up to 5 [WORD] units per line

z = up to 4 caesuras, the number of options being
contingent on line-internal occurrences of]]]

What these two correspondence rules for words and phrases make a matter of deepest compositional principle is a perception that any native speaker or reader can readily confirm. Poets working in historical eras prior to modernist and postmodernist experimentation do not violate fundamental linguistic givens; rather they create extra, optional orderings within the patterns already present in the language at large. This principle gains special force in Milton's verse because of his frequent use of words of more than one syllable. If these must bear the stress contours in the verse that they take in English speech, as the correspondence rules specify, polysyllabic words should emerge as vital indicators of the meter encoded in the abstract verse design. In Seymour Chatman's cogent formulation, they will prove to be "meter-fixing."[13]

The first two correspondence rules hold unproblematically for the metrical placement of very many polysyllabic words and phrases in the lines of *Samson Agonistes*. Proper names, for example, are always placed so as to fix the meter; thus the reader knows to say Dálila (229–), Mánoah (329–), Phílistine(s) (251–), but Philístian (39, 42, 216, 482, 722, 831, 1371, 1655, 1714). Since most of the polysyllables occur, moreover, in ten- or eleven-syllable lines with a perceptible pattern of rising rhythm (weak-strong ordering of stress contrasts), this body of evidence resoundingly confirms the case for iambic pentameter as Milton's verse design. Here is a sampling of the simplest type of instances:

Divine Prediction; what if all foretold (44)
Immeasurable strength they might behold (206)
To matchless valour, and adventures high (1740)

Polysyllabic words in *Samson Agonistes* do not always exhibit a directly meter-affirming relation to a presumptive iambic pentameter verse design, however. One reason for this is the existence of some historical differences in how stress was assigned to certain lexical words in Milton's day and in our own. Although stress is one of the most tenacious features of language structure, *Oxford English Dictionary* entries verify that some words were introduced into English from French or Latin marked with their stress assignment in those languages, which they retained into later periods until speakers of English naturalized them further by giving them an English stress assignment. Here are some illustrations (boldface marks lexical stress):

This unfreqúented place to find some ease (17) [from freqúent, v.]
Betray'd, Captív'd, and both my Eyes put out (33) [from captíve, v.]
From intimate impúlse, and therefore urg'd (223) [from Lat. impúlsus]
Full of divine instínct, after some proof (525) [from Lat. instínctus; cf. 1545]
Most shines, and most is ácceptable above (1052)[14]

There is also the historical difference registered in so-called stress doublets, words that could take either of two stress assignments at an earlier date in English but now can take only one. *Samson Agonistes* contains the following stress doublets with their accompanying metrical uncertainty for a present-day reader: the noun *éxploits | explóits* (32, 525, 1492), the adverb *ádverse | advérse* (192), the noun *préscript | prescrípt* (308), the verb *gángrene | gangréne* (622; signaled as such by *Webster's International Dictionary*), the verb *impórtune | importúne* (775, 797), the adverb *cóntrary | contráry* (973), the adjective *éxpert | expért* (1044), the noun *cómrades | comrádes* (1162), and the noun *díscharge | dischárge* (1573).

However, as has been well recognized since Bridges, the major source of metrical uncertainty regarding polysyllables in Milton's heroic verse is the high incidence of elision, to which I have already referred. Although more technically precise terms (synaloepha, syneresis) are available, I am content to use Bridges's term *elision* as long as I am understood to mean by it the prosodic collapsing of two contiguous syllables into one, under phonetic conditions that hold at large in ordinary English and make the resulting compound pronounceable (though not necessarily pronounced by every reader) as the single syllable it now counts for by being matched to a single position in the verse design.

While pronounceability by a speaker of English is its defining feature, elision has its textual signals also; in *Samson Agonistes* these include the apostrophe and shortened spellings like "embattelld" (130) or "Deprest" (1698) as marks of contraction. The 1671 print of the drama marks no fewer than 484 elisions, or metrical coassignments of two syllables of the language to one verse position, and by my analysis an unsignalled additional 395 elisions or metrical coassignments, all of them satisfying the criterion of pronounceability, require to be made in conformity both with the principle that linguistic stress assignment in polysyllabic words is preserved, not wrenched by the positioning they are given in a poetic line and with the linguistic evidence of other kinds that the basic verse design of *Samson Agonistes* is iambic pentameter. Obviously statistical evidence of such magnitude resists rehearsal here. Instead I will give an informal account of the local sound environments in word and phrase structure where Milton can and often does exercise the option of elision. Consider the following lines that could count straightforwardly as iambic pentameter if the vowels pronounceable as a single syllable (here marked with boldface) were elided, that is, coassigned to a single metrical position:

> For this did the Angel thrice descend, for this (361) [= th'Angel]
> Afford me assassinated and betray'd (1109) [= m'assassinated]
> Defie thee to the trial of mortal fight (1175) [= tri'al]
>
> *Chalybean* temper'd steel and frock of mail (133) [= Chalybe'an]
> Ordain'd thy nurture holy as of a Plant (363) [= holy'as]
> Unmanly, ignominious, infamous (417) [= ignomini'ous]
>
> Soften'd with pleasure and voluptuous life (534) [= voluptuous]
> To lesson or extenuate my offence (767) [= exten'uate]
> Tacit was in thy power; true; and thou bear'st (430) [= pow'r]

The first group of lines above exhibits the aurally simplest type of elision; two contiguous vowels blend into a single vowel sound under metrical co-assignment. The next two groups illustrate the phenomenon that Bridges called "consonantalization," that is, two contiguous vowels under metrical coassignment blend their independent sound values into what he rather impressionistically termed "y-glide" (the second group) and "w-glide" (the third group). Y-glide is a common type of Miltonic elision, w-glide less so.[15]

The phenomenon of consonantalization can be regarded as a type of elision intermediate between that of contiguous vowels with no intervening consonant and that of two vowels with an intervening consonant. In English, pronounceable elision can take place across the following consonants: the sonorants comprising the aspirant |h| (even more easily if it is unvoiced), the liquids |l|, |bl|, and |r|, and the nasals |m|, |n|, and |nd|; additional sites include the fricatives |v|, |s|, and |s = z|. At a number of points in *Samson Agonistes* the verse design calls upon all of these possible environments for elision as a means of actualizing lines that fit the iambic pentameter norm. Here are single illustrations of each (again with the site of elision marked in boldface):

> v|h|v: To the hazard of thy brains and shattered sides (1241) [= th'hazard]
> v|l|v: Miraculous yet remaining in those locks (587) [= Mirac'lous]
> v|bl|v: This day will be remarkable in my life (1388) [= remark'ble]
> v|r|v: Then who self-rigorous chooses death as due (513) [= rig'rous]
> v|m|v: And he in that calamitous prison left (1480) [= calam'tous]
> v|n|v: She's gone, a manifest Serpent by her sting (997) [= man'fest]
> v|nd|v: Mangle my apprehensive tenderest parts (624) [= tend'rest]
> v|v|v: True slavery, and that blindness worse then this (418) [= slav'ry]
> v|s|v: To gloss upon, and censuring, frown or smile (948) [= cens'ring]
> v|s = z|v: The close of all my miseries, and the balm (651) [= mis'ries]

In concluding this overview of the role of elision in *Samson Agonistes* it is fair to say that, while in certain instances this feature produces metrical uncertainty, its much more common effect is to conform the linguistic material of a verse instance to an iambic pentameter norm, even by multiple applications of elision within a single line. Here are typical examples:

> Should *Israel* from *Philistian* yoke deliver (39)
> Which many a famous Warriour overturns (542)
> With touch aetherial of Heav'ns fiery rod (549)
> Offering to combat thee his Champion bold (1152)
> To appear as fits before th'illustrious Lords (1318)

Among other kinds of meter-fixing polysyllables, compound words and phrases occupy a significant place even though their rhythmic effects are made more complex by the succession of two primary lexical stresses that they frequently incorporate. When Milton places compounds inside a verse—that is, neither at beginnings nor at endings in pentameter lines—he standardly respects the rule of stress reduction in spoken English that leaves only one lexical stress of a compound construction at full, primary strength. That is to say, he positions compounds so as to produce least disruption and most reinforcement for the patterning set by his verse design. Thus:

Lower then bondslave! Promise was that I (38)
      s   w

In wedlock a reproach; I gain'd a Son (353)
  s w

As with compound nouns, so too with the line-internal placement of compound adjectives. In English at large these are subject to a phrasal stress reduction rule that requires the noun they modify to take primary stress and the stress values of the compound adjective to adjust accordingly. Milton's compound adjectives are so positioned as to maximally affirm an iambic rhythm:

Heav'n-gifted strength (36)
 w   s w   s

first created Beam (83)
 s   ws w s

self-displeas'd (514)
 s   w s

oft-invocated death (575)

w s w   sw   s

seven-times-folded shield (1722)

s   w   s   w   s

The point holds likewise for compound verbs with monosyllabic first members and for monosyllabic verb + particle constructions. The general effect of the rule of phrasal stress assignment that governs them in English is to locate primary stress as close to the end of the phrase as possible. Thus the predicted metrical placement for both types would be w s, and this prediction is confirmed by the bulk of examples of these constructions in *Samson Agonistes.* From among numerous instances I cite:

subserve (57)

w   s

withstand (127)

w   s

withdrew (192)

w   s

shipwreck'd (198)

w   s

o'erwhelm (320)

w   s

pull'd up (141)

w   s

draw nigh (178)

w   s

put out (33)

w   s

cut off (1157)

w s

Thus far I have focused on the considerable resources afforded by polysyllables for pattern making in the English language and Milton's use of these to signal and sustain iambic pentameter as the basic compositional norm of *Samson Agonistes.* These and other practices of his need to be formulated in further correspondence rules for matching syllables of words and phrases to positions in the verse design. Before I do this, however, it is equally necessary to make an adjustment in the formulation of the verse design to allow for the option of variable line lengths that Milton exercises in 254 of the 1758 lines of his drama. Again the scope of the evidence makes feasible only a summary of the systematic result of applying the same poly-syllabic placement and elision rules in the nonpentameter lines. The result is eight two-foot iambic lines, seventy three-foot iambic lines (with another ten lines adding a feminine ending to the third foot), eighty-three four-foot iambic lines (with another six lines adding a feminine ending to the fourth foot), and twenty-eight six-foot iambic lines (with another one adding a femi-nine ending to the sixth foot). In all, 242 of the 254 nonpentameter lines concur with the pentameter lines, that vast majority of 1042, to confirm that the comprehensive verse design of *Samson Agonistes* consists of line units whose iambic feet range in number from two to six, with the single further option of a feminine line ending. This comprehensive verse design and the two correspondence rules stated thus far can be combined as follows:

comprehensive $_x$[[PHRASE $_y$[word] . . . [word]]]] [[phrase[word . . .]]]
verse design for ___ ___ ___ ___ ___ ___ ___ ___ ___ (∥)$_z$ ___ ___ ___ (___)
Samson Agonistes $_m$[[[w s | w s | w s | w s |w   s| w s (w)]]]
[[PHRASE [WORD]] . . . [[PHRASE [WORD]]]] [[PHRASE [WORD]] . . . [WORD]]]]

Values of variables: x = up to 5 [[PHRASE]] units per line
                       y = up to 3 [WORD] units per line
                       z = up to 4 caesuras, the number of options being
                             contingent on line-internal occurrences of]]]
                       m = 2 to 6 feet per line, with the option of 1 extra
                             weakly stressed syllable at line end

Here are some illustrations of the meter-fixing operations of polysyllabics, compound words, and elision (unsignaled instances in boldface) in the dra-ma's nonpentameter lines:

O're worn and soild (123)
La**bour**ing thy mind (1298) [two-foot lines]

Puts forth no vi**sual** beam (163)
Consolatories writ (657) [three-foot lines]

Sails fill'd, and streamers waving (718)
He all thir Ammunition (1277) [three-foot lines with (w)]

And to those cruel enemies (642)
Or was too much of self-love mixt (1031) [four-foot lines]

(Which way soever men refer it) (1017)
With inward eyes illuminated (1689) [four-foot lines with (w)]

Changest thy countenance, and thy hand with no regard (684)
And condemnation of the ingrateful multitude. (696) [six-foot lines]

But I Gods counsel have not kept, his holy secret (497) [six-foot line with (w)]

I now state my next pair of correspondence rules, which formulate procedures for matching syllables of the verse instance with positions of the verse design:

Correspondence Rule 3—Matching Syllables with Verse Design Positions: Pair the stressed syllable of the core [WORD] of the last [[PHRASE]] in the verse line with the rightmost s position to which it can be matched, making allowance for any following syllables grouped with this [WORD] in its [[PHRASE]]. Then proceed leftwards by matching syllables one by one to each position until a mutually exhaustive pairing with one of the specified options for the length of a line is obtained. Successful matching occurs when the relative stress contrasts in the linguistic material of the verse line, as assigned by the rules of English speech, correlate with respective s (more strongly stressed) and w (more weakly stressed) positions of the verse design.

Correspondence Rule 4—The Elision Option: If the process of matching fails because there are too many syllables for the number of available positions and/or there is no general fit of stress-bearing syllables with s positions in the verse design, look for possible application of one or more options for elision that allow two syllables to be coassigned to one position in the phonetic environments denoted by v|v, v|h|v, v|l|v, v|bl|v, v|r|v, v|m|v, v|n|v, v|nd|v, v|v|v, v|s|v, v|s = z|v. Then resume application of Correspondence Rule 3.

As stated, however, Correspondence Rules 3 and 4 are both too rigid and too limited to specify how the range of Milton's poetic practice in *Samson Agonistes* satisfies the comprehensive verse design with which I have been working. Another pair of rules analogous to Rule 4, the Elision Option, is needed to provide for the set of permissible variations from a perfect, sing-song metrical pattern that Milton in part found in the iambic pentameter verse written by his English predecessors and in part contributed through the singularities of his own compositional practice. The separate provisions of Correspondence Rule 5 detail the series of options for metrical variation that apply generally in Renaissance iambic pentameter. Option (a) permits an isolated stress reversal—that is, one not repeated in the next foot—following a phrase break at any point in a line. This powerful option can be made to license further and further departures from perceptible iambic rhythm by relaxing its specified constraints. Even in its most stringent form, stated in (a) below, it encompasses the common license of line-initial

stress reversal as well as stress reversal following a caesura, which can potentially affect any position in a line, given the frequency of phrase breaks
as I have defined them:

Correspondence Rule 5—Standard Options for Metrical Variation in
Iambic Pentameter:

(a) A [WORD] stress may depart from an iambic pattern of stress contrasts and pair with the
w position immediately after a [[PHRASE]] break at a foot division. Condition: This option will
not be taken twice in succession within a single line.

Examples: [[[Rifted]] [[the [Air],]]] [[[[clamouring]]] [[their [god]]] [[with [praise]]]] (1621)
        [[[(w s)   ‖   (w   s)

         [[[Ease]] [[to the [body]]] [[some,]]] [[[none]] [[to the [[mind]]]] (18)
         [[[(w   s)   ‖ (w   s)

         [[Then who [[[self]-[rigorous]]]] [[[[chooses]] [[[death]]] [as [due]]]] (513)
          ‖ (w   s)

A more permissive form of (a) is (a') below, with a pair of illustrations:

(a') A [WORD] stress may depart from an iambic pattern of stress contrasts and pair with the
w position immediately after a [[PHRASE]] break that cuts across a foot division. Condition: This
option will not be taken twice in succession within a single line.

Examples: [[Not [[flying],]]] [[but [[fore-casting]] [[in what [[place]]]] (254)
         (w ‖ s) (w   s)

        [[Thy [[Son]]]] [[is [[[rather]]] [[slaying] them]]]]; [[[that [[outcry]]] (1517)
                (w ‖ s) (w s)]]]

Further options (b) and (c) provide for the common license of temporarily
suspending the audible rhythm of stress contrasts in iambic pentameter:

(b) One s position may pair with an unstressed syllable before a [[PHRASE]] break with no
intervening [WORD]. Condition: This option will not be taken twice in succession within a
single line.

Examples: Lower then bondslave! [[[[Promise]] was]] [[that I]] (38)
                         (w   s) (w s)]]

        Of Heathen and profane, [[thir [[carkasses]]] (693)
                      (w   s)(w s)

        [[[[Consolatories]]]] [[writ,]]] (657)
        [[(w s)(ws)(w   s)

        [[(For so [[from such as] [[[nearer]]] [[stood]]]] [[we [[heard)]]] (1631)
         [[(w s) (w   s) (w   s)

(c) One s position per line may pair with an unstressed syllable after a [[PHRASE]] break with no intervening [WORD]. Condition: This option will not be taken twice in succession within a single line.

Examples: [[Like a [[wild][[Beast],]]] I am content to go. (1403)
          [[(w   s) (w   s)

          Toucht with the flame: [[on thir [whole][[Host]]] I flew (232)
          [[||(w   s)

Rare lines exercise both options, (b) and (c), compounding metrical complexity through weak runs of syllables in two successive feet:

[[She was not][the [prime][[cause]]]], but I my self, (234)
[[(w   s) (w   s) (w   s)

In mortal strength! [[[And oh [what not]][in [man]]] (349)
              ||(w   s)   (w   s)

Two distinctively Miltonic practices in composing verse to an iambic pentameter norm in *Samson Agonistes* remain to be formalized as a final pair of correspondence rules. One goes to a felt extreme but yields just four examples; it is the provision for the so-called "double anapests," also found in rare instances in *Paradise Lost* and *Paradise Regained*, that momentarily supplant iambic stress contrast with their variant duple rhythm.

Correspondence Rule 6—A Miltonic Option—The "Double Anapest": One w position in a line may be filled by a [WORD] stress flanked by two weakly stressed syllables on either side, with the front pair of syllables immediately adjoining the beginning of the line.

The four instances of double anapests in *Samson Agonistes* are:

[[But the [[heart]]][of the[[Fool],]]] (298)
[[(w   s) (w   s)

[[As a [[lingring][[[disease],]]]] (618)

[[To the [[Spirits]]][of [[just][[men]]] [[long][oppress'd]]]] (1269)
[[(w   s) (ws)   (w   s) ||

[[For his [[people]] [of [[old;]]] [[what [[hinders][now?]]] (1533)
[[(w   s) (w)(s) (w   s) ||

Only Weismiller, so far as I know, attempts to explain the Miltonic double anapest which, as he remarks, has "drawn uneasy comment from prosodists for the last two hundred years." Noting that this rhythmic effect across line positions 1–5 or 6–10 is "very common in Italian verse" (not just in *versi sciolti*), he suggests that it is tolerable there because "all syllables in Italian verse are read as equal-timed."[16] Significantly, the reason is not what Mil-

ton's English ear may have led him to infer—a uniquely permissible relax-
ation of the basic metrical principle of rhythmic contrast produced by
alternating stresses.

The other distinctively Miltonic practice in composing to an iambic
pentameter norm in *Samson Agonistes* is, in my analysis, the exclusion of
the so-called headless line as a metrically permissible option. I know that my
analysis will be controversial, for other English Renaissance poets allowed
themselves to write iambic pentameter lines with the first w position un-
filled by any linguistic material, and Milton did so himself in *L'Allegro, Il
Penseroso,* and *Lycidas.* He also writes twelve lines in *Samson Agonistes*
that appear to be candidates for analysis as headless iambics, three of them
rendered further metrically ambiguous by optional feminine line endings
(asterisked here). They are:

Prison within Prison* (153)
To the bodies wounds and sores (607)
As on entrails, joints, and limbs (619)
To black mortification* (622)
Comes this way sailing* / Like a stately Ship (713–14)
Great among the heathen round (1430)
In the camp of Dan (1436)
That no second knows nor third (1701)
All is best though we oft doubt / What th'unsearchable dispose (1744–45)
Oft he seems to hide his face (1749)

But if these lines are headless iambics, and the headlessness option is formulated as a correspondence rule for Milton's compositional practice in
Samson Agonistes, the result will be tantamount both to accepting Bridges's
judgment that the work has no self-consistent verse design and to confounding systematic metrical analysis as decisively as did Sprott's monosyllabic
feet (which were actually contrived as means for dealing with some of these
lines). I reject formulation of an option of headless iambic lines—de facto
trochaics—as rhythmically destructive of the otherwise coherent and audible interplay of securely iambic pentameter lines varied by the frequently
exercised option of feminine line endings and the more rarely exercised
option of different line lengths. Milton in my view was far too astute a poet
not to recognize that de facto trochaic line beginnings in any intermixture
with feminine line endings would erode and finally undo the perceptibility
of an iambic pentameter base on which an appreciation of the verse design
of *Samson Agonistes* vitally depends.[17] There are alternative ways of dealing
with these problematic lines and others that share certain of their features;

they can be analyzed as instances of expressive rhythmical ambiguity or unmetricality, as I shall now show.

2

In pervasive senses the dynamic of iambic rhythm informs the drama of *Samson Agonistes:* weakness before strength, no way to strength but through weakness, and the advent of strength in a stroke, as a beat that signals the imposition of purposive order from above and beyond, whether by the stress assignment rules of English or through a human coming to insight and re-solve.[18] Milton's prefatory argument states that the "Catastrophe"—etymologically, the downturn of the drama—will be brought on by Samson's "coming to the Feast before the Lords and People, to play or shew his strength in thir presence" as the Philistine powers have required and as he has become "at length perswaded inwardly that this was from God" (pp. 3, 5). Milton's preface, moreover, equates the "power" of this drama with the two-fold raising "pity and fear, or terror" and tempering or reducing to "just measure" of "those and such like passions . . . with a kind of delight, stirr'd up by reading or seeing those passions well imitated" that makes tragedy superior to "all other Poems." As these binary passions work toward realiza-tion through the binary poetic rhythm, weakness comes to align with pity and the pitiable, strength with fear and fearsomeness, even the terrifying.

Weakness typifies the initial condition of all the main personages in *Samson Agonistes*—Samson himself, Manoa, Dalila, and even and especially the Chorus, who are not exempted by their role as observers. The question of Samson's weakness and strength, however, is categorically of a higher order. He and his story became the defining norm for all judgments about the weakness and strength of the other characters. If they are for him, like his fellow Danites, Manoa and the Chorus, they can evolve toward true strength even if at varying rates and irregular paces. But if they are against him, like the two Philistines, they can never do this. Any ostensible strength will prove never to have been there at all, as in the case of Harapha, who enacts a kind of failed stress reversal. Or the weakness will prove spurious, revealing nothing but an unnatural and denaturing strength that imperils Samson's own; this proves to be the case of Dalila in the metrical typology cultivated and reinforced by the rhythms of Milton's verse.

This metrical typology operates through expressive variations upon the pervasive pentameter base rhythm—very considerably through feminine line endings, also through stress placements that create complex and even unmetrical lines. In general these variations are fully perceptible and self-signaling, as I will show. But I want to begin with a more encrypted feature of the metrical typology: a result of Correspondence Rule 5(c), which comprises a sequence of four syllables of increasing stress value, from the lightest to the strongest, two so-called unstressed, two so-called stressed. This combination, a characteristic of English Renaissance metrical style, has been called the "superiamb," after its formal pattern of paired weak syllables followed by paired strong ones.[19] A hunt for the superiambs of *Samson Agonistes* yields twelve instances, the first a usage by Samson, and the others used in descriptions of his prodigious actions and their effects. Placed end to end, as I arrange them here, the superiambs of *Samson Agonistes* tell an intelligible if disjointed story through some of its high points, marking with their stepped pulsations the singular course of this superhero from redoubled weakness (his fault, Dalila's betrayal) to redoubled strength (of body and resolve): "for with joint pace" (110); "And the same end" (232); "on thir whole Host" (262); "Like a tame Wether" (538); "From the dry ground" (583); "As a League-breaker" (Harapha's accusation, 1184); "As a league-breaker" (Samson's attestation of his mistreatment by the Hebrews, 1209); "Be of good courage" (1381); "Like a wild Beast" (1403); "As at some distance" (1550); "By his own hands," (1584); "As thir own ruin" (1684).

Both superhero and normative center, Samson is pivotal to a symbolics of rhythm that sustains a complex study in suspensefulness—whether weakness will be succeeded by strength—and he is so first and foremost because his divine gift of past, lost strength was forfeited by himself. I will analyze excerpts from his opening soliloquy and from his great monody, identifying those features and connotative effects of versification that define, respectively, the strong and the weak speaking styles and the strong and the weak lyric styles of *Samson Agonistes*. My purpose in doing this is not only to substantiate my claim that Samson sets all the standards for what is expressively and prosodically right in this drama but also to open discussion of how the versification bears on two perennial interpretive issues: the sincerity of Dalila's attempt to reconcile with Samson and the extent of the unreliability to be charged against the Chorus.

Samson's opening soliloquy thematizes his strength as certified before his birth by two descents of an angel—proof that he, "a person separate to God," was "Design'd for great exploits" (30, 32), the line-initial stress reversal, the elision, and consonant clusters signaling the onset of the muscular prosodic style that belongs truly to Samson alone. The same sound features dominate the next lines in which he derides his present condition with deep contempt:

> Betray'd, Captiv'd, and both my Eyes put out,
> Made of my Enemies the scorn and gaze;
> To grind in Brazen Fetters under task

With this Heav'n-gifted strength. O glorious strength
Put to the labour of a Beast, debas't
Lower then bondslave! Promise was that I
Should *Israel* from *Philistian* yoke deliver;
Ask for this great Deliverer now, and find him
Eyeless in *Gaza* at the Mill with slaves.   (33–41)

The compacted rhythmical energy of this passage is produced by its strongly
ending pentameter lines clogged with clustered consonants and rife with
marked and unmarked elisions (the latter here in boldface) as well as by a
density of lexical stresses in clustered verbals and compounds that override
foot breaks.

Yet an entropic pull toward metrical ambiguity affects even this heroic
verse in its three next-to-last lines. "I" at line end completes a masculine
ten-syllable line only through rhetorical promotion to some level of stress,
and "find him" two lines later is a certain instance of a feminine line. And
what of "deliver," the intervening line ending? It will not finish a pentameter but, rather, another feminine line unless an optional elision—deliv'r—
joins to make a third with the two earlier meter-fixing ones in the same line.
The rhythmical effect of "deliver" here proliferates throughout the drama
in dozens of lines ending in similarly stressed lexicals, the most frequent of
which is "power(s)" (see lines 745, 798, 1054, and 1367). Is this masculine
"pow'r" or feminine "power"? At each occurrence metrical ambiguity aug-
ments expressiveness. Here the ambiguity anticipates Samson's soon overt
declaration, "Suffices that to me strength is my bane" (63), climaxing a passage of self-reproach that mingles the massed consonants of the muscular
style with the highly contrastive metrical symbolism of feminine line endings, weakly stressed line endings, and weakly stressed line beginnings
(marked in boldface):

Whom have I to complain **of but my** self?
Who this high gift of strength commi**tted to me**
In what part lodg'd, how eas**ily bereft me,**
Under the Seal of silence **could not** keep,
But weakly to a woman must reveal **it,**
O'recome with import**unity and** tears.
O impotence of mind, in body strong!   (46–52)

Samson's first soliloquy markedly genders the binary rhythmical contrast of
weakness and strength, reenforcing it with the further sound effects of the
alliteration on "weakly" and "woman" and the pun linking "importunity"
with "impotence." The stage is set, thus early, for the eventual confrontation
of Samson with Dalila.

Between this soliloquy and that scene, however, the gendered difference of line endings undergoes considerable complication. The consistent
connotation of a feminine line ending is that of faltering or of undercutting
an assertion, but always with the speaker fully cognizant of doing this. Thus
feminine endings register self-disparagement (235–36: "Who vanquisht
with a peal of words (O weakness!) / Gave up my fort of silence to a
Woman"); criticism of another (221: "The daughter of an Infidel: they knew
not"); uncertainty about oneself (182: "To visit or bewail thee, or if better");
uncertainty about an outcome (506: "Or th'execution leave to high dis-
posal"). Feminine endings also register incongruity (120–21: "As one past
hope, abandon'd, / And by himself given over"), impropriety (441: "Besides
whom is no God, compar'd with Idols"), the extraordinary (167: "By how
much from the top of wondrous glory"), and the fleetingness of joy or pleasure (354: "And such a Son as all Men hail'd me happy"; 550: "I drank, from
the clear milkie juice allaying"). As such, the multivalent associations of
feminine endings provide an important key to Manoa's character in particular. His success in making the transition from weakness to strength is extremely belated. The expressive dynamics of line rhythms shows what holds
Manoa up. His speeches employ feminine line endings for speaking to so
many conjoint but incompatible purposes—from berating and cherishing
Samson to decrying Philistine idolatry to affirming that Samson's sight will
return and that he will ransom his son—that both his development and his
actions founder for a long while in incoherence and irresolution. In this
state Manoa reaches maximal metrical and dramatic complexity at line 579:
"Better at home lie bed rid, not only idle"—an address to Samson that he
means and does not mean in equal measure. Manoa's incoherence and irresolution vanish only when he trains his attention on learning the full story of
Samson's self-immolating vengeance on the Philistines and hails what for
him is a clarifying resolution of the deeply vexed issues of God's and Samson's due honor; this is also precisely the juncture at which he at last displays consistent clarity and control in his use of feminine line endings
(1508–96, 1709–25).

But what long remains rhythmically uncertain in Manoa's case, the
question of how to interpret his character, is never left in doubt in Dalila's
case at the level of the drama's prosody. At the levels of discursive speech
and action I think the interpretation of her character can be treated as an
open question; I have done so in my teaching, probing how far her appeal
to Samson registers as sincerely caring and reconciliatory. Such an approach
takes Dalila's weakness as genuine, the result of painfully divided loyalties,
and her reaction to Samson's rejection of her as a sudden strength born of
her need to recoup her life without him—a strength which she either never

imagined she had or never thought she would have to call upon. Any sense
of an open question, however, is closed by the consistent and cumulatively
damning connotations of the prosody with respect to Dalila. Once the muscular style has been established as both definitive and normative for Samson, its compounded elements work to evoke a castrating female when
Samson accuses Dalila to Manoa even before she appears (consonant clusters and unmarked elisions in boldface):

> Thrice she assay'd with flattering prayers and sighs,
> And amorous reproaches to win from me
> My capital secret, in what part my strength
> Lay stor'd, in what part summ'd, that she might know
> . . . .
> Yet the fourth time, when mustring all her wiles,
> With blandisht parlies, feminine assaults,
> Tongue-batteries, she surceas'd not day nor night
> To storm me over-watch't, and wearied out.   (392–95, 402–05)

There is not a feminine line ending in this run of descriptive lines, but
when Dalila enters upon the scene she speaks in lines with frequent, expressive feminine endings and elisions (marked in boldface) that slur key ethical
and psychological terms as if she took them lightly: "With doubtful feet and
wavering resolution / I came, still dreading thy displeasure, Samson," "if
tears / May expiate," "My penance hath not slack'n'd, though my pardon,"
"conjugal affection / Prevailing over fear and timerous doubt / Hath led me
on desirous" (732–33, 735–36, 738, 739–41). This entering speech climaxes
in a metrical ambiguity at the end of line 745, "what amends is in my
power." Is Dalila's power unelided and feminine, or elided and masculine?
Has Samson's earlier description done her wrong? As if directly answering
that question, Samson responds to Dalila in a line so constructed that his
redoubled "out" or his unelidable epithet for her, "Hyaena," makes it unmetrical: "Out, out, Hyaena, these are thy wonted arts" (748). There is an
obviously metrical possibility, "Hyaena, out," which he does not take, thus
violating the limits of the verse design while violently expressing that she is
the violator who must be excluded.

Dalila returns with a new rash of feminine line endings and slurring
elisions on key ethical and psychological terms—one w-glide and two
y-glides on "extenuate," "easier," and "Curiosity": "Yet hear me Samson;
not that I endeavour / To lessen or extenuate my offence," "The easier
towards me," "Curiosity, inquisitive, importune / Of secrets, then with like
infirmity" (766–67, 772, 774), lodging her conjoint accusation and appeal to
Samson in the expressively rhythmed lines (unmarked elisions and feminine

endings in boldface): "Nor shouldst **thou have** trusted that to womans frailty / E're I to thee, thou to thy self wast cru**el**" (783–84). But additionally amid these softened touches she promotes the word "weakness" from the feminine position at line end that she first gave it—"First granting, as I do, it was a **weakness**" (773)—and gives it full meter-fixing weight in her verse, thereby assertively thematizing the gendered complex of domestic and ethical questions that pivot for her and Samson on the vocabulary of strength and weakness: "Was it not **weakness** also to make known / . . . Wherein consisted all thy strength and safety? / To what I did thou shewdst me first the way" (778, 790–91):

> Let weakness then with weakness come to parl
> So near related, or the same of kind,
> Thine forgive mine; that men may censure thine
> The gentler, if severely thou exact not
> More strength from me, then in thy self was found.   (785–89)

Dalila oddly positions "forgive" as a stress reversal, a departure from the rhythmical pattern although a permissible one, and she more oddly places "not" as an extra eleventh, feminine syllable at a line break where it is an absolutely crucial term. She also begins to mass consonant clusters in seeking to set herself and Samson on a par in weakness and strength. In the symbolics of the prosody, Dalila makes a bid for full gender equality.

Samson's immediate response, in two lines with feminine endings, is rhythmically shaky but dotted with masculine consonant clusters: "That malice not repentance brought thee hither, / By this appears; I gave, thou say'st th'example" (821–22). Most significantly in terms of metrical typology, he takes control of the word "weakness," himself moving it from a stress reversal to a meter-fixing position in three successive lines while also now using feminine line endings only to deride or denounce Dalila:

> Thou wilt renounce thy seeking, and much rather
> Confess it feign'd, **weakness** is thy excuse, [stress reversal]
> And I believe it, **weakness** to resist [meter-fixing]
> Philistian gold: if **weakness** may excuse, [meter-fixing]
> What Murtherer, what Traytor, Parricide,
> Incestuous, Sacrilegious, but may plead it?
> All wickedness is **weakness**: that plea therefore [meter-fixing]
> With God or Man will gain thee no remission.   (828–35)

Samson's exercise of dominance in making "weakness" a term without further positive sense in their exchanges leaves Dalila bereft of any feminine resources that can be made to matter to Samson or register with him. Femi-

nine resources now will only serve her for purposes of show or emotional
venting. She herself registers both his voiding of the valence of her gender
and her continued resistance to him in five lines that begin to stake her full
and now open claim to the muscular masculine style and to a public heroism
that is the equal of Samson's among her own people. Dalila begins, "Since
thou determinst weakness for no plea / In man or woman, though to thy
own condemning" (843–44), with a second line that is unmetrical unless
"woman" is elided, rhythmically cut down to size, exactly the sort of move
that she wants to contest. She does so by moving now to appropriate the
muscular style expressly to her own situation, slipping a single feminine line
ending in among a threesome of firmly end-stopped pentameters with their
elisions and clotted consonants:

> Hear what assaults I had, what snares besides,
> What sieges girt me round, e're I consented;
> Which might have aw'd the best resolv'd of men,
> The constantest to['] have yielded without blame.   (843–46)

How outrageous a self-heroizing Dalila is to Samson shows in the new
rash of feminine line endings that he appropriates to himself, as exclusive
vehicles for his astonishment and anger at her temerity (873–903). But she
challenges his emotionally expressive monopoly on feminine line endings
by using them herself again to make one last appeal for reconciliation. In
prosody no less than in psychology or ethics, Dalila will accept no masculinist double standard. But her renewal of feminine forms of address merely
enrages Samson to a fresh sense of what he excoriates as her "smooth hypocrisie" (872), her "warbling charms" (934). He remains implacable, dismissing her in two lines in the muscular style proper to him alone by the drama's
metrical typology. The first of these presses the limits of metrical complexity
with a nearly unpronounceable required elision, "wid'whood," which is also
by far the earliest suggestion of Samson's intuition that he will die avenging
himself upon more Philistines than the woman he now divorces in Old Testament style: "Cherish thy hast'n'd widowhood with the gold / Of Matrimo-
nial treason, so farwel" (958–59). What is more, the prosodic texture of
Dalila's last response to Samson strongly confirms his repeated charge that
she is not his feminine complement but, rather, his self-masculinizing adversary who seeks to overmatch his strength and his heroic glory with her
own:

> But in my countrey, where I most desire,
> In *Ecron, Gaza, Asdod,* and in *Gath*
> I shall be nam'd among the famousest
> Of Women, sung at solemn festivals

Living and dead recorded, who to save
Her countrey from a fierce destroyer, chose
Above the faith of wedlock-bands, my tomb
. . . .
Not less renown'd then in Mount *Ephraim*,
Jael, who with inhospitable guile
Smote *Sisera* sleeping through the Temples nail'd.   (980–90)

Besides its dense consonant clusters largely comprised of Philistine names
and its key elision compounded with alliteration in the significant sequence
"Smote *Sis'ra* sleeping" that supplies Dalila with her present prototype of
how a woman secures heroic stature, these lines and others surrounding
them are remarkable for their single feminine line ending, "famousest." It
does appear on the full rhythmical evidence of her speeches that Dalila can
turn feminine and masculine line endings on and off at will; with her they
are not straightforwardly expressive. This last one, "famousest," is itself an
ostensible coinage by which Dalila signifies her self-willed reconstitution of
herself in a strength that will have owed nothing to Samson except its occasion of triumphant exercise. This is exactly what Samson finally makes of
himself and his strength vis-à-vis the entire host of Philistines, subterfuge
and indirection not excluded in either case. But prosodically the cases of
Samson and Dalila are firmly distinguished; it is he who is normative in his
maleness and she who moves beyond all bounds in making of herself an
antagonist who can both weaken him and challenge his embodiment of
strength with her own. Thus it is that the Chorus signal their perception of
Dalila's approach in a sequence of two expressively unmetrical lines that,
like her presence finally, can find no accommodation in the verse design of
the drama: "Comes this way sailing / Like a stately Ship" (713–14).

I have claimed that Samson's metrical style is normative not only for
the dialogue by which character development and interaction occur in this
drama but also for the lyrical verse which he and the Chorus, but no other
characters, utter. I have also suggested that the question of the unreliability
of the Chorus is bound up with their lyric performance, the extent to which
they meet or fail to meet the norms for such utterance set by Samson. These
assertions now require some substantiation, and I wish to begin discussion
with the pointers regarding the Chorus in the preface to *Samson Agonistes*.
Here Milton is strongly concerned to distinguish the lyric forms and practices of his Chorus from anything that will count as ordinary stanzaic verse.
His Chorus is to be loosed or set free (the root meanings of "Apolelymenon")
from such set, conventional, repeating patterns as those of "Strophe, Antis-
trophe or Epod," and instead employ "all sorts" of "measure of Verse,"
which Milton terms "Monostrophic" (in a sense apparently close to the

present-day term *through-composed,* or *durchkomponiert,* used to characterize song-text settings that employ a continuous rather than a recurring
melodic development). I take Milton to include in "all sorts" of "measure of
Verse" the Chorus' varying recourse to lines of different lengths, as well as
the need for compositional units that prove, in Milton's emphatic words,
"material," "essential to the Poem," which I understand to mean effectively
and expressively keyed to the drama of Samson. If the Chorus' compositional units come to resemble stanzaic divisions, Milton nevertheless stipu-
lates that they "be called *Allaeostropha,*" literally, another kind of stanza,
which takes this little passage of definition back to a norm of "*Monostrophic,*
or rather *Apolelymenon*" lyric form (p. 5).

Samson's first soliloquy sets the precedent for the functional lyric deployment of short lines and freed-up forms in the drama: "O dark, dark,
dark, amid the blaze of noon, / Irrecoverably dark, total Eclipse / Without
all hope of day" (80–82). Three lines herald the onset of the monostrophic
lyric mode—the first a pentameter rendered complex by three caesuras and
repeating form at the lexical level only; the second a pentameter rendered
differently complex by the metrically requisite elision of "Irrecov'rably" and
the rare stress reversal in its fourth foot ("total"). The third line is regular
but has only six syllables, the first short line among many subsequent ones
to swing the drama away from its pentameter base. Soon there follows a
triad of trimeter lines, enjambing the syntax of one sentence to end by filling
a base line of pentameter. This is a nonce compositional unit, and in its
rhymelessness and lack of other recurrent elements it is clearly no stanza:
"The Sun to me is dark / And silent as the Moon, / When she deserts the
night / Hid in her vacant interlunar cave" (86–89).

Samson's first soliloquy likewise demonstrates how the monostrophic
lyric mode is to be "material," "essential to the Poem" through its stretches
of highly variable line lengths. Theirs is the content and the measure of the
utmost that speech can pit against silence at a given juncture of high emotion or great incertitude. This remains the distinctive expressive function of
the short lines: they symbolize all the speech that can be won or wrung at
the extremity, the boundary of muteness imposed by the limits of mystery
or suffering. These symbolics are borne out in Samson's great monody (606–
51) at the nadir of his desolation after Manoa's visit and his pitifully weak
offer to rescue Samson into dependency in the paternal household. Samson's monody labors to articulate the anguish of his realization that emotional pain far exceeds bodily pain. He dwells for a stretch on wishing this
were not so, during which two unmetrical lines—"To the bodies wounds
and sores" (607), "As on entrails, joints, and limbs" (619)—expressively register that Samson is dealing in counterfactuals, not reality. Two more unmet-

rical lines—"But must secret passage find" (611), "To black mortification" (622)—evoke that pain beyond pain which triggers despair of life. The unreduced polysyllable draws full attention to its three-way pun on "mortification": the deadening of living tissue (necrosis), the shaming that nullifies self-respect, and the mortal effects of both in the extreme. With their weak onset runs of unstressed syllables (in boldface below), the subsequent irregular alternations of short and long lines operate like relay points for the almost inexpressibly painful contents of Samson's mortification and the death wish to which this has brought him: "**I was his** nursling once and choice delight," "**Under his** special eie," "**But now hath** cast me off as never known, / **And to those** cruel enemies," "**Nor am I in the** list of them that hope" (633, 636, 641–42, 647). Highlighting this lyric mode by its differences from ordinary dialogue, Samson declares to his father the same hopelessness of his state in heavily endstopped, jogtrot lines of maximally actualized stress contrasts, with a single stress reversal on "nature" as the only sign that life could hold any appeal or meaning for him:

> That these dark orbs no more shall treat with light,
> Nor th'other light of life continue long,
> But yield to double darkness nigh at hand:
> So much I feel my genial spirits droop,
> My hopes all flat, nature within me seems
> In all her functions weary of herself;
> My race of glory run, and race of shame,
> And I shall shortly be with them that rest.   (591–98)

Despite the rhymelessness of this passage, it betokens what the stanzaic mode of lyric in *Samson Agonistes* might sound like—that is, if Milton had authorized any such thing, which the preface shows he expressly did not do. Hence Samson relegates such heavy-handed sound effects to dialogue. This, however, is not what the Chorus does—and, hence, their unreliability as observers and commentators. They use short lines more mundanely, more easily, more cheaply in the sense of being much less hard won from the limits of utterance in pain or mystery. They are the ordinary humans of this drama. Their great difference from Samson announces itself in the contrast between his compositional unit beginning "The Sun to me is dark" and their "This, this is he; softly a while, / Let us not break in upon him / . . . With languish't head unprop, / As one past hope abandon'd, / And by himself given over; / In slavish habit, ill-fitted weeds / O're worn and soild" (116–17, 119–23). Although short lines predominate here, they abound in prolixity and overspecificity about Samson's posture and clothing. Besides the signaled elisions, moreover, the unsignaled ones required by the meter give these prosaic lines a heightened colloquialism—Let's not, giv'n o'er, hab't—an effect that the meter sustains as the Chorus speaks his name: "Can this be hee, / That H'roic, that Renown'd, / Irr'sistible Samson?" (125–26). Merely external description of Samson continues in their next series of short lines, rendered more prosaic by their recourse to rhyme—"And weaponless himself," "Adamantean Proof; / But safest he who stood aloof," "Thir plated backs under his heel" (130, 134–35, 140). When the Chorus next proceeds to turn Samson's predicament to moral commonplace (151–75), it is a warrantable conclusion from the metrical typology that they are not producing the freed-up short lyric lines envisaged in Milton's preface. Instead, these ostensible short lines virtually fall into pairs as sententious long lines, the twelve- and fourteen-syllable units of so-called poulters' measure with their heavily actualized stress contrasts and caesuras:

> Which shall I first bewail, Thy Bondage or lost sight (150–51)
> Prison within Prison Inseparably dark? (152–53)
> The Dungeon of thy self; thy Soul Imprison'd now indeed, (156, 158)
> For inward light alas Puts forth no visual beam (162–63)
> O mirror of our fickle state, The rarer thy example stands (164, 166)
> Since man on earth unparallel'd Strongest of mortal men (165, 168)

Significantly Samson is unaware that the Chorus in this attempted lyric has been describing and addressing him; he remarks: "I hear the sound of words, thir sense the air / Dissolves unjointed e're it reach my ear" (176–77).

The Chorus' second lyric (293–329) transposes the question of their reliability most obviously to the plane of logic. They begin by declaring both God's justice and God's justifiability in human terms and then proceed to undermine this declaration with a series of concessions, qualifications, and accusations. Atheists cannot be convinced but atheists are fools; skeptics cannot be convinced but they want to bind God by human laws of reason and political obligation, from which he is not only exempt but from which he can exempt humans for his own purposes. There is no other way, the Chorus says, to think about God's role in the marriage of Samson. "Down Reason then, at least vain reasonings down" (323); the refrainlike line draws them to their self-contradictory conclusion. The Chorus in this second lyric does manage access to the content that Samson had shown to be normative for this type of utterance: thought and feeling brought so close to the edge of mystery as to be barely articulable. Yet their resources of expression remain prosaic, bound in sententiousness, as can be heard in their repeated reversions to rhymed line endings and heavily actualized stress contrasts: "For of such Doctrine never was there School, / But the heart of the Fool, / And no man therein Doctor but himself" (297–99). They even produce their first stanzalike moralization within this purportedly *"Allaeostrophic"* drama:

> Regardless of his glories diminution
> Till by thir own perplexities involv'd
> They ravel more, still less resolv'd,
> But never find self-satisfying solution.   (303–06)

Some of the same perceptions hold for the prosodic style of the Chorus' third lyric (654–99), except that they have just heard Samson's great monody of despair and self-evacuation. Now they begin to apply their colloquial elisions and their tidy habit of rhyming to a meditation on God's doings.[20] All at once the effect is no longer either colloquial or tidy (elisions in boldface): "That thou towards him with hand so va**ri**ous, / Or might I say contrar**ious**" (667–68), "**Th**e Angelic orders and infe**ri**our creatures mute, / Irrational and brute. / Nor do I name of men the common rout, / That wand'ring loose about" (672–75), "But throw'st them lower then thou didst exalt them high, / Unseemly falls in human eie" (689–90). The rhymes are not tidy because they tie lines of widely different lengths, and do so only in the minimal unit of a pair. These elisions work to keep metrically complex lines from becoming unmetrical, and the new sound texture pervades what I earlier called the sententious long line of twelve syllables, which is now more aptly styled the labored line: "Changest thy countenance, and thy hand with no regard" (684); "Or to **th**e **u**njust tribunals, under change of times, / And condemnation of **th**e **i**ngrateful multitude" (695–96). The Chorus of the third lyric is still capable of qualifications that lead into self-contradiction or something perilously like it, but here they register the difficulty of the distinction they are trying to sustain with regard to God's visitations— "Though not disordinate, yet causless suffring" (701) in a line of great metrical complexity. "Just or unjust, alike seem miserable, / For oft alike, both come to evil end" (703–04), they generalize, and in the next breath pray that Samson may be the exception they have nowhere else found reason to imagine in this lyric: "Behold him in this state calamitous, and turn / His labours, for thou canst, to peaceful end" (708–09). The two line-terminal occurrences of "end" here (704, 709) are the opposite of a rhyme; they reinforce the discordant impact of the mystery of human suffering on a patly providential worldview. And the Chorus has found its way to lyric articulation of such mystery and suffering through their sympathetic identification and Samson.

By the end of the third choral lyric, all of the dramatic development that bears on the question of the Chorus' unreliability has taken place. They confirm themselves as Samson's men—instruments of his interests and fellows of his passions insofar as their lyricism can keep pace. In that regard, the Chorus proves distinctly better at understanding Samson than at understanding God—or Dalila, for that matter. Their unreliability regarding the two latter subjects emerges in their regression to sententious rhymed verse, the ordinary English stanza forms that Milton had declared out of bounds for this drama, at two crucial junctures. At the first of these, the Chorus purports to have the last interpretive word on Dalila:

> Therefore Gods universal Law
> Gave to the man despotic power
> Over his female in due awe,
> Nor from that right to part an hour,
> Smile she or lowre:
> So shall he least confusion draw
> On his whole life, not sway'd
> By female usurpation, nor dismay'd.   (1053–60)

At the second of these, the Chorus purports to have the last interpretive word on God:

> All is best though we oft doubt,
> What th'unsearchable dispose
> Of highest wisdom brings about,
> And ever best found in the close.
> • • • • • • • •
> His servants he with new acquist
> Of true experience from this great event
> With peace and consolation hath dismist,
> And calm of mind all passion spent.   (1744–47, 1755–58)

In the second composition, the pair of quatrains above, there are details of metrical texture that additionally signal their failure as lyrics true to Milton's specifications in the preface of *Samson Agonistes*.[21] The first line is unmetrical without an initial elision, "All's best, though we oft doubt," though this metrical requirement only further heightens the banal jauntiness and singsong regularity of the following lines, as is also the case with the metrically required y-glide elision of "experience" in the second quatrain. What is more, the next two lines of the first quatrain, "What th'unsearchable dispose" and "Oft he seems to hide his face," are irreducibly trochaic and hence unmetrical within the iambic verse design as I have analyzed it. Interestingly, "What the unsearchable dispose" is an easily metrical line; yet the elision, "th'unsearchable," is marked in the 1671 printing. The clear implication from the prosody here is that these are failed lyric lines that the

Chorus of a drama named *Samson Agonistes* has no business offering as sententious closure.

Where, then, if anywhere do Milton's criteria for monostrophic, freed-up composition achieve realization in the Chorus' lyric utterance? Put otherwise, is the Chorus ever a reliable source for allaeostrophic measures "material to the Poem"? On the evidence of the metrical symbolics of *Samson Agonistes* I would point to two highly likely passages, both significantly lyrics about Samson, the Chorus' most reliable subject, spoken from Samson's own perspective. One is the imposing passage beginning "Oh how comely it is and how reviving" at line 1268—a through-composed sequence of what amounts to free verse held to an iambic norm only by the usual expedients of elision, feminine line endings, and variable line lengths. An especially effective, freed-up feature of this passage is the uncertainty the Chorus induces about where its lyric mode modulates to spoken dialogue. Does this occur at line 1297 or 1300 or 1307? The rhythmic fluidity seems anticipatory of opera. The other passage is a compositional unit (1697–1707) that admits the Chorus' penchant for rhyme while distributing its occurrence irregularly across a series of varying line lengths and rhythms. It expressively uses near unmetricality, the perhaps unpronounceable elision, "begott'n," at line 1699 and outright unmetricality at line 1701 to evoke the boundary-shattering anomaly of Samson's at once self-willed death and self-willed return to his life of prodigious feats of strength:

> So vertue giv'n for lost, [6 syllables, a rhyme]
> Deprest, and overthrown, as seem'd, [8 syllables, b rhyme]
> Like that self-begott'n bird [6 syllables, c rhyme; is elision pronounceable?]
> In the *Arabian* woods embost, [6 syllables, a rhyme; elision required]
> That no second knows nor third, [7 syllables, c rhyme; unmetrical trochaics]
> And lay e're while a Holocaust, [8 syllables, a rhyme]
> From out her ashie womb now teem'd, [8 syllables, d rhyme]
> Revives, reflourishes, then vigorous most [10 syllable, a rhyme; elision]
> When most unactive deem'd, [6 syllables, b rhyme]
> And though her body die, her fame survives [10 syllables, e rhyme]
> A secular bird ages of lives. [6 syllables, e rhyme; elision]

Here, I would affirm, the metrical symbolics cue the reader to identify the most reliable choral summation on the superhero of *Samson Agonistes*. Here the Chorus evokes the phenomenon of Samson as mysteriously true—in the sense of being self-identical—to the etymology of his name, meaning 'solar,' 'sun-like,' 'fiery,' and they do so without any references to the divine, or the human, or the natural that so often elicit platitudes from them. They lyrically transpose what Manoa in their wake utters as tautology in the dialogue:

"*Samson* hath quit himself / Like *Samson*" (1709–10). In this pity-inducing, fear-inducing, and finally terror-inducing tragedy that Milton projects for the reader in his preface, what remains the consistently and comprehensively human element is the superb achievement of its versification.

University of Chicago

NOTES

1. All *Samson Agonistes* quotations are cited from the Scolar Press facsimile, John Milton, *Paradise Regain'd,* . . . *To which is added Samson Agonistes* (1671; Menston, Eng., 1968), although I parenthetically supply modern line references in the text because the lineation in this first edition is erratically numbered.

2. Robert Bridges, *Milton's Prosody* (Oxford, 1921), pp. 46–66.

3. S. Ernest Sprott, *Milton's Art of Prosody* (Oxford, 1953), pp. 131–32.

4. James Holly Hanford, *A Milton Handbook* (New York, 1947), p. 324.

5. F. T. Prince, *The Italian Element in Milton's Verse* (Oxford, 1954), chaps. 3–5; quote from p. 132.

6. Milton, *Of Education,* in *Complete Prose Works of John Milton,* vol. 2, ed. Ernest Sirluck (New Haven, 1959), pp. 404–05; preface to *Samson Agonistes,* pp. 4–5.

7. Edward R. Weismiller, "Studies of Style and Verse Form in *Paradise Regained,*" vol. 4 of *A Variorum Commentary on the Poems of John Milton,* ed. Walter MacKellar (New York, 1975), p. 274.

8. O. B. Hardison, Jr., *Prosody and Purpose in the English Renaissance* (Baltimore, 1989), chap. 4. Hardison also considers the rhymelessness of *versi sciolti* to be its most influential feature in the eventual emergence of blank verse (pp. 83–85). His other prototype for English iambic pentameter is "the verse combining syllable count and rhyme that emerged in the high Middle Ages and became standard for the romance languages" (p. 53); Chaucer in the *Canterbury Tales* is the first English poet to have responded to this prototype and his lines "can be scanned either as syllabic or as iambic pentameter" (p. 55).

9. Paul Kiparsky, "The Rhythmic Structure of English Verse," *Linguistic Inquiry* VIII (1977): 189–247, and "Stress, Syntax, and Meter," *Language* LI, no. 3 (1975): 576–616, refining foundational work in so-called generative metrics by Morris Halle and S. Jay Keyser, "Chaucer and the Study of Prosody," *CE* XXVIII (1966): 187–219, and *English Stress: Its Form, Its Growth, and Its Role in Verse* (New York, 1971). The concepts of verse design and verse instance derive from Roman Jakobson, "Closing Statement: Linguistics and Poetics," in *Style in Language,* ed. Thomas Sebeok (Bloomington, Ind., 1960), pp. 364–66.

10. There is a possible fourth instance in the short-lined verse: "Renders them useless, while / With winged expedition" (1282–83), but, as my discussion of the Chorus in the latter half of this essay will clarify, I regard many of their verses of this type as tentative forms in their struggle to hit upon a lyric style that will do justice to the phenomenon of Samson.

11. Weismiller, "Studies of Style," pp. 274–75.

12. When I refer to the stress assignment rules for English words and phrases I mean the Main Stress Rule and its associated rules, the Alternating Stress Rule, the Compound Stress Rule, and the Nuclear Stress Rule as developed in generative phonology. See Noam Chomsky and Morris Halle, *The Sound Pattern of English* (New York, 1968); *Contributions to*

Generative Phonology, ed. Michael Brame (Austin, 1972); George Lakoff, "The Global Nature of the Nuclear Stress Rule," *Language* XLVIII, no. 2 (1972): 285–303; and *Essays on the Sound Pattern of English*, ed. Didier L. Goyvaerts and Geoffrey K. Pullum (Ghent, 1975). Other relevant considerations are raised by Joseph C. Beaver, "Current Metrical Issues," *CE* XXXII (1971): 177–97, and "The Rules of Stress in English Verse," *Language* XLVII, no. 4 (1971): 586–614.

13. Seymour Chatman, *A Theory of Meter* (The Hague, 1964), further elaborated by Roger Fowler, "What Is Metrical Analysis?," *The Languages of Literature* (London, 1971), p. 143, who defines "metrical set" as "the psychological reflex of verse design: the disposition of a reader, variable according to his experience and to the metrical regularity of the poem in question, to impose a certain reading on it."

14. As recorded in the *OED*, the rest of the set for *Samson Agonistes* comprises forecást (254; a verb so pronounced in the sixteenth and seventeenth centuries); edíct (from Lat. edíctum), cómbatant (344), Crystálline (547; a Latinizing pronounciation of a Greek loan word used by Milton, Gray, and Shelley); remédiless (648; so pronounced in the fourteenth to seventeenth centuries with a long e sound for the stressed vowel), contést (noun stressed identically to the verb contést until the eighteenth century).

15. Bridges, *Milton's Prosody*, pp. 19–25. For a mild protest against this admittedly unphonetic terminology, see Robert O. Evans, *Milton's Elisions* (Gainesville, Fla., 1966), pp. 5–6.

16. Weismiller, "Studies of Style," p. 270. For other double anapests, see *PL* IV, 597; V, 750; VI, 34, 866; VII, 527; VIII, 299; XI, 79, 377; and *PR* I, 175, 361; IV, 597. In order to cover these instances from *PL* and *PR*, the end of Correspondence Rule 6 must read "immediately adjoining either the beginning of the line or a line-medial caesura."

17. There is an enlightening analogy to be drawn here with Milton's elision practices in *Samson Agonistes*. Clearly he recognized how pervasive his use of elision was, and in strict compensation he all but eliminated the complementary phonetic option of diaresis, or making one syllable in speech count for two in verse. He permits himself only occasiön (425) and evasiöns (842)—an astonishing showing in view of the frequency with which diaresis is metrically utilized by other English Renaissance poets.

18. The autobiographical resonance with Milton's *Second Defense* remains compelling: "There is a certain road which leads through weakness, as the apostle teaches, to the greatest strength. May I be entirely helpless, provided that in my weakness there may arise all the more powerfully this immortal and more perfect strength. . . . For then I shall be at once the weakest and the strongest. . . . By this infirmity may I be perfected, by this completed" (*A Second Defence of the English People*, trans. Donald Mackenzie, in *Complete Prose Works*, vol. 4, ed. Don M. Wolfe (New Haven, 1966), pp. 589–90.

19. The term is due to Kiparsky, "Stress, Syntax, and Meter," 594.

20. For a discussion that adumbrates certain of my findings and contradicts others, see Keith N. Hull, "Rhyme and Disorder in *Samson Agonistes*, " in *Milton Studies* XXX, ed. Albert C. Labriola (Pittsburgh, 1993), pp. 163–81. Hull analyzes rhyme as participating expressively in the thematizing of "turbulence" as well as order, concluding that Milton's deployment of this feature heightens the "radical uncertainty" that such recent critics as Joseph Wittreich and Stanley Fish have taken to be the underlying principle and effect of this drama.

21. A further notable feature of these quatrains is that they are in the so-called "ballad meter" or "common meter" of cross-rhymed, octosyllabic tetrameter stanzas in which sixteenth-and seventeenth-century English hymnodists, not excluding Milton periodically from the 1620s to the 1650s, versified Psalm texts. See Margaret P. Hannay, " 'Psalms done into metre': The Common Psalms of John Milton and of the Bay Colony," *CL* XXXII, no. 3 (1983):

19–29. My analysis of the versification of *Samson Agonistes* indicates that Milton considered the communal assurances and the common-denominator pieties associated with common meter as generically inadequate for lyrics about the *sui generis* superhero, Samson. The rigorous application of the principle of decorum ("the grand master peece to observe") is typically Miltonic and implies no retrospective, blanket disparagement of his English Psalms as such.

"VIGOROUS MOST / WHEN MOST UNACTIVE DEEM'D": GENDER AND THE HEROICS OF ENDURANCE IN MILTON'S *SAMSON AGONISTES*, APHRA BEHN'S *OROONOKO*, AND MARY ASTELL'S *SOME REFLECTIONS UPON MARRIAGE*

Mary Beth Rose

I

THE LATE SEVENTEENTH century in England is often called the age of the failed epic. As its traditionally defined task, the epic celebrates the civilizing components of military conquest. Perhaps not surprisingly, epic idealizations did not convince a culture in which all power relations involving hierarchy and subjection were being eagerly scrutinized and violently redesigned. Indeed, literary representations of the heroic in the Restoration indicate that the experience of civil war and its aftermath robbed "slaughter and gigantic deeds" (*PL* XI, 659) of much of their charisma.[1] Traditional forms of male heroics—concerned with movement and adventure, rescue, exploration, and conquest—characteristically survive in overblown, grandiose versions, as in the heroic drama; or parody, as in *Hudibras*.[2] The most famous epic poem of the period, *Paradise Lost*, decides that marriage is the truly significant human endeavor and wages a full-scale attack on military glory as flashy, anachronistic, and trivial:

> Since first this Subject for Heroic Song
> Pleas'd me long choosing, and beginning late;
> Not sedulous by Nature to indite
> Wars, hitherto the only Argument
> Heroic deem'd, chief maistry to dissect
> With long and tedious havoc fabl'd Knights
> In battles feign'd; the better fortitude
> Of Patience and Heroic Martyrdom
> Unsung; or to describe Races and Games,
> Or tilting Furniture, emblazon'd Shields,
> Impreses quaint, Caparisons and Steeds;

83

Bases and tinsel Trappings, gorgeous Knights
At Joust and Tournament; then marshall'd Feast
Serv'd up in Hall with Sewers, and Seneschals;
The skill of Artifice or Office mean,
Not that which justly gives Heroic name
To Person or to Poem. Mee of these
Nor skill'd nor studious, higher Argument
Remains.   (IX, 25–43)

In this passage Milton does not simply attack the phallic heroics of action; he also announces his intention to transform radically its traditional idealizations of violent conquest. He proposes an alternative and, he argues, superior dimension of heroic identity: that which privileges not the active confrontation with danger, but the capacity to endure it—to resist and suffer with patience and fortitude, rather than to confront and conquer with strength and wit. "Thou hast not half the power to do me harm / As I have to be hurt," Emilia declares triumphantly to Othello (v, ii, 163–64); or, on a less defiantly victimized but equally self-assured note: "They also serve who only stand and wait."[3]

Indeed, Western culture reveals an ongoing preoccupation with both the phallic heroics of action and the heroics of endurance. With its multiplicity of sources, including Seneca and the Stoics, the lives of the Catholic saints, the continuing popularity of medieval treatises on the art of dying, Patient Griselda stories, and the careers and tribulations of both Protestant and Jesuit martyrs related to Renaissance audiences, the heroics of endurance is not so clearly gendered as the heroics of action, and includes both sexes among its protagonists.[4] Yet it is striking that the terms that constitute the heroics of endurance are precisely those terms used to construct the Renaissance idealization of woman: patient suffering, mildness, humility, chastity, loyalty, and obedience.

In this essay I analyze the ways in which modes of heroic identity intersect with conceptions of gender in late seventeenth-century England. I treat heroic subjectivity not simply, or even necessarily, as a kind of behavior, psychology, or morality, but rather as a position in a structure: specifically, as a gendered positioning of the self in relation to pleasure and power. Considering the prominence of the heroics of endurance in the late seventeenth century, I argue that, when viewed together, three Restoration texts—Milton's *Samson Agonistes* (1671), Aphra Behn's *Oroonoko* (1688), and Mary Astell's *Some Reflections Upon Marriage* (1700)—reveal a self-conscious effort to revalue and transform the male heroics of action. From Milton's text to Astell's, the construction and performance of the heroic are accomplished increasingly in terms that are, if ambiguously, nevertheless predominantly, gendered female. All three texts deconstruct the phallic heroics of action by presenting a sustained critique of physical strength as the source of male privilege; and all three texts focus on compromised agency, or agency inscribed in contradictions, as the defining condition of the heroic. This condition is represented first in the hero's position of being seduced into slavery; and second in the relation of the hero's slavery to marriage.

II

In *Samson Agonistes*, the hero first appears as a blind slave, a condition that defines him throughout the play, demanding interpretation. Scholars have defined slavery in terms of power and property relations, variously exploring the slave's alienation and domination. Recently, Orlando Patterson has argued that "archetypically slavery was a substitute for death in war." Emphasizing the ways in which a dishonored acquiescence in physical powerlessness was all that stood between the slave and death, Patterson demonstrates how that violence disenfranchised slaves from the symbolic economy of the culture as well:

Slaves differed from other human beings in that they were not allowed freely to integrate the experience of their ancestors into their lives, to inform their understanding of social reality with the inherited meanings of their natural forebears, or to anchor the living present in any conscious community of memory.[5]

I will return to the peculiar ways in which the texts I am considering use the condition of slavery to interpret violence and death. Here I would like to stress that, when we are first introduced to Samson, his slavery makes manifest his alienation from his own past. Indeed, that the hero is bereft of a usable past, a "community of memory," becomes an informing structural principle of the play.

As Mary Ann Radzinowicz has shown, in a bold revision of the Judges narrative, Milton begins his play where earlier tragedies, such as those by Shakespeare and Marlowe, end: that is, with the defeated hero. Whereas in *Dr. Faustus* or *Macbeth* we witness the entirety of the hero's courageous if doomed trajectory, in *Samson Agonistes* the hero's exploits have become a remembrance of things past, recited, rather than enacted, as a choral lament.[6] At the beginning of the play, the Chorus encounters Samson paralyzed, "dead more than half," and trying to reconcile his divine genealogy and fabled exploits with the horror of his present life. Appalled at the concrete, physical spectacle of fallen might (soiled clothes, drooping head, foul odor, blank eyes), the Chorus exclaims:

O change beyond report, thought, or belief!
· · · · · · · ·
    Can this be hee,
That Heroic, that Renown'd,
Irresistible *Samson*? whom unarm'd
No strength of man, or fiercest wild beast could withstand;
Who tore the Lion, as the Lion tears the Kid,
Ran on embattled Armies clad in Iron,
And weaponless himself,
Made Arms ridiculous.
· · · · · · · ·
Which shall I first bewail,
Thy Bondage or lost Sight,
Prison within Prison
Inseparably dark?
Thou art become (O worst imprisonment!)
The dungeon of thyself.   (117, 124–31, 151–56)

To the Chorus Samson is fallen, his legendary career over. As the passage just quoted makes clear, this conviction comes from a concrete conception of Samson's heroic identity as grounded in his physical strength and warlike victories over his enemies: a traditional phallic heroics of action. Yet, as he makes clear in the invocation to Book IX of *Paradise Lost*, Milton, concerned with a "better fortitude," finds this conception of the heroic inadequate and deluded.[7] In Samson's long opening soliloquy, recited before the Chorus enters the scene, the hero does not so much lament the loss of his strength as interrogate its meaning, asking,

    But what is strength without a double share
Of wisdom? Vast, unwieldly, burdensome,
Proudly secure, yet liable to fall
By weakest subtleties, not made to rule,
But to subserve where wisdom bears command.
God, when he gave me strength, to show withal
How slight the gift was, hung it in my Hair.   (53–59)[8]

Far from elegiacally recalling his past exploits, Samson in fact rejects his past, finding it unusable: "to mee strength is my bane" (63). Indeed the text is ambiguous at several points about whether or not Samson still possesses his fabulous physical might (173–74, 586–87); clearly this manifestation of his legendary heroism is no weapon against present misery. As the opening soliloquy indicates, Samson's heroic career has entered a new phase, a reflective phase that interests Milton much more than the performance of amazing feats. Paralyzed, Samson himself revalues his past by ruminating upon his present compromised agency. Is he the betrayer of his own mission, or helplessly abandoned by God; self-enslaving or seduced into slavery; actor or acted upon; male or female?

The last twenty years or so of research have revealed an economy of gender in the Renaissance based on hierarchy—the male is superior and commanding, the female inferior and subordinate—and binary opposition— his unity and coherence clarify her dispersal and fragmentation; his identification with the soul underscores and transcends hers with the body; his mobility demands her stasis; his speech is animated by her silence. Simply viewed, these connective chains become embodied in representation by active male subjects and passive female objects. As I hope to show, critical analysis reveals the complex ways in which these binary oppositions break down, both from self-generated discursive contradictions and from the empirical evidence of historical experience. Nevertheless these prescriptive binaries remain operative norms and, as such, become informing principles in Renaissance representations of gender relations.

Renaissance courtesy literature and other discourses about gender prescribe the aristocratic male role as that of political leader, warrior, sportsman, and poet; while the aristocratic female, even when educated and accomplished, must serve primarily as the inspiration of masculine endeavor and the provider of (preferably male) heirs through whom property is legitimized and transmitted. Similarly, in the more middle-class households, domesticity is seen to depend upon the male as the public figure, provider, and determiner of meaning, linked to the female as wife and mother, ideally characterized by her adherence to the now notorious trio: silence, chastity, and obedience. It is an economy in which, as ideally conceptualized in all classes of society, women have symbolic power while men have direct agency.

Given the ubiquitous deployment of these norms throughout Renaissance texts, Samson as hero in Milton's play clearly inhabits a subject position gendered female. It is not simply that Samson bitterly taunts himself as effeminate. As slave to the Philistines, he also occupies the passive position of object of the hostile gaze, subject to his enemies' mocking scrutiny and literally rendered helpless by blindness to return the predatory look: "Betray'd, Captiv'd, and both my Eyes put out, / Made of my Enemies the scorn and gaze" (34–35). Second, he explicitly conflates his present slavery with his former position as husband ("Foul effeminacy held me yok't / Her Bondslave," 410–11). By thus inscribing himself within a burgeoning seventeenth-century critique of marriage that equated wifehood with slavery, Samson by implication defines himself as a wife.[9] Further, Samson's gifts from God bind him to silence, inscribed in Renaissance discourses as a female virtue. Whereas men characteristically are found wanting in terms of insufficient eloquence, Samson's crime is "shameful garrulity" (491), one of the most frequently denounced female transgressions.

But what does it mean when the "strongest of mortal men" (168), the phallic hero *par excellence,* occupies a female position, one that, like the Chorus, we tend to regard negatively as vulnerable, passive, and subjected—all Renaissance meanings of the word *effeminate?*[10] I argue that, rather than representing the loss of his heroic identity, Samson's slavery and passivity are constituent of it. Thus the gendered shifts in Samson's identity do not simply signify a descent from former greatness; the deconstruction of his hypermasculinity instead represents a shift in the mode of conceptualizing heroic experience itself.

The components of this shift, and its painfulness, become apparent in the despairing exchange between Samson and his father, Manoa. Upon first entering the scene, the father does not recognize his son (331–36). Manoa's subsequent shocked lament about Samson's condition reveals that his view of his son's heroic identity resembles that of the Chorus: that is, he evaluates Samson's worth according to his effectiveness as a hero of action:

> O miserable change! is this the man,
> That invincible *Samson,* far renown'd,
> The dread of *Israel's* foes, who with a strength
> Equivalent to Angels' walk'd thir streets,
> None offering fight; who single combatant
> Duell'd thir Armies rank't in proud array,
> Himself an army. (340–46)

The ensuing miscommunication between father and son is awful; it takes shape as conflicting interpretations of and allegiances to the hero's past. Upon perceiving his son's blindness and despondency, Manoa loudly bewails his betrayed fatherhood, blaming God. In reply, Samson tries desperately to dwell on his disastrous marriage, emphasizing in no uncertain terms what is important to him. But Manoa denies his son's view of the source of his own misery, dismissively uttering one of the less memorable Miltonic lines, "I cannot praise thy marriage choices, Son" (420). The father thus willfully misses the significance of his son's plight, implicitly defining as trivial Samson's preoccupation with his marriage and emphasizing instead Samson's failure as destroyer of the Philistines and liberator of the Israelites. At this point the Chorus colludes with Manoa's insistent erasures of Samson's past. Until Dalila physically enters the scene, forcing a confrontation, the Chorus refuses either to comprehend or even to acknowledge the significance of Samson's marriage. When, with bitter sorrow, the hero angrily recounts his virtual castration at the hands of his wife (530–40), demanding a response, the Chorus anxiously offers, "Desire of wine and all delicious drinks, / Which many a famous Warrior overturns, / Thou couldst repress" (541–43). But Samson's sufferings are not about alcoholism. He desperately replies, "But what avail'd this temperance, not complete / Against another object more enticing?" (558–59). Now Manoa interjects. Vowing to ransom Samson, he expresses hope in the shape of a wild fantasy of the return of his son's former heroic style.[11] Ignored, Samson realizes that returning to his father's house will turn him into a kind of useless wife, sitting "idle on the household hearth, / A burdenous drone; to visitants a gaze, / Or pitied object" (566–68). Thus the exchange between Manoa and Samson creates the most agonized moment of loss in the play, concluding with Samson wishing for death (594–98) and the Chorus vehemently protesting the injustices of God (668–704).

Manoa and the Chorus are not simply repressed and oblivious; they are also anachronistic in their conception of heroism. As Samson tries repeatedly to tell them, the arena of significance—the arena in which he has endeavored and failed—is not military conquest, but marriage. As is often pointed out, one of the major revisions of Judges in the play is Milton's decision to have Samson and Dalila be married. Indeed, Joseph Wittreich has shown that all of Milton's alterations of the source material amount to an intensification of concern with marriage and deliverance.[12]

Milton's representation of marriage as heroic in the play (as well as in the divorce tracts and in *Paradise Lost*) continues, and perhaps sums up, a century of Protestant commentary in which the public dignity and cosmic significance of marriage are vehemently asserted. As many scholars have shown, during and after the Reformation and coinciding with the centralization of the nation-state, English Protestants developed both political and religious discourses that compared the organization and structure of authority in the family to that of the church and the state.[13] Rather than distinguishing sharply between personal and public concerns and subordinating the former to the latter, this discourse attempts to equate spiritual, public, and private realms by analogizing the husband to God and the king, the wife to the church and the kingdom. As Carol Pateman sums up, "During the political ferment of the seventeenth century . . . conjugal relations and the marriage contract were as central to political debate as the relation between king and subject and the social contract. . . . The terms . . . of the two contracts were used to argue about the proper form of marriage and political rule."[14]

The analogy between the state and the family is, of course, an ancient invention rather than an English Protestant one; but in Renaissance England the Protestants dramatized it with newly elaborated detail and intensity. Arising in part as an attempt to overthrow the prestige of celibacy, Protestant sexual discourse proliferated in a large quantity of widely publicized sermons and tracts idealizing "holy matrimony" as the most critical endeavor of a person's entire spiritual, personal, and public life. Whether the Protestants stress the obstacles or the rewards inherent in marriage, the crucial point becomes their consensus that this relationship constitutes the arena in which the individual can struggle and meet death or defeat, triumph or salvation. To quote Alexander Niccholes, writing in 1615, for example, "Marriage is an adventure, for whosoever marries, adventures; he adventures his peace, his freedom, his liberty, his body; yea, and sometimes his soul too." Furthermore, undertaking this quest, "the means either to exalt on high to preferment, or cast down headlong to destruction," becomes "this one and absolutely greatest action of a man's whole life," requiring the unwavering commitment characteristic of the hero and assuming the properties of inevitable destiny: "as theron depending the future good or evil of a man's whole after-time and days." Marriage is a perilous odyssey, a voyage on a dangerous sea, "wherein so many shipwreck for want of better knowledge and advice upon a rock."[15]

Unlike earlier, doctrinal commentary on the subject, Protestant discourse dwells upon the heroic marriage as a lived relationship. As I have argued at length elsewhere, this detailed focus on sexual and domestic behavior tends to analogize public and private life and to grant them equal importance. Almost as an unacknowledged corollary, the discourse of companionate marriage moves toward a conception of mutuality between husband and wife, thus bringing to light potential contradictions that challenge the principles of hierarchy and subordination characterizing the distribution of authority in patriarchal marriage.[16] Consequently such issues as whether or not a couple needs parental consent in order to marry, or the precise nature and extent of wifely obedience (to name two problems besetting Samson's marriages) become particularly vexed.

Discussions of individual choice of a spouse and the often contradictory need for parental consent in marriage present compelling examples of the double-mindedness of heroic marital discourse. In 1624 the Jacobean Vicar of Banbury, William Whately, declares not untypically that a couple need not obey their parents—"in not suffering them to marrie in the Lord, but offering to force them marrie against the will of God"—only to declare shortly thereafter that a couple marrying without parental consent lives in sin until "they have procured an after-consent, to ratify that which ought not to have been done before the consent."[17] Similarly, wifely obedience is lionized ("By nature woman was made man's subject"),[18] while at the same time material is provided for its subversion: women should never obey husbands who urge them to do "what is forbidden by God."[19] Furthermore, while wives' subjection is absolute (rising against husbands is the equivalent of rising against God), some writers encourage women not only to disobey, but actively to seek to correct, erring husbands.[20] And subjection that is conceived as absolute and natural is nevertheless defined as merely temporal, temporary: "Her place is indeed a place of inferiority and subjection, yet the nearest to equality that may be."[21]

However one assesses heroism and delegates moral responsibility in *Samson Agonistes,* I wish to emphasize the ways in which these issues are dramatized in the conflicted terms of heroic marital discourse. Linking the public and private spheres, Samson himself justifies his marriages in terms of his divine assignment:

> The first I saw at *Timna,* and she pleas'd
> Mee, not my Parents, that I sought to wed,
> The daughter of an Infidel: they knew not
> That what I motion'd was of God; I knew
> From intimate impulse, and therefore urg'd
> The Marriage on.   (219–24).

Notably, the doubts and ambiguities surrounding Samson's marriages are here couched in the problematic terms of the need for parental consent. Further, Samson and Dalila become embroiled in disputes about the boundaries between the public and private spheres and about wifely obedience and subordination. Dalila first attempts to seduce the blinded Samson with declarations of her love and promises of domestic security, possibilities that she ironically presents both as subversive of his public life and as imprisoning (for example, lines 790–819). When Samson responds with rage, she next asserts loyalty to her people as a reason for betraying her husband. Interestingly, Dalila manipulates the ambiguities in the rhetoric of wifely subordination, hinting that to obey Samson would be to do "what is forbidden by God": "It would be to ensnare an irreligious / Dishonorer of Dagon: what had I / To oppose against such powerful arguments?" (860–62). Samson protests with an absolutist definition of wifely obedience, eliding the ambiguities that in fact characterize that concept. He replies that, according to the rules of marriage, *he* has become her country, her world: "Being once a wife, for me thou wast to leave / Parents and country" (885–86). Rebuffed, Dalila proudly avenges and defends herself in similarly absolutist terms as a celebrated woman, "who, to save / Her country from a fierce destroyer, chose / Above the faith of wedlock-bands" (984–86).

In constructing her argument, Dalila speciously subordinates the private to the public sphere ("To the public good / Private respects must yield," 867–68). From Samson's point of view and, indeed, from the construction of the play, Dalila's final outrage is to claim a space for herself in the public sphere. Yet Samson also diminishes the importance of the private sphere, which, as we have seen, is distinguished in heroic marital discourse as having equal significance with the public, to which it is analogously yoked. Evading the complex terms of the heroic marriage upon which he had previously relied ("I was no private," he insists with contempt, "but a person rais'd / With strength sufficient and command from Heav'n / To free my Country," 1211–13), Samson ignores his own (and the play's) insistent knowledge of the central significance of his marriages to his heroism and identity.[22]

In their antagonistic manipulations of Protestant marital discourse, Samson and Dalila both fall prey to the contradictions that are already embedded in its terms. With the inconsistency of self-interest, each attempts to purify and simplify what is muddy and complex. Indignant and confused, the Chorus responds to Samson and Dalila's wrathful marital encounter with a fierce, frustrated assertion of absolute male superiority:

> But virtue which breaks through all opposition,
> And all temptation can remove,
> Most shines and most is acceptable above.
> Therefore God's universal Law
> Gave to the man despotic power
> Over his female in due awe,
> Nor from that right to part an hour,
> Smile she or lour:
> So shall he least confusion draw
> On his whole life, not sway'd
> By female usurpation, nor dismay'd.   (1050–60)

In its lack of logic, this passage recalls Thomas Hobbes's assertion that the only reason for a husband's superiority in marriage is that no one can obey two masters: in short, there is no natural reason. If marital politics were to follow nature, the power and knowledge of mothers would allow them to retain their (naturally) superior position.[23] Closer perhaps to Milton is John Locke's recognition that a husband and wife, "though they have but one common concern, yet having different understandings, will unavoidably sometimes have different wills too; it therefore being necessary that the last determination—i.e., the rule—should be placed somewhere, it naturally falls to the man's share, *as the abler and the stronger*" (my emphasis).[24] Locke unambiguously cites superior physical strength as the natural basis

of male privlege; but, as we have seen, strength is precisely the heroic quality that *Samson Agonistes* deconstructs, subjecting its meaningfulness to
angry and bewildered scrutiny.

Interestingly, in Protestant discourse, the necessary virtue required of
the marital hero of either sex is not physical strength, but patience.[25] After
witnessing Samson's encounter with the Philistine blowhard Harapha,
whose cowardly bullying exposes traditional phallic heroics as no more than
parody, the Chorus finally realizes that a new mode of heroism is called
for. Dismissing "the brute and boist'rous force of violent men / Hardy and
industrious to support / Tyrannic power" (1273–75), Samson's contemporaries announce that

> Patience is more oft the exercise
> Of Saints, the trial of thir fortitude,
> Making them each his own Deliverer,
> And Victor over all
> That tyranny or fortune can inflict,
> Either of these is in thy lot,
> *Samson*, with might endu'd
> Above the Sons of men; but sight bereav'd
> May chance to number thee with those
> Whom patience finally must crown.   (1287–96).

Patience in the face of inevitable affliction; the moral prestige such
affliction grants the sufferer, who is personally chosen by God to endure;
obedience, humility, fortitude: the qualities privileged in the heroics of endurance are the same as those used to construct the Renaissance idealization
of woman. These parallels would at first seem odd in a text so framed by,
and embedded in, masculine constructs as *Samson Agonistes* is. As Michael
Lieb points out, despite the Chorus' idealization of Samson as a patient
sufferer, he is no saint: "The outcome of his *agon* with Harapha is one that
moves him to an ultimate act of glorious and triumphant violence."[26] Second, however problematic traditional male heroics turn out to be, Manoa
delivers a ringing endorsement of Samson's death by praising his legendary
exploits. In my reading of the play, Manoa's tautological view ("Nothing but
well and fair" and "*Samson* hath quit himself / Like *Samson*, and heroicly
hath finish'd / A life heroic," 1723, 1709–11) presents a denial and revision
of reality; but the father's eloquence at least renders ambiguous the nature
of the son's heroic identity by insisting on the need for interpretation. Several other factors also would seem to cast doubt on granting a positive valence to the female in this play. I refer to the rampant misogyny that
inscribes Dalila and characterizes many of the choral mutterings (for ex-

ample, lines 710–24), as well as the curious fact that Milton excises Samson's mother, who plays such a critical part in Judges—a rather drastic revision of the source.[27] Further, in the argument, Milton suppresses mention of Samson's encounter with Dalila, which is arguably the central event of the play. Like his creations in designated moments of their struggles, Milton, when introducing his play and framing its action for the reader, fails to acknowledge the existence of the relationship that he has in fact endowed with multidimensional levels of meaning. Instead he presents the reader with a world composed solely of fathers and sons.

As it is wont to do, however, the repressed returns. While beyond one early mention of "both my parents" (26), Samson's mother disappears from Milton's story, God is represented as a mother: "I was his nursling once and choice delight," Samson explains, "His destin'd from the womb, / Promis'd by Heavenly message twice descending" (633–35). And "the self-begott'n bird" (1699), the phoenix as image of regeneration and renewal with which the Chorus counters Manoa's version of Samson's death is, of course, decisively gendered female:

> From out her ashy womb now teem'd,
> Revives, reflourishes, then vigorous most
> When most unactive deem'd,
> And though her body die, her fame survives
> A secular bird ages of lives.   (1703–07)

Thus at the end of the play, Manoa and the Chorus present rival versions of heroism that compete with each other in gendered terms. As his father's insistent idealization makes clear, Samson's bringing down the pillars of the theater on himself and the Philistines represents a desirable revival (in theological and political terms) of his phallic strength; and Manoa's concluding view commands assent. In contrast, as noted earlier, for the majority of the action Samson performs his heroic identity while occupying a female position. That Milton represents Samson's female heroics as the location of significance in the play is clarified not only by the quantity of time spent focusing on this condition as the meaningful one, but also by the Chorus' eloquent valorization of heroic patience and fortitude (quoted above), that, as noted, is formulated in female terms.

I find the ending of the play unsettling and disturbing, and I am arguing that Milton concludes with two distinctively gendered heroic positions that are represented as rivals and never reconciled. This troubled (and troubling) irresolution is articulated in the frequent debates about the hero's compromised agency that run throughout the play. To what extent has he participated in his own demise, to what extent has he been helplessly be-

trayed, seduced and abandoned into slavery? Interestingly, in those passages where Samson contemplates himself or is contemplated as an object
of seduction, the seducer is sometimes Dalila, sometimes God (for example,
198–210, 359–61).[28] However we interpret the hero's relation to his own
death—whether as a suicide or as a glorious regenerative feat—John
Locke's designation of the component that clinches the definition of the
slave presents an unerring description of Samson's heroic position as he
lowers the pillars of the temple on the Philistines and himself: "Whenever
he finds the hardship of his slavery outweigh the value of his life, it is in his
power, by resisting the will of his master, to draw on himself the death he
desires. This is the perfect condition of slavery."[29] Ironically, despite his
urgent glorification of Samson's masculinity, Manoa himself is responsible
for complicating the gender of his son's legend by bringing him "Home
to his Father's house" (1733) and turning him into a statue. Interestingly,
aestheticization (often as a monument) is frequently the fate of sacrificial
women in Renaissance literature.[30] We can recall that the living Samson had
emphatically refused immobilization in his father's house, using contemptu-
ous imagery of idle wifehood to underscore his resistance (566–68). Thus
Samson's final heroic position—the subject position embodying penultimate
significance—is that of a woman and a slave.

III

In Aphra Behn's *Oroonoko*, the creation of the heroic position as female and
its juxtaposition with slavery are more explicitly and centrally explored. The
story presents a problematic critique of late seventeenth-century English
colonialism, with a particular emphasis on the slave trade. It is divided both
chronologically and geographically into two parts. The first presents the
hero as an honored warrior-prince in his African home, a country called
Coramantien, where his happiness with his beloved, Imoinda, is disrupted
when the king (his grandfather) desires Imoinda, seizes her, and eventually
sells her into slavery, telling Oroonoko she is dead. In the second half, the
hero is himself sold into slavery and is transported to the English colony,
Surinam, where he meets the English narrator, joyfully discovers and re-
unites with Imoinda, stages a doomed rebellion, and dies.

Oroonoko was written in 1688, at a time when the project of imperial
expansion and the slave trade in England were thriving. As scholars have
shown, there was an antislavery debate (although not couched in modern
terms) in the late seventeenth century; but *Oroonoko* only arguably can be
called an abolitionist text.[31] As noted, the African hero and his adored wife
are both duplicitously betrayed into slavery, suffer outrages, and die horribly trying to escape their English masters. Aristocratic Coramantiens be-

lieve that the degradation of slavery is worse than death (p. 27).[32] Yet, as an African prince, Oroonoko himself trades in and owns slaves unambivalently, as a matter of right. Laura Rosenthal has demonstrated that slavery more often appears in this text as a class entitlement, rather than human injustice. She argues convincingly that Behn seems to mandate the slavery practiced by the aristocratic Africans, who win their slaves in battle and trade them as part of a gift economy that Behn sentimentally and conservatively idealizes. On the other hand, the author's critique of English slave-trading practices takes the form of a royalist condemnation of the greed and brazenness characterizing the Whiggish merchant forces that propel colonialism.[33]

Moreover, the narrator's own conflicted relation to slavery disturbingly qualifies the consistency of her critique. While struggling to escape the structures of Eurocentrism by sympathizing with Oroonoko and Imoinda and indignantly rejecting the outrages perpetrated upon them by the English, that sympathy and indignation are in fact deeply divided. The narrator's attitudes toward Oroonoko's blackness present a strong example of her ambivalence. Here is one instance of many in which she rhapsodizes about the prince's physical magnificence on one level while undercutting her praise with unacknowledged distaste on the other: "He was adorn'd with a native Beauty, so transcending all those of his gloomy Race, that he struck an Awe and Reverence, even into those that knew not his Quality; as he did into me, who beheld him with surprize and wonder, when afterwards he arrived in our World" (p. 6).[34] Oroonoko, then, is a very difficult text to sort out in ideological terms. An ambivalent critique of colonialism and slavery, a Eurocentric exposure of Eurocentrism, the text is also complicated by its close relation to Behn's biography and the fact that the narrator herself is clearly a surrogate for the author. By contextualizing Behn's novella among contemporary cultural narratives about slavery and women, along with the biography of Behn herself, Margaret W. Ferguson has cogently summed up these complexities as follows: "Behn's professional and economic interests deviated just enough from those we may ascribe to England's dominant male property owners and investors in the colonies to provide a fascinating example of a female author oscillating among multiple subject positions and between complicity with and critique of the emergent institution of New World slavery."[35]

What form does heroism take in a narrative so fractured by ambivalence? In attempting to locate the heroic in Behn's text, it is useful to examine the many important ways in which Oroonoko resembles Samson Agonistes. Like Milton's play, Oroonoko conjoins the female subject position with slavery and compromised agency and presents the combination as the defining condition of heroism, simultaneously idealizing and scrutinizing the heroics of endurance. As in the earlier text, *Oroonoko* stakes the hero's original claim to audience attention by creating him as a traditional male military champion: "from his natural inclination to Arms, and the Occasions given him . . . he became, at the Age of seventeen, one of the most expert Captains, and bravest Soldiers that ever saw the Field of *Mars:* so that he was ador'd as the wonder of all that World, and the Darling of the Soldiers" (p. 6). However, the narrative does not sustain the idealization of these phallic qualities, which prove wholly inadequate and are destined never to be realized. In the African half of the story, Oroonoko's military abilities are represented rather obliquely, a point to which I will return. In the Surinam half of the story, during his career as a slave, his identity as a hero of action, like Samson's, is reduced to performing feats like a circus strongman to amuse his captors (pp. 50–59). Indeed, when Oroonoko stages an abortive, doomed, slave rebellion, it occurs in the text directly following the narrator's account of his strongman antics (pp. 50–60). Given the hero's dignity, fierceness, and charisma in generating the rebellion, combined with his ineffectuality in pulling it off, the rebellion tends in its violent inconsequence to resemble those brave and remarkable but politically insignificant feats. Again like Samson, Oroonoko tells his secrets to a woman (the narrator), and he is (repeatedly) seduced. Further, he too occupies a female subject position, particularly when enslaved. Much of his time as a slave is spent in the narrator's household, being diverted and entertained: "He liked the Company of us Women much above the Men" (p. 46).[36] Indeed Oroonoko could be seen to be enacting Samson's dreaded fantasy of being a useless wife, "idle on the household hearth." As the narrator explains when accounting for Oroonoko's agitation in captivity, "Though he suffer'd only the Name of a Slave, and had nothing of the Toil and Labour of one, yet that was sufficient to render him uneasy; and he had been too long idle, who us'd to be always in Action, and in Arms. He had a Spirit all rough and fierce, that could not be tam'd to lazy Rest" (p. 47). As in *Samson Agonistes,* the hero's strength proves his bane. Finally, like Samson's, Oroonoko's death bears a close and ambiguous relation to suicide.

Like Milton's, Behn's is an angry and irresolute text, rather than an elegiac one. Just as her predecessor does, Behn presents a hero with a lost past composed of high status and military achievement; and, like *Samson,* *Oroonoko* neither focuses intensely upon, nor mourns the disappearance of, these glories. As discussed above, in *Samson Agonistes* the hero's magnificent exploits (with the exception of the denouement) are always already over. In contrast, the structure and story of *Oroonoko* are half-slave, half-free, with the betrayal of the hero taking place almost exactly in the middle. Distinctly divided into two parts, in which the prince loses his country and his birthright and becomes a slave, the text would seem to present another good example of the ways in which the enslaved hero is deprived of a usable past. More interesting for purposes of this discussion, however, are the links between the subject positions the hero inhabits during his freedom and his slavery.

In contrast to Samson's original, horrific appearance in the play, Oroonoko begins as a handsome, brave, famous soldier, and he remains one for the first half of the story. While the narrator describes Oroonoko's valiance at length, however, most of the dramatized incidents represent his paralysis. This attenuation of traditional male heroics is in fact applicable to both halves of the story, not simply the second, when the hero is enslaved in Surinam. His African adventures primarily concern his thwarted love for Imoinda. Oroonoko's grandfather is the king in Coramantien; enchanted by Imoinda's beauty, the impotent old man seizes her for his own while Oroonoko is off hunting. Although the African kinship system makes it especially difficult for Oroonoko to defy his grandfather, the narrative nevertheless indicates that defiance is an option that the prince rejects:

It was objected to him, That . . . Imoinda being his lawful Wife by solemn Contract, 'twas he was the injur'd Man, and might, if he so pleas'd, take Imoinda back, the breach of the Law being on his Grandfather's side; and that if he cou'd circumvent him, and redeem her . . . it was both just and lawful for him so to do. (P. 14)

Oroonoko instead responds to Imoinda's loss by proving "pensive, and altogether unprepar'd for the Campaign . . . he lay negligently on the ground, and answer'd very little" (p. 23). Later, he "laid himself on a Carpet, under a rich Pavilion, and remained a good while silent," vowing "that henceforth he would never lift a Weapon, or draw a bow" (pp. 27–28). The point is not that these are the conventional postures of a melancholy lover, but that Behn is interested in exploring heroic agency as paralyzed, grieved, and oppressed. Oroonoko often figures in the narrative as the passive object of the admiring, awe-struck gaze (pp. 6, 30, 39, 41). And his most frequent posture by far is not that of the valiant male conqueror, but of the female object of seduction. In Coramantien he is seduced out of his grief for Imoinda (whom his grandfather tells him is dead) and into slavery; on the slave ship he is seduced into remaining alive with lying reassurances of freedom; in Surinam he is seduced into believing that he and Imoinda will be released, into believing he won't be whipped, and into believing he will be killed, rather than forced to endure further indignities.

Oroonoko's identity as a phallic hero of action is suggestively attenuated in the African half of the novel, then; but the conditions of the heroic as Behn envisions them are starkly and unmistakably revealed during the hero's captivity in Surinam and in the manner of his death. His death occurs in an extended episode of prolonged agony, in which he leads the unsuccessful slave revolt, is deserted by all of the other slaves, kills the pregnant Imoinda in a suicide pact, then fails to kill himself and is captured, tortured, and hideously dismembered by the English colonists.

Why does Oroonoko not kill himself, rather than letting himself be killed?[37] At one point he names revenge as his motive for remaining alive after Imoinda's death (pp. 70–73); yet he neither avenges his enemies nor takes his own life. Instead he lies paralyzed by his wife's dead body until his captors discover him. At this point, readers may find themselves wishing that the hero would release himself from further betrayal and torment. Yet, like Job, he refuses to curse God and die. We can recall that, according to Locke, the ability to commit suicide when captivity becomes intolerable is the "perfect condition of slavery." Thus by resisting suicide, Oroonoko resists self-definition as a slave. This argument is borne out by the fact that a model of the heroics of endurance which valorizes the patient suffering of unspeakable pain is twice singled out for praise by the narrator. The first instance is a description of the proud and horrifying mutilations that the warriors among the native American Indians who inhabit Surinam are seen to inflict upon themselves:

Being brought before the old Judges, now past Labour, they are ask'd, What they dare do, to shew they are worthy to lead an Army? When he who is first ask'd, making no reply, cuts off his Nose, and throws it contemptibly on the ground; and the other does something to himself that he thinks surpasses him, and perhaps deprives himself of Lips and an Eye: so they slash on till one gives out, and many have dy'd in this Debate. And it's by a passive Valour they shew and prove their Activity. (P. 58)

Stating that "For my part, I took 'em for Hobgoblins, or Fiends, rather than Men," the narrator with characteristic obliquity assures the reader that the Indians' self-violence presents "a sort of Courage too brutal to be applauded by our *Black* Hero; nevertheless, he express'd his Esteem of 'em" (p. 58). However, referring later to Oroonoko's own beatings, woundings, and dismemberments, she states, "I have a thousand times admired how he lived in so much tormenting Pain" (p. 68). And as the penultimate representation of greatness, the narrator presents Oroonoko's death with admiring awe as a spectacle of the endurance of grotesque and humiliating pain:

He had learn't to take Tobacco; and when he was assur'd he should die, he desir'd they would give him a Pipe in his Mouth, ready lighted; which they did: And the Executioner came, and first cut off his Members, and threw them into the Fire; and after that, with an ill-favour'd Knife, they cut off his Ears and his Nose, and burn'd them; he still smoak'd on, as if nothing had touch'd him; then they hack'd off one of his Arms, and still he bore up, and held his Pipe; but at the cutting off of the other Arm, his Head sunk, and his Pipe dropt and he gave up the Ghost, without a Groan, or a Reproach. (P. 77)

Oroonoko's heroic agency, then, is manifested in the nonsuicidal (and so nonslavish) endurance of suffering; the one resolution he keeps is that "he would stand fix'd like a Rock, and endure Death so as should encourage them [i.e., his captors] to die" (p. 77). Yet Oroonoko *is* a slave and, being human property, cannot escape what Carole Pateman defines as "the contradiction inherent in slavery, that the humanity of the slave must necessarily be simultaneously denied and affirmed."[38] This contradiction is, of course, applicable (with some qualifications) to seventeenth-century women, who were also simultaneously considered both property and persons. Oroonoko's inscription in contradiction becomes apparent when the components of his heroism are broken down in gendered terms. The ambivalent conditions that define the heroic in this text are fully revealed when Oroonoko's destiny is compared with, and elaborated by means of, those of the two women with whom he shares the stage: Imoinda and the narrator.

As has been analyzed extensively elsewhere, the narrator's position in the text is one of discursive incoherence, particularly in her attitudes and behavior toward Oroonoko. Thus while reciting the events of the hero's death with appalled outrage, the narrator also unwittingly clarifies her own complicity in it. Although she claims a special friendship with Oroonoko and Imoinda, among the English colonists, she is the major protagonist in the plot to seduce the royal slaves from thoughts of their freedom. The narrator confides that she assured Oroonoko of his eventual freedom and then speaks with dismay of his being "fed . . . from day to day with Promises" (p. 45), as though she were not one of the offenders. Afterwards she confesses, seemingly with no sense of disparity, that she in fact spied on him and schemed against his freedom: "I was obliged, by some Persons who fear'd a Mutiny . . . to discourse with [him] and to give him all the Satisfaction I possibly could" (p. 46); and that she came to mistrust him: "I neither thought it convenient to trust him much out of our view, nor did the Country, who fear'd him" (p. 48); and, later, "We were possess'd with extreme Fear, which no Persuasions could dissipate, that he would secure himself till night, and then, that he would come down and cut all our Throats" (p. 68). Finally, seemingly (and oddly) to exonerate herself, she confesses to abandoning him twice, in instances when he is tortured and at last killed: "For I suppose I had Authority and Interest enough there, had I suspected any such thing, to have prevented it" (p. 68).[39]

Oroonoko and the narrator, then, each possess compromised and strained agency. As noted, Oroonoko is paralyzed by the obvious contradiction that, like a woman, a slave is property while simultaneously remaining a human being. The narrator implicitly recognizes her connections to the hero when she links what she considers to be the inferiority of her female authorship with Oroonoko's destiny as a slave. For example, at exactly the point when the hero is renamed "Caesar" (being renamed and so possessed is the fate of women and slaves), she remarks, "His Misfortune was, to fall in an obscure World, that afforded only a Female Pen to celebrate his Fame" (p. 40). In the final words of the story, she announces cryptically, "Thus died this great Man, worthy of a better Fate, and a more sublime Wit than mine to write his Praise" (p. 78). However, identifying with the female position of the slave, the narrator, as discussed above, also identifies with and participates in the European structures that oppress him and, presumably, herself.

Like the narrator, the hero is both slave and slave-master. While his position as an owner is explicit before he himself becomes a slave, Oroonoko enacts his conflicted identity with painful clarity when he kills his wife. As scholars like Patterson have pointed out, one of the characteristics of slavery is the slave's lack of control over kinship ties.[40] In this sense, as Charlotte Sussman cogently argues, Oroonoko's killing of Imoinda, which also includes aborting their child, proves an act of mastery, a resistance to slavery. The gruesomely ironic fact—that Oroonoko can assert mastery only in this destructive and self-destructive sense—points in a circular fashion back to his slavery. Sussman makes the interesting point that Oroonoko acts out this duality when confronting his captors over his wife's dead body: cutting flesh from his own throat, he imitates slitting Imoinda's; disemboweling himself, he "recalls that he has just effectively aborted Imoinda's child. . . . Thus, the sign of Oroonoko's courage to choose a noble death over the shame of slavery is also a repetition of the sign of his absolute possession of wife and child." Yet, "the code of nobility that Oroonoko writes on his own body signifies his power over a woman, not his emancipation from slavery."[41]

If the ambivalent conditions characterizing Oroonoko's identity and agency as owner and slave are displaced onto the white female narrator, Imoinda also enacts displaced parts of her husband's heroic identity: namely, his slavery. Like the narrator's, Imoinda's explicitly female destiny clarifies the multiple meanings of the heroics of endurance. As Ferguson and Sussman have made clear, it is the black slave/wife who unambiguously bears the symbolic brunt of powerlessness in the text. At critical points in the narrative (during the slave revolt, for example), Imoinda shows herself capable of courageous deeds; she is the only slave who attacks a white male ruler. Indeed, Ferguson has argued convincingly for a causal relation be-

tween Imoinda's physical courage and her death.[42] But the major significance of her actions is her willingness to die at her husband's hands, a scene
which the narrator describes as follows: "He told her his Design, first of
killing her, and then his Enemies, and next himself, and the Impossibility
of escaping, and therefore he told her the Necessity of dying. He found the
heroick Wife faster pleading for Death, than he was to propose it, when she
found his fix'd Resolution . . . for Wives have a respect for their Husbands
equal to what any other People pay a Deity" (pp. 71–72).

When describing Imoinda's marriage, the narrator romanticizes her
subordinate condition as accepted without ambivalence, even joyfully. But
Behn also directly connects the violence that defines all slavery with Imoinda's sexuality, including, by implicit extension, female sexuality in general.
In Africa, kidnapped by the doting grandfather, Imoinda occupies the status
of possession even before she literally becomes a slave. We have already
seen how her death at her husband's hand embodies all the tragic ironies of
slavery. There is also an earlier, very telling conflation of violence, female
sexuality, and slavery. After his capture, Oroonoko befriends his owner,
Trefry, and, learning that Trefry is suffering from unrequited love of a slave
and not yet knowing that the slave is Imoinda, Oroonoko asks Trefry why
he does not simply rape the object of his desires. Trefry replies, "I have
been ready to make use of those Advantages of Strength and Force Nature
has given me: But Oh! she disarms me with that Modesty and Weeping, so
tender and so moving, that I retire and thank my Stars she overcame me.
The Company laugh'd at his Civility to a Slave" (pp. 42–43).

IV

With this conflation of the woman/wife and the slave as vulnerable to sexual
violence, Aphra Behn represents male dominance based on physical
strength as a figure for all oppression. While in Behn's text the conjunction
is implicitly articulated and ambivalently qualified in multifaceted representations, in Mary Astell's Some Reflections Upon Marriage, the conflation of
the woman/wife and the slave is directly and systematically developed in
impassioned polemic. As noted, Behn manages with self-serving sentimen-
tality to sever the single white woman narrator's more powerful position
from that of the black, married slave; further, in Behn's narrative structure
Imoinda's story is crucial, but decentered. Astell's text is also divided between a single woman narrator (in this case Astell herself) who is not disem-
powered and a married woman who is by definition a slave. But in Astell's
text, the wife/slave is the central figure. No longer displaced, no longer met-
aphorical, her identity is now literal; she has become the hero.

If the defining condition of slavery is that it presents the only alternative to death, then the conflation of the wife and the slave could be seen as structurally imperfect. Locke, for example, argues that the public and private spheres are distinguished precisely by the fact that the husband, *unlike* the sovereign, does not possess the power of life and death over his wife.[43] Nevertheless, Patterson's analysis of the slave as a "social nonperson," or Pateman's of the wife and the slave as each civilly dead, demonstrates the power and cogency of the analogy when extended beyond the literal. Like Milton, when defining the configurations of power and desire in marriage, Astell draws on decades of Protestant discourses that analogize marriage to the state, linking the public and private spheres. Interestingly, when defining the married woman in no uncertain terms as a slave, Astell attacks Milton:

Patience and Submission are the only Comforts that are left to a poor People, who groan under Tyranny, unless they are Strong enough to break the Yoke, to Depose and Abdicate, which I doubt wou'd not be allow'd of here [i.e., in marriage]. For whatever may be said against Passive-Obedience in another case, I suppose there's no Man but likes it very well in this; how much soever Arbitrary Power may be dislik'd on a Throne, Not *Milton* himself wou'd cry up Liberty to poor *Female Slaves,* or plead for the Lawfulness of Resisting a Private Tyranny. (Pp. 28–29)[44]

Astell and Milton are political opposites: he is a Puritan radical and regicide who, despite ambivalence about hierarchy, buttresses male superiority; she is a conservative, monarchist, high Anglican Tory, who (inconsistently, given her use of the family-state analogy) protests male superiority in the private sphere.[45] Interestingly, just as they do in *Samson Agonistes,* the contradictions in *Some Reflections* emerge through the representation of the problematic concept of wifely obedience (as we have seen, in Behn's text this tricky issue is romanticized and its contradictions self-consciously erased).

Although she concludes her polemic with an idealized version of heroic female patience, in the passage quoted above Astell is not recommending obedience and patience as heroic, but rather is defining them as limiting, indicating lack of empowerment. The mixed message is forcefully apparent in her consideration of the constraints on female agency. On the one hand, she argues that women have no agency in the marriage market: "A Woman indeed can't properly be said to Choose, all that is allow'd her, is to Refuse or Accept what is offer'd" (p. 23). On the other hand, she herself has pointedly chosen *not* to marry. And in later sections of her essay, she asserts that women do have a choice in the selection of mates:

She who Elects a Monarch for Life, who gives him an Authority she cannot recall however he misapply it, who puts her Fortune and Person entirely in his Power; nay even the very desires of her Heart according to some learned Casuists, so as that it is not lawful to Will or Desire any thing but what he approves and allows, had need be very sure that she does not make a Fool her Head, nor a Vicious Man her Guide and Pattern, she had best stay till she can meet with one who has the Government of his own Passions and has duly regulated his own Desires, since he is to have such an absolute Power over hers. (Pp. 32–33)

This hypothesis of a good husband in effect deconstructs itself, as Astell dwells so insistently on the unequal power relationships that define marriage. Notably, no examples of good marriages appear in the text. Second, Astell employs the traditional feminist argument that women suffer not from essential, gendered inferiority, but from lack of an education and the options it introduces: "But, alas! what poor Woman is ever taught that she should have a higher Design than to get her a Husband?" (p. 66). After marriage, a woman "has nothing else to do but to Please and Obey" (p. 59); further, "she who can't do this is no way fit to be a Wife" (p. 60). The not-so-subtext of this analysis is that, given the construction of marriage as a tyranny, no woman is fit to be a wife. To put this proposition another way, wifehood is not suitable for any woman.

Why, then, do women consistently go about surrendering the little agency they have, however compromised, in order to get married? That men and women should be attracted to one another simply is not a possibility for Astell. Sexual desire, so critical and passionately destructive in Milton's text and Behn's, becomes trivial, foolish, vain delusion in Astell's. In her most ferocious foray against the heroics of endurance, she exposes the connection between passive obedience and seduction. She delivers a brilliant, devastating attack on courtship as idolatrous and deceptive, designed to induct women into a life of servitude: "he may call himself her Slave a few days, but it is only in order to make her his all the rest of his Life" (p. 25). With dramatically restrained rage, Astell presents a most unrelenting exposure of the contempt for women that lies behind male courtship, with its abstract, insistent idealizations: "For nothing is in truth a greater outrage than Flattery and feign'd Submissions, the plain English of which is this: . . . 'We who make the Idols, are the greater Deities; and as we set you up, so it is in our power to reduce you to your first obscurity, or to somewhat worse, to Contempt' " (pp. 25–26). In imagery that recalls *Samson Agonistes*, she concludes that "a Blind Obedience is what a Rational Creature shou'd never Pay" (p. 87).

Astell's analysis of the dynamics of seduction leads her, like Milton and Behn, to recognize physical strength as the misguided source of male dominance. Rather than mourning male valor as sadly lost, she attacks the idea of the supposed superiority of male strength with unspeakable, classist glee:

It were ridiculous to suppose that a Woman, were she ever so much improv'd, could come near the topping Genius of Men, and therefore why shou'd they envy or discourage her? Strength of Mind goes along with Strength of Body, and 'tis only for some odd accidents which Philosophers have not yet thought worthwhile to enquire into, that the Sturdiest Porter is not the Wisest Man. As therefore the Men have the Power in their Hands, so there's no dispute of their having the Brains to manage it. . . . Do not men generally speaking do all the great Actions and considerable Business of this world, and leave that of the next to the Women? . . . Justice and Injustice are administred by their Hands, Courts and Schools are fill'd with these Sages; . . . Histories are writ by them, they recount each others great Exploits, and have always done so. . . . Indeed what is it they can't perform, when they attempt it? (Pp. 91–92)

Having thoroughly undercut the traditional bases of the male heroics of action, Astell has little choice but to propose an alternative subjectivity grounded in endurance. That heroism is distinctly female: "For she . . . who can be so truly mortify'd as to lay aside her own Will and Desires, to pay such an entire Submission for Life, to one whom she cannot be sure will always deserve it, does certainly perform a more Heroic Action than all the famous Masculine Heroes can boast of" (p. 93). Yet Astell's exposure of the humiliating, oppressive, and compromising conditions defining this martyrdom has been potent enough to mitigate its claims for approval. At one point she does envision equality between the sexes, although interestingly not in the marriage relation, but in the public sphere: "She will discern a time when her Sex shall be no bar to the best Employments, the highest Honor . . . provided she is not wanting to her self, her Soul shall shine as bright as the greatest Heroe's" (p. 88).

V

Astell does not develop this visionary insight. Like Milton's and Behn's, her argument implies that only revolutions can change the existing interrelations of gender and power; and, like Milton and Behn, she finds that revolutions fail. Like *Samson Agonistes* and *Oroonoko, Some Reflections Upon Marriage* is a text extraordinary for its anger and despair. All three texts begin with the premise that the heroics of action is ineffectual, outdated; and none mourns the demise of traditional, phallic glory as the legitimate form of the heroic. Instead, all three propose an alternative heroics of endurance, that, while idealized with varying intensity in each, is shown in all to incur terrible costs. Indeed this heroism is presented at best as ambivalent and compromised, at worst as bitter and scathing. Elaborated in terms of seduction, marriage, and slavery, the heroic attains its purest form in Astell's text when the wife and the slave literally become the same person, who is also the figure of major significance: that is, the hero. Each text presents a central figure who is seduced into slavery and paralyzed, caught between being identified with, and opposed to, other central figures. This contradictory position, conflated in each case with slavery, is also and always a female position, the position of the woman. In *Samson Agonistes, Oroonoko,* and *Some Reflections Upon Marriage,* it becomes the situation of the hero, forming the combination of factors that defines and constitutes heroic experience.

The Newberry Library, Chicago

NOTES

I would like to thank the American Council of Learned Societies for the fellowship that made possible the completion of this essay.

1. For an analysis of the fortunes of the epic in its relation to politics and history during the Restoration, see Nigel Smith, *Literature and Revolution in England: 1640–1660* (New Haven, 1994), especially chapt. 7, pp. 203–49. Arguing that the civil war created a "process of transformation in which epic and heroic language was made to refer to inward states of human constitution and consciousness" (p. 203), Smith traces the ways in which the epic's dialogue with history keeps changing epic structure and plot. He concludes that "The Civil War had proved the decadence of aristocratic martial, honour culture, and after 1660 traditional epic was no longer possible" (p. 233).

All citations from Milton's poetry are from John Milton, *Complete Poems and Major Prose,* ed. Merritt Y. Hughes (Indianapolis, 1957), and are cited in the text by book and/or line number.

2. See Michael Wilding, *Dragons Teeth: Literature in the English Revolution* (Oxford, 1987), pp. 173–204. Wilding comments that, "although past civil wars had later found epic treatment, the contemporary slaughter of fellow-countrymen could have little appeal" (p. 173). He goes on to demonstrate the antimilitary critique of traditional heroics in *Paradise Lost* and *Hudibras,* "the two most famous heroic poems of the Restoration."

3. William Shakespeare, *Othello,* ed. M. R. Ridley (London, 1958). The Milton quotation is from *Sonnet XIX.*

4. See Reuben A. Brower, *Hero and Saint: Shakespeare and the Graeco-Roman Tradition* (New York, 1971), and John Steadman, *Milton and the Renaissance Hero* (Oxford, 1967).

5. Orlando Patterson, *Slavery and Social Death: A Comparative Study* (Cambridge, Mass., 1982), p. 5. Also see William D. Phillips Jr., *Slavery from Roman Times to the Early Transatlantic Slave Trade* (Minneapolis, 1985).

6. Mary Ann Radzinowicz, "The Distinctive Tragedy of *Samson Agonistes,*" in *Milton Studies* XVII, ed. Richard S. Ide and Joseph Wittreich (Pittsburgh, 1983), pp. 249–50.

7. For an account of other seventeenth-century texts that, in contrast to Milton's play, glorify Samson as a military hero, see Joseph Wittreich, *Interpreting Samson Agonistes* (Princeton, 1986), esp. pp. 103–105. Wittreich argues that Milton's play undertakes a reevaluation of heroism, but he (Wittreich) tends to define the heroic in moral terms: for example, "Milton's Samson is no villain, to be sure, but he *is* deeply flawed and thus ambiguous in his heroism" (italics his). Also see Steadman, *Milton and the Renaissance Hero,* p. 27.

8. For an invaluable analysis of what he terms Milton's "theology of strength," see Michael Lieb, *The Sinews of Ulysses: Form and Convention in Milton's Works* (Pittsburgh, 1989), pp. 98–138. Lieb traces Milton's appropriation of the Old Testament tradition of conceptualizing strength as a manifestation of God's power and wisdom and the New Testament transvaluation of that concept into a paradoxical new form of strength as spiritual, rather than physical, and perfected in weakness: that is, in the patient endurance of affliction and suffering.

9. See Carole Pateman, *The Sexual Contract* (Stanford, 1988), p. 120.

10. See Alan Sinfield, *Cultural Politics—Queer Reading* (Philadelphia, 1994), p. 15, who provides a good assessment of the ways in which effeminacy in the Renaissance was connected not with male homoeroticism, but with heterosexuality and, particularly, with men who behaved or felt in what would normally be considered a "female" manner.

11. Compare Lieb, *Sinews of Ulysses*, p. 124, who observes that, "Where Manoa errs, of course, is in assuming that the full return of strength can be realized without appropriate suffering." What Manoa offers is rest, but "it is indeed the rest of escape."

12. See Wittreich, *Interpreting*, pp. 62–80.

13. The bibliography on the relations of the family and the state in the Renaissance has become extremely large. I offer only a few titles, many of which can lead the reader to other materials. While widely debated, Lawrence Stone's *The Family, Sex and Marriage in England 1500–1800* (New York, 1977), remains invaluable. Also see Jack Goody, *The Development of the Family and Marriage in Europe* (Cambridge, 1983); Gordon J. Schochet, *Patriarchalism in Political Thought: The Authoritarian Family and Political Speculation and Attitudes, Especially in Seventeenth-Century England* (Oxford, 1975); Margaret J. Ezell, *The Patriarch's Wife: Literary Evidence and the History of the Family* (Chapel Hill, N.C., 1987); Susan Dwyer Amussen, *An Ordered Society: Gender and Class in Early Modern England* (Oxford, 1988), p. 314; and Frances E. Dolan, *Dangerous Familiars: Representations of Domestic Crime in England, 1550–1700* (Ithaca, 1994).

14. Pateman, *Sexual Contract*, p. 90.

15. Alexander Niccholes, *A Discourse of Marriage and Wiving* (London, 1615), in *Harleian Miscellany*, vol. 2, ed. William Oldys (1808–13), pp. 162, 159, 164, 159, 161.

16. See Mary Beth Rose, *The Expense of Spirit: Love and Sexuality in English Renaissance Drama* (Ithaca, 1988), pp. 116–31, and "Where Are the Mothers in Shakespeare? Options for Gender Representation in the English Renaissance," *Shakespeare Quarterly* (Fall 1991): 291–314.

17. William Whately, *A Care-Cloth* (London, 1624), pp. 33–34.

18. John Dod and Robert Cleaver, *A Godlie Forme of Householde Government* (London, 1635), p. 149.

19. William Gouge, *Of Domesticall Duties* (London, 1622), p. 328.

20. See, for example, Gouge, *Of Domesticall*, pp. 295, 328, and Dod and Cleaver, *A Godlie Forme*, sig. o6r.

21. Gouge, *Of Domesticall*, p. 356.

22. Compare John Guillory, "Dalila's House: *Samson Agonistes* and the Sexual Division of Labor," in *Rewriting the Renaissance: The Discourses of Sexual Difference in Early Modern Europe*, ed. Margaret W. Ferguson, Maureen Quilligan, and Nancy Vickers (Chicago, 1986), pp. 106–22, and "The Father's House: *Samson Agonistes* in Its Historical Moment," in *Re-Membering Milton: Essays on the Texts and Traditions*, ed. Mary Nyquist and Margaret W. Ferguson (New York, 1988), pp. 148–76.

23. Thomas Hobbes, *Leviathan*, ed. Michael Oakeshott (New York, 1962), pp. 152–153.

24. John Locke, *The Second Treatise of Civil Government*, in *Two Treatises of Government*, ed. Thomas I. Cook (New York, 1947), p. 161.

25. See, for example, Gouge, *Of Domesticall*, p. 241, and Whately, *A Care-Cloth*, pp. 80–82.

26. Michael Lieb, *Milton and the Culture of Violence* (Ithaca, 1994), p. 260.

27. Compare Jackie DiSalvo, "Intestine Thorn: Samson's Struggle with the Woman Within," in *Milton and the Idea of Woman*, ed. Julia Walker (Urbana, 1988), pp. 211–29.

28. Compare *Paradise Regained*, the companion text to *Samson Agonistes*, in which Christ unproblematically inhabits the position of female hero, defined by his absolute resistance to being seduced. In further contrast, Christ ends by peacefully (unambivalently) returning home to his mother's house, although we know he will not remain there.

29. Locke, *Second Treatise*, p. 133.

30. Compare Rose, *The Expense of Spirit*, pp. 93–127, for a relevant discussion of the fates of Zenocrate in Marlowe's *Tamburlaine*, Desdemona, and the Duchess of Malfi.

31. See Laura Brown, "The Romance of Empire: *Oroonoko* and the Trade in Slaves," in *The New Eighteenth Century: Theory, Politics, English Literature*, ed. Felicity Nussbaum and Laura Brown (New York, 1987), pp. 41–61; and Moira Ferguson, *Subject to Others: British Women Writers and Colonial Slavery, 1670–1834* (New York, 1992), pp. 3–49.

32. All citations from *Oroonoko* are taken from the edition edited by Lore Metzger (New York, 1973).

33. Laura J. Rosenthal, "Owning Oroonoko: Behn, Southerne, and the Contingencies of Property," in *Renaissance Drama*, n.s. 23 (1992): 25–58.

34. For essays that deal with the complexities of the relation of skin color to conceptions of race in the early modern period, see *Women, "Race," and Writing in the Early Modern Period*, ed. Margo Hendricks and Patricia Parker (London, 1994), Kim F. Hall, "Guess Who's Coming to Dinner? Colonization and Miscegenation in *The Merchant of Venice*," *Renaissance Drama* XXIII (1992): 87–111; and Margo Hendricks, "Managing the Barbarian: *The Tragedy of Dido, Queen of Carthage*," *Renaissance Drama* XXIII (1992): 165–88.

35. Margaret Ferguson, "News from the New World: Miscegenous Romance in Aphra Behn's *Oroonoko* and *The Widow Ranter*," in *The Production of English Renaissance Culture*, ed. David Lee Miller, Sharon O'Dair, and Harold Weber (Ithaca, N.Y., 1994), pp. 151–89. Compare her "Juggling the Categories of Race, Class and Gender: Aphra Behn's *Oroonoko*," in *Women, "Race" and Writing*, pp. 209–24, and "Transmuting *Othello*: Aphra Behn's *Oroonoko*," in *Cross-Cultural Performances: Differences in Women's Re-Visions of Shakespeare*, ed. Marianne Novy (Urbana, Ill., 1993), pp. 15–49. For further valuable discussion of the ideological complexity of the text, see Brown, "The Romance of Empire," pp. 41–61, and Moira Ferguson, *Subject to Others*, pp. 27–49.

36. For a brilliant analysis of Oroonoko's vulnerability to being entertained, see Robert L. Chibka, " 'Oh! Do Not Fear a Woman's Invention': Truth, Falsehood, and Fiction in Aphra Behn's *Oroonoko*," in *TSLL* XXX, no. 4 (Winter 1988): 510–37.

37. For further discussion of this point, see Moira Ferguson, *Subject to Others*, 40–45.

38. Pateman, *The Sexual Contract*, p. 60.

39. Compare Margaret Ferguson, "Juggling," pp. 214–15, where she traces the narrator's inconsistent use of personal pronouns when she (the narrator) uneasily seeks to identify herself both with the slaves and the colonialists.

40. Patterson, *Slavery and Social Death*, p. 13. See also Phillips, *Slavery from Roman Times*, pp. 6–14.

41. Charlotte Sussman, "The Other Problem with Women: Reproduction and Slave Culture in Aphra Behn's *Oroonoko*," in *Reading Aphra Behn: History, Theory, and Criticism*, ed. Heidi Hutner (Charlottesville, Va., 1993), p. 220.

42. Ferguson, "Juggling," p. 222; Ferguson, "Transmuting," p. 35; and Sussman, "The

Other Problem," pp. 212–33. I am also grateful to Carolyn Swift, who was the first to point out to me to the importance of the fact that Imoinda wounds the governor.

43. See Locke, *Second Treatise*, pp. 161–63.

44. All citations come from Mary Astell, *Some Reflections Upon Marriage, Occasion'd by the Duke and Dutchess of Mazarine's Case; Which Is Also Consider'd.* 2nd ed. (London, 1703).

45. For astute analyses of the contradictions between and among Astell's feminism and her political and religious conservatism, see Ruth Perry, *The Celebrated Mary Astell: An Early English Feminist* (Chicago, 1986), pp. 150–69; and Catherine Gallagher, "Embracing the Absolute: The Politics of the Female Subject in Seventeenth-Century England," *Genders* I (March 1988): 24–39.

THE SECRET OF *SAMSON AGONISTES*

John Rogers

I T I S N O secret that the problem of *Samson Agonistes* that has most consistently provoked Milton's critics is the question of the presence of divine authority for Samson's final action, his destruction of both himself and the Philistine aristocracy at the festival of Dagon. As early as his 1651 *Defence of the English People,* Milton had raised the issue that would prove so central to his literary treatment of the story, the question of whether Samson's heroism "was instigated by God, or by his own valor."[1] Milton scholars have largely assumed that this query, which Milton had permitted to float unanswered in 1651, must have been given in *Samson Agonistes* a final, definitive solution. And it is the literary critical attempt to determine the content of that solution that has founded the conflicting schools of *Samson* criticism. The scholarly identification of the source of the "rousing motions" that impel Samson to tug and shake the pillars of the temple has established itself as a necessary labor for all the poem's critics: it is the task performed in the traditional assessment of Samson's divine authorization, as well as in the more recent revisionist evaluation of the hero's irrational, merely instinctive barbarity. I will not attempt here to adjudicate the conflict between these increasingly entrenched positions; I will pursue rather an understanding of the function of what all critical parties must concede to be the evident ambiguity of Milton's representation of Samson's final action. If the larger problem of the divine or instinctive cause of Samson's action presents itself as this poem's central interpretive riddle, then we might profitably approach the meaning of that riddle by way of its manifestation within the poem's own plot. I refer to the poem's explicitly narrativized mystery, of unquestionable interest to the fictional characters, to which Samson refers as his "capital secret": "in what part my strength / Lay stor'd, in what part summ'd" (394–95). The theological question of the instigating source of Samson's action finds a narrative embodiment in the question of the source and location of Samson's strength: whether that strength is literally "stor'd" in the "capital" part of Samson's body, his hair, or whether it is merely "summ'd" there, a divinely derived power that has its corporeal summation, or simple testamentary ornament, in the champion's glorious locks. I will examine the secret buried in the hero's body not necessarily as a secret whose positive content can finally be revealed, but one whose status *as* secret is central to the theological, and, I will suggest, the ideological, import of Milton's poem.

I

With its focus on the hero's "capital secret," *Samson Agonistes* muses over the same riddle worried by the Philistines in the Book of Judges, who in their desire to rein in Samson press Delilah to ascertain "wherein his great strength lieth" (xvi, 5).[2] The writers responsible for the Judges text may have been a little puzzled themselves, as we will see, about the proper answer to this question. But at a central moment in the Judges version of the Samson myth, that puzzle finds a straightforward solution: Samson's great strength lies in his hair, and, as a consequence, according to Samson, "if I bee shaven, my strength will goe from me, and I shall be weake" (Judg. xvi, 17). But Samson's secret, however plain, retreats in *Samson Agonistes* to the occulted status it possessed for the Philistines. In its preliminary attempts to answer that riddle, Milton's poem points us toward the mythic location of Samson's bodily strength at the heart of the original folktale. Samson, for example, laments near the poem's beginning that God, "when he gave me strength, to show withal / How slight the gift was, hung it in my Hair" (58–59). And other characters, no less unenlightened, will continue throughout the poem to reproduce this physiological understanding of Samson's strength: the giant Harapha speaks of Samson's "boist'rous" locks (1164), and Manoa, after Samson's death, will praise "those locks, / That of a Nation arm'd the strength contain'd" (1493–94). But Samson comes to reject this archaic identification of his hair as the literal container of strength. Responsive to the Protestant, specifically Calvinist, discomfort with this key feature of the Samson myth, Milton follows the many biblical exegetes who felt compelled to qualify the tale's overwhelming suggestion of the bodily source of Samson's power.[3] Samson's strength had an immediate and ongoing source in the will of God, who perpetuated that strength daily only as long as Samson adhered to his Nazarite pledge. For the normative Calvinist annotators of the Geneva Bible, Samson loses his strength, then, "Not for the losse of his hair, but for the contempt of the ordinance of God, which was the cause that God departed from him."[4]

It is the Reformer's elevation of the source of Samson's strength, from the self-contained body of the hero to the immediate will of an arbitrary God, that Milton not only inherits but actually incorporates into the narrative of his poem. If the hero can be said to develop over the course of *Samson Agonistes*, then one of the components of that "regeneration" is surely his accedence to the dominant Protestant reinterpretation of the source of his strength. That moment of conversion occurs in the confrontation with Harapha, who, as Michael Lieb has persuasively argued, "affords Samson the opportunity to reaffirm his faith in the true source of power, God Himself."[5] Teasing out the logical absurdity of the mythical location of strength in hair, Harapha dismisses what he calls Samson's "magician's art,"

> which thou from Heaven
> Feign'd'st at thy birth was giv'n thee in thy hair,
> Where strength can least abide, though all thy hairs
> Were bristles rang'd like those that ridge the back
> Of chaf't wild Boars, or rufff'd Porcupines.   (1134–38)

Harapha's reductio here, his hyperbolic elaboration on the unlikely inherence of force in the lifeless excrescence of hair, however chafed or ruffled, presses Samson into a new understanding of the provenance of physical force.[6] He responds to Harapha's taunt with an unequivocal declaration of what the poem presents as its orthodox understanding of the hero's power:

> I know no spells, use no forbidden Arts;
> My trust is in the living God who gave me
> At my Nativity this strength, difflus'd
> No less through all my sinews, joints and bones,
> Than thine, while I preserv'd these locks unshorn,
> The pledge of my unviolated vow.   (1139–44)

His strength, Samson declares, is not localized magically in his hair, where, as Harapha seems rightly to have noted, "strength can least abide." God has instead diffused his strength at his birth throughout his entire body and preserved that strength on the condition of Samson's preservation of his Nazarite locks, since, as the Calvinist theologian William Perkins had explained, "God promised strength but with a commaundement, that [Samson] should be a Nazarite to the end."[7]

This reorientation of the ontology of strength is sudden and, in marking the point at which the hero relinquishes all claims for the autonomy and integrity of his body, the most recognizable sign that Samson has submitted himself to a new and uncompromising theocentric cosmos. This theological transumption draws even more force from the poem's reassessment of the nature of the "pledge" of Samson's "unviolated vow": there lies an assumption throughout Milton's text that Samson's "pledge" is not simply, as the Book of Judges and its Calvinist interpreters had assumed, his vow to uphold the Nazaritical codes of bodily purity. His pledge, much more abstractly, appears in this poem to have been a vow—one mentioned nowhere in Judges or the other texts on the Nazarate—not to reveal the *secret* of his source of strength. Samson's failure, from the vantage of this even more sophisticated formulation of the source of his power, was not the simple violation of his pledge to keep his hair intact. It was instead an act of "Shameful garrulity" (491), the disclosure of a divine secret for which the poem offers many synonymous formulations: Samson, we are told, exposed his willingness to "divulg[e] the secret gift of God" (201), to "profan[e] / The mystery of God giv'n . . . under pledge / Of vow" (377–78), "Presumptuously" to "publish" "his holy secret" (497–98), to "unbosom[] all [his] secrets" (879), to "commit[] / To such a viper [as Dalila] his most sacred trust / Of secrecy" (1000–02).[8] To authorize this translation of Samson's pledge from a vow of purity to a vow of secrecy, Milton appears to have relied on the original meaning of the name for Samson's consecrated status. To be a Nazarite (from the Hebrew *nazir*, "separate") is by definition to be secret (from the Latin *secretus*, "separated," "hidden").[9] Milton would have found further justification for his treatment of Samson's pledge in the rhetorical elaboration of Nazaritic secrecy already performed in the Judges text. When Samson's father Manoah presses to know the Angel of the Lord who has announced the conception of his son, that mysterious angel secretes the knowledge of his divinity from its human interpreters: "Why askest you thus after my name, which is secret" (Judg. xiii, 18). The secrets withheld by the story's divine agents adumbrate the secret Samson will need later to keep, and Milton locates in the Scripture's silent coupling of reticent man and withholding God the secret of his hero's miraculous feats of strength.

In these curious reformulations of the pledge, the origin of Samson's strength is cleansed entirely of its association with the autonomous physical body and the self-willed bodily behavior of the hero. The God whose overwhelming power and inscrutability the hero must come to acknowledge in Milton's text is a silent, unsearchable God whose sacredness is founded on his secretness. This is a God whose outlines Milton was able to sketch, with varying degrees of intensity and commitment, throughout his career. In *Eikonoklastes*, Milton would condemn the man who "takes upon himself perpetually to unfold the secret and unsearchable Mysteries of high Providence" (V, p. 272). He would extend this protection of divine privacy to *Paradise Lost*, when the otherwise garrulous Raphael thinks to hesitate before "unfold[ing] / The secrets of another World, perhaps / Not lawful to reveal" (V, 568–70). And in *Christian Doctrine* Milton would praise not only those angels who do not *reveal* such secrets, but those "good angels [who] do not *look into* all the secret things of God" (XV, p. 107, emphasis mine). This God of secrets whom Milton would champion with disconcerting frequency is capable not only of withholding the rational justification of his actions from his subjects; he can also compel them, as he does with Samson, to keep some secrets of their own. This God, in other words, is the nominalist God of Calvin whom this same Milton, writing not as pious believer but as rational theologian, had spent so much of his career struggling to reject.

"Just are the ways of God," asserts the Chorus for a brief moment in a colloquy with Samson, "And justifiable to men" (293–94). This ringing declaration of divine justice, preceding with terrible irony a competing claim for God's transcendence of justice, law, and reason (307–25), does not surface here to announce this poem's commitment to theodicy. It works instead to remind us of the core Miltonic faith in divine accountability so ostentatiously absent throughout all the other lines of *Samson Agonistes*. The special status of this poem as the most puzzling work in the Miltonic canon is due in no small part, of course, to the antagonism between its predominantly nominalist theology and the explicit theology of rational justifiability that forms the basis of *Paradise Lost* and *De doctrina Christiana*. In spite of the momentary defenses of divine secrecy cited above, the logical foundation of those texts, in which Milton asserts the ways of God as publicly justifiable, cannot support such a phenomenon as a "holy secret." The incommensurability of Milton's *Samson* with the other late works has been both defended and denied in a number of ways. It has been variously argued, for example, that Milton actually came to embrace the dread God of Calvin in his final poem; that he intended its embarrassing theology to be read ironically, the hero's final action subjected to the reader's condemnation; and that Milton succeeds in converting Samson to his own anti-Calvinist, free-will theology despite the theological recalcitrance evidenced everywhere by the Chorus and even Samson himself.[10] My own contribution to the solution of the theological mystery that surrounds this poem will rest on an analysis of Milton's representation of that phenomenon that proves so mysterious to the fictional characters themselves: the secret connection between Samson's body and his strength.

In the confrontation with Harapha, Samson enjoys the poem's sanction, at least provisionally, when he accedes to the Calvinist displacement of all power and will onto the deity. But it is nonetheless important that Samson's claim for his strength's dependence on the arbitrary judgment of a secretive God is not the poem's only theologically creditable etiology of human power. Milton's poem offers, if not a reasoned argument against, then at least a show of rhetorical resistance to the orthodox demotion of Samson's hair to a sign, rather than a source, of his strength. *Samson Agonistes* effects this resistance by exploiting a potentially contradictory moment in the Judges version of the ancient story of Samson. It is generally accepted that the folktale on which the Samson tale is based focuses on the magical powers embodied in the strong man's hair. The deuteronomic authors, however, long before their Calvinist successors, superimposed upon the beginning and ending of the original story the narrative of Samson's mysterious, "secret" conception and of his Nazarite vow; they attempted to harness that myth of organically magical human strength to a more seemly exemplum of the pious man's virtuous submission to an arbitrary religious code.[11] The redactive authors did not, however, successfully remodel all of the story's archaic mythical components. A particular narrative detail, one that somehow escaped revisionary deletion, clings fast to the story's end in the Judges text; and this surviving remnant of the ancient tale can reasonably be said to erode any interpreter's insistence on God's absolute control over his champion's strength: "the haire of his head," we are told in the Judges narration, "began to grow again after that it was shaven" (xvi, 22).[12] The story's revisors, as we might expect, neglect to develop this folkloric thread that persists in investing magical power in the strands of Samson's hair. They move instead to subordinate Samson's potentially autonomous physical regeneration to the arbitrary will of God. Samson's strength is not officially returned until he makes his appeal, at the temple, for the renewed strength required at the story's end: "O God, I beseeche thee, strengthen me," Samson prays (xvi, 28). But the present text of the Bible retains nonetheless the ancient detail of the hair's regrowth. And while the revised tale soon goes on to imply God's voluntary agency in the re-empowerment of Samson, that startling sentence works inevitably to arouse suspicions of an alternative explanation for the explosion of power with which Samson concludes his life: Samson may well regain his strength for the simple and unexceptional reason that his hair, the only obvious source of his strength, grows back.

Quick to recognize the potentially dangerous theology embedded in this odd detail, the annotators of the Geneva Bible provide a marginal gloss for xvi, 22 that warns readers not to heed its narrative implications: "Yet had he not his strength againe till he had called upon God, and reconciled himself." Given Milton's reproduction of the generally Calvinist emphasis on the Nazarite pledge, we might reasonably expect Milton, too, to emphasize the scriptural focus on the deity's agency behind the massive power displayed at the temple. But nowhere in *Samson Agonistes* does Milton suggest, like the Geneva commentators or the Judges redactors before them, that the hero regains his strength when "he called upon God"; nor does Milton ever state, or even imply, that Samson at the temple, his head bowed either "as one who pray'd, / Or some great matter in his mind revolv'd" (1637–38), is requesting the return of his physical prowess. Milton's Samson, quite to the contrary, makes clear *before* his arrival at the temple that his body is already experiencing its resurgence of strength, which is "again returning with my hair / After my great transgression" (1354–55). If the poem can be seen anywhere to thwart its own acceptance of the orthodox Calvinist reading of the Samson myth, it is surely in this unmistakable gesture of resistance to the chronology of the return of the hero's strength. Violating the explicit logic of cause and effect established by the deuteronomic author of Judges 16, Milton has clearly and carefully unhinged the return of Samson's strength from the critical moment at the temple. Exploiting the embarrassing folkloric remnant left untouched by the biblical writers, Milton loosens the official dependence of Samson's power upon the arbitrary will of God. Manoa, a little later, will voice a theological compromise when he conjectures that God has *"permitted* / His strength again to grow up with his hair" (1495–96; my emphasis). But Manoa's invocation of divine permission, a theological category Miltonic theology carefully distinguishes from direct divine action, surely fails to crush Samson's personal strength beneath the weight of God's omnipotence.[13] The realignment of Samson's strength with the length of his hair, one discouraged both by the redacted biblical text and its early modern Protestant exegetes, simply removes divine power from the realm of arbitrary will and restricts it to the far less exalted realm of ongoing and impersonal natural process. This realignment begins as well to undermine any orthodox location of Samson's strength in his obedient observance of a pledge, whether that pledge is one of purity, secrecy, or both. Through this inversion of the established chronology of the return of Samson's strength, Milton, I believe it can be said, begins to undo the authoritative voluntarism to which Samson had acceded and reinvests Samson's body as a viable, perhaps even noble, origin of power. In this extraordinary complication of the mystery charging Samson's boisterous locks, or what the poet himself had in 1642 called Samson's "puissant hair," Milton has forced the tale of Samson to reveal a new secret.[14]

II

The puzzle of his own body, and of human bodies in general, teases Milton's Samson in his magnificent opening monologue. In order to understand the ultimate function of the competing ontologies of heroic strength that mark this poem, I propose we turn to the first corporeal riddle Samson addresses, the question of his sight. Much as Samson, Manoa, Harapha, and the Chorus are all concerned to pinpoint the location of strength in a part of Samson's body, so also the blind Samson questions the Creator's curious localization of visual strength in the eyes:

> Since light so necessary is to life,
> And almost life itself, if it be true
> That light is in the Soul,

She all in every part; why was the sight
To such a tender ball as th' eye confin'd?
So obvious and so easy to be quench't,
And not as feeling through all parts diffus'd,
That she might look at will through every pore?   (90–97)

In this surprisingly syllogistic analysis that questions the nature and extent of visual sentience, Samson in lamenting his blindness is clearly making a case for all the injustices that beset the human organism. Scholars have identified a source for Samson's critique here of the justice of the Creator's organization of the parts of the body. The Latin Father Arnobius, whom Milton cites throughout his career, had formulated perhaps the first version of Samson's fascinating query: "From what kind of material have the inner parts of men's bodies been formed and built up into firmness? . . . Why, when it would be better to give us light by several eyes, to guard against the risk of blindness, are we restricted to two?" Arnobius does not, as these questions might lead us to suspect, proceed to justify God's seemingly irrational organization of the "parts of men's bodies." His perspective is not theodicial, but fideistic, as he quickly moves to argue that Christ "bade us abandon and disregard all these things . . . and not waste our thoughts upon things which have been removed far from our knowledge."[15] With this final appeal to the inaccessibility of divine wisdom, Arnobius may be responding to a similarly nominalistic argument in Paul, who issues a related defense of the Creator's isolation of the senses in the body's most vulnerable organs: "If the whole body were an eye, where were the hearing? If the whole were hearing, where were the smelling? But nowe hath God disposed the members every one of them in the body at his owne pleasure" (1 Cor. xii, 17–18). The body has not been organized, for either Paul or Arnobius, along lines rationally accessible to human understanding. To yearn for the animate perceptivity of the "whole body," to question the reason behind the awkward division of labor among the body's parts, is to pursue a dangerous critique of God's secrets. The Pauline and Arnobian formulas for the limitations of human understanding, and the corollary acceptance of the illogical manner in which "God disposed the members . . . in the body," are of course only two of countless precedents for this poem's pietistic demotion of reason and rational divinity. Milton calls on the entire tradition of such fideism when producing Samson's claim, uttered just a few lines before his querulous account of visual percipience, "I must not quarrel with the will / Of highest dispensation, which herein / Haply had ends above my reach to know" (60–62).

This rehearsal of *Samson*'s proto-Calvinist, nominalist filiations is, at least, one way to define the theological parameters of Samson's startling

inquiry—one no doubt close to Milton's heart—into the scandalous irratio-
nality of the organization of the human body. But it is not, I think, the only
way to understand the function of the poem's opening speech. Given the
explicit interest this text has exhibited in the contradictory accounts of the
constitution of Samson's body, we should not be surprised to discover that
Milton may be alluding to more than just the pious fideism of an Arnobius
or a Paul. He can also be seen to tap another, no less authoritative, response
to the recognition of the illogical organization of the body's members. Milton may have found in the Gospel of Luke what seemed a rejection of Paul's
sanguine acceptance of God's demarcation of the frail human organism "at
his owne pleasure."[16] Far from acquiescing to the erratic logic of divine
pleasure, Luke suggests that the "whole body" of the enlightened believer
might actually be capable of vision: "The light of the body is the eye: therefore when thine eye is single, then is thy whole body light" (Luke xi, 34).
Read literally, Luke's contribution to the theology of the body's members
offers a more attractive perspective on the limitations of ocular vision. This
is in fact the compensation the blind Milton himself requested in the second
invocation in *Paradise Lost:* "So much the rather thou Celestial Light / Shine
inward" (III, 51–52). But where Milton the blind bard was seeking the traditional internal illumination of the Spirit, his Samson has in mind a far more
radical illumination that fills with sensible light the actual physical body.
Far from courting blasphemy by quarreling with the will of highest dispensation, Samson might actually have a scriptural sanction for his fantastic
desire that sight, like feeling, could be "diffus'd" "through all parts . . . /
That she might look at will through every pore."

If Milton was, as I suspect, more than casually interested in alternative
modes of physical vision, he would not have needed to rely solely on Scripture for the authorization of Samson's imaginative investment in a more
perfect body. There were seventeenth-century natural philosophers no less
interested than Samson in the possibility of the homogeneous dissemination
of percipience throughout the human organism. The natural philosopher
Margaret Cavendish, whose affinity with Milton's own science I have described elsewhere, asserts the astonishing idea that the human body does in
fact already enjoy a panorganismic capacity for perception: "though Man, or
any other animal hath but five exterior sensitive organs, yet there be numerous perceptions made in these sensitive organs, and in all the body; nay,
every several Pore of the flesh is a sensitive organ, as well as the Eye, or
the Ear."[17] Few of Cavendish's philosophical contemporaries would have
concurred that man, at least as his body is presently constructed, can look
at will through "every several Pore of the flesh." But the physician William
Harvey had argued, in his *De motu cordis* of 1628, that other creatures,

whose bodies were less complexly organized than man, did possess this ideal state of homogeneously diffused organic sentience. In his celebrated revelation of the circulation of the blood, Harvey digresses to discuss those remarkable creatures—he calls them "Plant animals"—in whom he can distinguish no "distinct and separate" organs, whether heart or otherwise: "such as are *Palmer-worms* and *Snails,* and very many things which are ingender'd of putrefaction and keep not a *species,* have no *heart,* as needing no impulsor to drive the nutriment into the *extremities:* For they have a body *connate* and of one piece, and indistinct without members." Animals, like worms and snails, that are "ingender'd of putrefaction and keep not a species"—born, in other words, of spontaneous generation—are for Harvey constituted of "one piece, and indistinct without members." Their crucial vital functions are not consigned to the "tender ball" of a vulnerable organ like the heart, "for instead thereof they use their whole body, and this whole creature is as a *heart.*"[18]

Far from a dangerous critique of the way in which "God disposed the members every one of them in the body," the question Samson forwards concerning an ideal state of total-body percipience touches upon a reasonable form of bodily organization that may, if we credit Harvey, actually have a basis in at least some corners of the creation.[19] In *Paradise Lost,* Milton himself had indulged Samson's fantasy of a body that escaped the vulnerable hierarchies of human corporeal order. Samson, the man "with a strength / Equivalent to Angels" (342–43), in many ways simply reproduces the desire for the angelic body that charges Milton's epic:

> For Spirits that live throughout
> Vital in every part, not as frail man
> In Entrails, Heart or Head, Liver or Reins,
> Cannot but by annihilating die;
> Nor in thir liquid texture mortal wound
> Receive, no more that can the fluid Air:
> All Heart they live, all Head, all Eye, all Ear,
> All Intellect, all Sense, and as they please,
> They Limb themselves, and colour, shape or size
> Assume, as likes them best, condense or rare.   (VI, 344–53)

Unlike the "cumbrous flesh" of humans, the angelic body is "uncompounded," not a compound of separate elements, but constituted by a single, homogeneous "Essence pure" (I, 424–28). Unlike "frail man," whose capacity for perception has been organized entirely into distinct and therefore vulnerable organs, angelic bodies are not "Vital" exclusively "In entrails, Heart or Head, Liver or Reins" (VI, 345–46). Like the bodies of palmer-worms, they are "indistinct without members," embodying in their entirety the function of one vital organ as fully as any other. No less "all Heart" than Harvey's glorious "Plant animals," Milton's angels also live "all Eye," embodying Samson's powerful desire to "look at will through every pore" in a perpetual act of enlightened perception.[20]

To voice a desire, as Samson does, for an uncompounded, homogeneously constituted body is also to voice a call, as Harvey, Cavendish, and a number of Milton's monistic contemporaries did, for a new ontology of bodily matter. Like the ingeniously embodied angels of *Paradise Lost*, Samson's fantasized body functions, in fact, as a narrative extension of Milton's own radical ontology of substance, the theological doctrine, worked out at such length in chapter 7 of the first book of *Christian Doctrine*, of the inseparability of the body and soul. There Milton puts forward what may be the most conceptually daring of all his theological heresies: "Man is a living being, intrinsically and properly one and individual, not compound or separable, nor, according to the common opinion, made up and framed of two distinct and different natures, as of soul and body, but that the whole man is soul, and the soul man, that is to say, a body, or substance individual, animated, sensitive, and rational" (XV, p. 41).[21] By declaring the whole man "animated" and "sensitive," Milton is not here proposing the visual percipience of every inch of human flesh. But this exuberant definition of the monistic human frame seems at the very least a wishful account of the mortal human body, in which, as Milton knew, the organs of sensation and reason are all too easily sundered from the vulnerable body and rendered lifeless. Milton's monistic declaration does, however, in stressing the absolutely uncompounded nature of divinized human flesh, read as a fairly accurate abstraction of the bodies of Milton's angels, and the body embraced in fantasy by the blind, disgruntled Samson.

Samson, as we have seen, had arrived in his confrontation with Harapha at an understanding of his strength that began to approach the ideal of homogeneity implicit in the philosophy of monism: his physical force was now to be seen as "diffius'd . . . through all [his] sinews, joints and bones." But that equitably diffused strength was nonetheless, within Samson's new orthodox conception of God's conditional bestowal of physical strength, contingent on divine favor. In the monistic theological analogue of that diffusion of strength, and in the monistic body for which Samson yearns at the poem's beginning, the dissemination of vital virtue throughout the entire human animal is never contingent upon the approving nod of a secretive God of Judgment. It is the unconditional prerogative of being human. When the monistic God of *Christian Doctrine* breathed "that spirit into man," and "moulded it in each individual, and infused it throughout" (XV, p. 39), he created a being whose inalienable divine properties could never be subject to divine arbitration.

Stephen M. Fallon has argued correctly that one of the most notable puzzles of the doctrinal component of *Samson Agonistes* is its failure to "fit the picture of the mature Milton's philosophy of substance."[22] It would in fact be impossible to assimilate Samson's soul, which dwells "Imprison'd now indeed, / In real darkness of the body" (158–59), to the otherwise enlightened world of Miltonic monism.[23] Except for the counterfactual fantasies we have heard Samson voice, the dominant theological tenor of *Samson Agonistes* is aggressively dualist, so much so, in fact, that Fallon is led to argue that Milton must have begun composition in the 1640s, before his formal elaboration of the monistic thesis. But *Samson Agonistes*, I think we can see, is nothing if not conscious of the doctrine of monism or its far-reaching conceptual implications. This poem, to be sure, resists forwarding the explicit monistic argument Milton carefully framed for the pages of *Christian Doctrine* and *Paradise Lost*. But this doctrinally secretive poem does open itself up to a suppressed theory of monism, not by means of careful Ramistic argument—that was the purpose of the theological treatise—but by means of the dialectical interplay of dualist argument and monistic figure. Through the potentially more potent vehicle of the explosive rhetorical figure Milton establishes the priority of his monistic materialism over what he could not help but think to be the conceptual tyranny of the Calvinist structure of divinity.

It is necessary now to determine the end for which *Samson Agonistes* incorporates so many hidden signifiers of Milton's radical ontology of matter. I propose we examine the purpose of the poem's monism by means of Milton's echo of a passage from his theological treatise. Samson, we remember, had begun his questioning of the confinement of sight "To such a tender ball as th' eye" with this opening condition: "if it be true / That light is in the Soul, / She all in every part" (91–94). In the *Christian Doctrine*, the Miltonic source for Samson's metaphysical construction, Milton employs this same conditional proposition to found one of his wilder conclusions concerning the materiality of the soul: "If the soul be equally diffused throughout any given whole, and throughout every part of the whole" ("si anima est tota in toto, et tota in qualibet parte"), then the human soul, he reasons, can only be "communicated to the soul by the laws of generation," imparted to the child by means of the generative seed of the parent, "or at least of the father" (XV, pp. 47–49). No passage of Scripture, Milton argues at considerable length, can "prove that each soul is severally and immediately created by the Deity" (XV, p. 49). The human soul is not "created daily by the immediate act of God"; it is the product rather of the "power of matter" itself (XV, pp. 43, 49). The "power which had been communicated to matter by the Deity" at the Creation is itself capable of generating the human soul, without any direct activity from an intervening God (XV, p. 53). Milton is willing elsewhere in the treatise to grant the premise of divine omnipotence. But the elaborate argument that constitutes the bulk of Milton's theology of divine power works more often than not to restrict the exercise of that omnipotence to the initial moment of Creation, permitting all other acts of generation to proceed by a more or less inviolable principle Milton calls the "general law of creation" (XV, p. 53). The rigorous theological argument for monism, to which Samson alludes in his opening monologue, forms the intellectual means by which Milton defends himself against the seemingly inescapable doctrine of omnipotence, and the awkward, Calvinist notes of voluntarism with which that doctrine seems so often to resound. Miltonic monism, by distancing the human soul from the creating deity, establishes a set of judicial restraints on divine power. Like his own rebel angels in *Paradise Lost,* for whom the theses of monism and omnipotence are logically incompatible, Milton writes often, in his theological prose as in his poetry, as one of those "who while they feel / Vigor Divine within them, can allow / Omnipotence to none" (VI, 157–59).

I have attempted to demonstrate a way in which *Samson Agonistes* depicts its hero pressing for a monistic philosophy of substance that the poem's dualist ontology cannot support. I have not yet accounted for the purpose behind Milton's systematic opposition of incompatible derivations of Samson's strength and incompatible ontologies of matter. What might be the function of Samson's fantasy of corporeal perfection in this poem which, by means of its Chorus, works otherwise to resign itself, in humble obedience, to the "unsearchable dispose" of the secretive Maker? By way of answering this question, I propose we enlist the help of a recent avatar of Samson's oppositional fantasy of the homogeneous body's panorganismic perceptivity. One of the most intriguing aspects of the critical philosophy of Gilles Deleuze and Félix Guattari has been the obscure theoretical entity they style the "Body without Organs."[24] Using as their model a schizophrenic's delusional belief in an entirely organless, limbless, but nonetheless vital human body, Deleuze and Guattari posit the fantasy of this Body without Organs as a "de-organized," nonhierarchical mode of being—one admittedly impossible fully to cultivate or even imagine—that functions as an immanent conceptual domain necessary for the successful subversion of almost any established authority. Like Samson in his opening monologue, Deleuze and Guattari forward the most exuberant formulation of this desire for organlessness in the halting form of a question:

Is it really so sad and dangerous to be fed up with seeing with your eyes, breathing with your lungs, swallowing with your mouth, talking with your tongue, thinking with your brain, having an anus and larynx, head and legs? Why not walk on your head, sing with your sinuses, see through your skin, breathe with your belly: the simple Thing, the Entity, the full Body, the stationary Voyage, Anorexia, cutaneous Vision, Yoga, Krishna, Love, Experimentation.[25]

The fantasy of "cutaneous Vision" and the massive percipience of "the full Body" is not, of course, geared to any straightforward expansion of physiological possibility. The intimately experienced external forces that seem to have "organized" the human organism work to signify for Deleuze and Guattari all the forms of hierarchical order and categorization that determine the operations of power in every facet of human existence. The impossible but necessary attempt to dismantle the hierarchical conception of the organized bodily self must precede any attempt to dismantle the forces of discursive authority they identify as "state philosophy," or ultimately to dismantle, they suggest, the state itself.

In a gesture that might remind us of the peculiarly Calvinist universe of *Samson Agonistes,* Deleuze and Guattari telescope all of the world's allied and unallied loci of authority into a single, demonizable embodiment of arbitrary power they call the "judgment of God." It is by means of the wicked "judgment of God" that the frail organs of the human body seem to have been disposed and organized so irrationally and arbitrarily. The individual's oppositional fantasy of the Body without Organs, or, as they come to denote it, the "BwO," is

opposed to the organism, the organic organization of the organs. The *judgment of God,* the system of the judgment of God, the theological system, is precisely the operation of He who makes an organism, an organization of organs called the organism, because He cannot bear the BwO, because He pursues it and rips it apart so He can be first, and have the organism be first. The organism is already that, the judgment of God.[26]

The hypothetical God forwarded by Deleuze and Guattari "cannot bear the BwO" because the individual's capacity to imagine a Body without Organs can unleash a subversive power so antihierarchical that it undermines God's entire system of judgment; it renders the fiction of a hierarchical cosmos governed by an absolutist deity irrelevant, inoperative. The fantasy of the Body without Organs facilitates an escape from the constraining network of the psychic, social, and political relations that present themselves as ineluctable truths, as facts as seemingly unimpeachable and inalterable as the order and function of the organs in the body created by God.

In their rhapsodic meditations on the Body without Organs, Deleuze and Guattari have opened themselves to the same type of criticism to which Samson, in his plaintive question concerning bodily organization, is vulnerable: the vision of the Body without Organs is without question a utopian vision, a fantasy that could not possibly be instituted to effect meaningful change. But the theoretical construct of the undifferentiated body seems nonetheless to be forwarded by the French theorists as if it were something approaching a useful tool for progressive political and social action. If a comparison of Milton's "uncompounded" monistic body and the "BwO" of contemporary French philosophy is warranted, the connection is due surely to the curious faith Deleuze and Guattari share with Milton in the potential political implications of the monistic fantasy of the de-organized body. The utopian theorizations of Deleuze and Guattari read today as a cultural by-product of the rebellion against the state in the Paris of 1968, much as the disestablishmentarian logic of Milton's monism is at least in part an intellectual response to the recentralized state in the years of the Stuart Restoration. *Samson Agonistes,* as I have noted, often seems committed to its restoration of the ontology of dualism that Milton himself had rejected, along with monarchic tyranny, well before the poem's composition. But there is a way in which this poem suggests, much like the texts of Deleuze and Guattari, that there exists a conceptual interdependence between the hierarchical logic of a dualist philosophy and the hierarchical logic of political oppression.[27] If Samson is compelled to end his days in a Philistine prison house, it is possible that a chief agent of oppression is his culture's intellectual propensity for dualism, the Chorus' belief that the soul "dwells" "Imprison'd . . . / In real darkness of the body" (158–59). By means of this rhetorical coordination of the political imprisonment of Samson with a dualist metaphysics of body and soul, Milton attributes to the misguided theology embraced by Samson and the Chorus a chief responsibility for their subjection to their Philistine oppressors.

In his preface to *Christian Doctrine,* Milton explained that he had devoted himself to his formal theology "because nothing else can so effectually wipe away those two repulsive afflictions, tyranny and superstition" (VI, p. 118). Milton does not in that treatise articulate with any specificity how a new monistic theology can wipe away the affliction of tyranny. But Deleuze and Guattari supply a useful elaboration of the way in which a thesis of monism can function as a displaced discursive counter to what may seem to be the excessively organized and inextricably intertwined bodies of a tyrannical Church and a tyrannical state. Christopher Hill has argued persuasively that the philosophy of substance Milton develops late in his life had an origin in the poet's partial, sometimes submerged political sympathy with the Levelers, Diggers, and Ranters, radical political groups of the 1640s and 1650s whose theorists, especially Overton, Lilburne, and Winstanley, were among the first in England to propose the monistic heresy.[28] In Samson's hesitant invocation of the monistic body Milton proposed in *Christian Doctrine*, we can hear, I think, a powerful, if brief, reengagement of the radical egalitarian utopianism of the poet's earliest forays into political speculation.

III

I turn now to the poem's problematic ending because it is here that the full implications of the contradictions concerning Samson's body, and especially the fantasy of the Body without Organs, make themselves known. Milton, much to the dismay of many of his critics, resists concluding his poem with the easily apprehended gestures toward divine voluntarism that characterize so much of the Chorus' discourse. Refusing to submit desire and instinct to the compelling, transcendent forces of the deity, Samson articulates his astonishing decision to attend the forbidden festival as if it were the consequence of a gradual physiological process: "I begin to feel / Some rousing motions in me which dispose / To something extraordinary my thoughts" (1381–83). The traditional reading of *Samson Agonistes* has identified those "rousing motions" as providential; the revisionist reading has deemed them unauthorized and purely instinctive; and some analyses, those with which I am most sympathetic, have described them as both.[29] But the agential ambiguity raised by these "rousing motions" is not necessarily a sign of absolute theological indecipherability. The central point of overlap between Samson's idiosyncratic sensation of motion and Milton's rational theology occurs at the theologically loaded adjective "extraordinary." In *Christian Doctrine*, Milton had clung to a residual orthodox belief in God's miraculous powers of intervention, naming God's capacity for voluntary intervention his "extraordinary providence" ("providentia Dei extraordinaria"), which is that power "whereby God produces some effect out of the usual order of nature" (XV, p. 95). Here, however, as if to shake off forever the vestiges of voluntarism that had shackled the argument of *Christian Doctrine*, Milton shifts this loaded adjective, "extraordinary," from God to God's creature, as if in imitation of the devolution of power at the heart of Milton's monistic account of Creation. The verb that names Samson's apprehension of these motions, "feel," locates this new knowledge of rousing motions in the space of the monistically divinized body, as "feeling" is that sense which is neither irrationally segregated to a vulnerable organ or subject to whimsical conditions, being definitively, as Samson stated in his opening speech, "through all parts diffus'd."

Samson had begun the poem with his yearning invocation of the monistic body, and it is just this image of a divinely infused Body without Organs that reappears after Samson's climactic act of destruction. In the poem's final and most elaborate burst of rhetorical energy, Milton recalls the promise of compensatory percipience made by Luke that Samson, at the beginning of the poem, had questioned:

> But he though blind of sight,
> Despis'd and thought extinguish't quite,
> With inward eyes illuminated
> His fiery virtue rous'd
> From under ashes into sudden flame,
> And as an ev'ning Dragon came,
> Assailant on the perched roosts,
> And nests in order rang'd
> Of tame villatic Fowl.   (1687–95)

In an extraordinary succession of similes, Milton characterizes Samson, the destroyer at his end of the "Lords and each degree . . . sit[ting] in order" (1607), as "an ev'ning Dragon" who has assailed the "nests in order rang'd / Of tame villatic Fowl." The being who had raged against the arbitrary ordering of sight and strength in the fragile receptacles of eyes and hair wreaks vengeance on the social and institutional manifestations of those irrational forms of order. "With inward eyes illuminated," Samson moves not only to destroy the irrationally organized body that had left him open to a punitive blindness and impotence; nor merely to destroy the carefully organized Philistine aristocracy, sitting in order of each degree; but to destroy the entire principle of arbitrarily determined organization, manifested throughout the bodily, religious, social, and political fabric of experience. Creating for himself, through suicide, an extravagantly literal Body without Organs, Samson strikes a blow at all the injustices perpetrated by that Deleuzian bogey, the judgment of God.

It is only at this point, once Milton has represented the destruction of the evils of order and organization, that he allows himself to indulge in a daringly liberated figuration of the redeemed being who thrives in the new organless, de-organized cosmos. The Chorus' shocking figure of the phoenix soars from the destruction of all the principles of hierarchical organization that Samson has crushed at the end of his life:

> Like that self-begott'n bird
> In the *Arabian* woods embost,
> That no second knows nor third,
> And lay erewhile a Holocaust,
> From out her ashy womb now teem'd,
> Revives, reflourishes, then vigorous most
> When most unactive deem'd.   (1699–1705)

We must take seriously, I think, the admonition of Dr. Johnson, who had written in *The Rambler* that "the grossest error" in *Samson Agonistes* "is the solemn introduction of the phoenix in the last scene."[30] In spite of Johnson's astute disapproval of what he must have adjudged the phoenix's theological impropriety ("it is so evidently contrary to reason and nature"), commentators have most typically attempted to demonstrate the decorous piety of Milton's comparison by invoking the association of the phoenix with the Crucifixion. But Milton's adjective here, "self-begott'n," can only with great difficulty be applied to the Son of God, whose "begetting" by the Father was such a consequential event in *Paradise Lost*. Milton's focus on that mythical bird's capacity for spontaneous generation reminds us, of course, much more of Satan than the Son, the Satan who boasted to Abdiel in heaven that the angels were "self-begot, self-rais'd, / By their own quick'n-ing power" (V, 860–61). William Harvey, in the passage from *De motu cor-dis* cited above, had identified those vermicular bodies without organs as beings born of spontaneous generation who "keep not a *species*," knowing no second or third. It is as if Milton here, revisiting the debate in heaven between Abdiel and Satan, were making a conceptual leap as fantastical as Harvey's. This final explosive figure seems almost to sanction Satan's claim that the angelic Body without Organs exists by right outside the arbitrary judgment of God. Milton's daring affirmation in *Samson Agonistes* of what may have been the grossest theological error in all of *Paradise Lost*—the heresy of angelic self-begetting—is not, of course, a rejection of the Creator of the monistic universe Milton described in *Christian Doctrine*.[31] It is a rejection, instead, of the theological voluntarism that had structured *Samson*'s dominant conception of God. Milton's image of the phoenix refigures Samson's "regeneration," which for the Chorus could only be the product of arbitrary divine will, as a process we might with justice call "spontaneous regeneration." The image of the phoenix suggests the possibility that Samson's alteration is the consequence less of divine impulsion than of the forces inhering, by right of divine Creation, within the inescapably physical, already divinized self.

We can discern the usurpation enacted here of a Calvinist voluntarism by Milton's own Arminian monism if we examine the function of one of the poem's most important words. As critics have noted, the "rousing motions" behind Samson's inscrutable change of heart are felt again when Milton writes of Samson, "His fiery virtue rous'd / From under ashes into sudden flame." Looking ahead to the image of the phoenix, Milton's loaded verb "rous'd" can be seen to retain a strong element of its original meaning, which was "to shake the feathers" or "to ruffle." But while Milton's verb does gesture ahead to the imminent figure of the phoenix, it is first and foremost the verb that names Samson's own action in his final moments at the temple: "but he though blind of sight . . . / His fiery virtue rous'd." In this more proximate alliance, the verb *rouse* here activates a closely related variant of its original meaning, which, when used intransitively of hair, meant "to stand on end." The satanic hero of Shakespeare's *Macbeth*, for example, recalls near the end of that play a time at which the hair on his skin "would . . . rouse and stir / As life were in 't" (5.5.12–13).[32] This crucial verb of material self-motion, with its roots in the autonomous activity of hair and feathers, returns us inevitably to that most intransigent element of the original Samson myth, the inherence of strength in the matter of his hair. We are reminded of the "rousing motions" that had earlier impelled Samson to attend the festival, and we are led, retrospectively, to identify the origin of those motions in the monistic bodily self. Although the implicit grammatical agent of that rousing was left in that phrase deliberately unclear, Milton's "rousing" cannot help but draw upon some of the autonomous virtue and power it possessed in his *Areopagitica*, in which that word was definitively aligned with the immensely liberatory strength inhering in Samson's hair: "Methinks I see in my mind a noble and puissant nation rousing herself like a strong man after sleep, and shaking her invincible locks" (IV, p. 344).

The ending of *Samson Agonistes* will no doubt always remain the most secretive element of this secretive poem, because Milton has so steadfastly resisted submitting the great conceptual problems of his poem to his own high standards of rational, argumentative discourse. As if to compensate for the fateful loquacity of his hero, Milton refrains from violating "the sacred trust of silence" deposited deep within the Samson story. Instead of tearing down the structure of voluntarism by means of intellectual argument, as he had throughout most of *Christian Doctrine* and *Paradise Lost*, Milton permits his final poem to undermine that oppressive theology by means of subversive metaphor. The phoenix invoked in *Samson Agonistes* is, as we have noted, self-begot. But Milton's particular figuration of that phoenix has risen from the ashes of an earlier image in the poem, the far more traditional, sacrificial representation of Samson's miraculous beginnings. At the annunciation of Samson's birth, "an Angel . . . all in flames ascended / From off the Altar, where an Off'ring burn'd, / As in a fiery column" (24–27). This self-immolating angel (who in Judges had kept his name a "secret") declares at the poem's opening Samson's heavenly paternity and announces the cruel, voluntarist theology of sacrifice that marks Samson at birth as an adherent to the arbitrary Nazaritic code. But in the concluding reappearance of this image of fiery ascension, the figure of the self-begotten phoenix, Milton works to release his hero from the debt immense of heavenly paternity. It is as if Samson were born again, self-quickened this time by the divine vigor of his own body, into the noninterventionist monistic universe Milton had in his other poetry and prose claimed as his own. The positive valuation given the fantastic freedom of self-begetting announces the poem's magical, perhaps impossible, desire to escape once and for all the dualist and voluntarist theology in which it would seem to be imprisoned. Instead of marshaling a final argument, in his final poem, against an inimical theological system, Milton simply watches it go up in smoke.

Yale University

NOTES

1. *The Works of John Milton*, 18 vols., ed. Frank Patterson et al. (New York, 1931–40), vol. VII, p. 219. All subsequent quotations from Milton's prose will be cited by volume and page number from this edition.

2. All scriptural quotations and marginal glosses are drawn from the Geneva translation, cited, unless otherwise noted, from *The Bible* (London: Robert Barker, 1608). Michael Lieb, *Sinews of Ulysses: Form and Convention in Milton's Works* (Pittsburgh, 1989), pp. 98–138, has argued for the importance of what he calls "the theology of strength" in *Samson Agonistes*. Discussing Samson's strength in the context of Milton's exchange with Salmasius, Lieb elaborates his thesis in his *Milton and the Culture of Violence* (Ithaca, N.Y., 1994).

3. For a description of the early modern reinterpretation of the source of Samson's strength, see Michael Krouse, in *Milton's Samson and the Christian Tradition* (Princeton, 1949), p. 75.

4. For a related argument for the nonphysiological cause of Samson's fall, see William Perkins, *The Workes of That Famous and Worthie Minister of Christ*, 3 vols. (London, 1608), vol. I, p. 752. William Gouge, *A Learned and Very Useful Commentary on the Whole Epistle to the Hebrewes*, 2 vols. (London, 1655), vol. II, p. 176, further amplifies the Genevan gloss: "*Samsons* hair being thus a sign of more than ordinary comeliness, purity and subjection, so long as, in testimony of his inward piety, that external Rite was observed, Gods Spirit continued his assistance to him, and gave that evidence thereof, his extraordinary strength. But when by a violation of that Rite be manifested his impure, disobedient and rebellious disposition against God, God took away his Spirit." Michael Lieb discusses Gouge's contribution to the theology of Samson's strength in *Sinews of Ulysses*, pp. 114–16.

5. Lieb, *Milton and the Culture of Violence*, p. 257.

6. Harapha appears here to reproduce the pained literalism of the Calvinist William Gouge, who is led in his 1655 *Learned and Very Useful Commentary*, vol. II, p. 175, to itemize the arguments against the inherence of strength in Samson's hair:

1. Hair is no integral or essential part of the body: it is a meer excrement.
2. It hath no stability in itself, as bones have: but is exceeding weak.
3. Hair draweth strength out of a mans body, as weeds out of the ground.

7. Perkins, *Workes* I, p. 752.

8. A related cluster of images, focusing not merely on secrecy but on silence, is composed of Milton's references to Samson's willingness to break the "Seal of silence" (50) and "violate the sacred trust of silence/ Deposited within" him (428–29).

9. I am grateful to Matthew Giancarlo for bringing my attention to some of the implications of *secret*'s derivation from *secretus*.

10. In response to Mary Ann Radzinowicz's argument for the consonance of *Samson Agonistes* with the rational theology Milton developed in *De doctrina Christiana*, in her *Toward "Samson Agonistes": The Growth of Milton's Mind* (Princeton, 1978), William Kerrigan has argued for Milton's late voluntarist rejection of reason in "The Irrational Coherence of *Samson Agonistes*," in *Milton Studies* XXII, ed. James D. Simmonds (Pittsburgh, 1987), pp. 217–32; Joseph Anthony Wittreich Jr. makes the strongest case for the ironic structure of the poem in *Interpreting Samson Agonistes* (Princeton, 1986); and Joan S. Bennett performs a subtle dialectical synthesis of all these readings in *Reviving Liberty: Radical Christian Humanism in Milton's Great Poems* (Cambridge, 1989), pp. 119–60.

11. Cuthbert Aikman Simpson, *Composition of the Book of Judges* (Oxford, 1957), identifies two successive hands in the Judges revision of the original tale. The earlier writer, "J1," he argues, is responsible for the narrative of Samson's miraculous birth, while "J2" "carried further the process, begun by J1, of depaganizing the legend by ascribing Samson's deeds of prowess to the energizing power of the 'Spirit of Jahveh,' and by explaining his uncut hair as being due to the fact that he was, by divine appointment, a life-long Nazirite" (pp. 53–54). This "theological updating" is also discussed by John G. Boling, *The Anchor Bible: Judges* (Garden City, N.Y., 1975), pp. 29–38.

12. John L. McKenzie, *The World of the Judges* (Englewood Cliffs, N.J., 1966), p. 156, argues that Judges xvi, 22 "shows how in popular tradition the connection between Samson's strength and his hair was magical. The Nazarite consecration has nothing to do with this conception, the original conception of the stories. When Samson's hair is long, his strength is proportionate to its length." Simpson, *Composition*, p. 63, notes this verse's inconsistency with the stress on "the immediate divine origin of Samson's strength." See also J. Alberto Soggin, *Judges: A Commentary* (Philadelphia, 1981), pp. 257–58.

13. Milton distinguishes between God's "permission" of sin and his direct causation of it in *Works of John Milton* XV, pp. 67–93. For a careful coordination of the modes of divine action represented in *Samson Agonistes* and *Christian Doctrine*, see Albert C. Labriola, "Divine Urgency as a Motive for Conduct in *Samson Agonistes*," *PQ* L (1971): 99–107. It should be noted that *Samson Agonistes* attempts nowhere to suggest, with William Gouge, in *Learned and Very Useful Commentary* II, p. 176, that Judges xvi, 22, points simply to a "sign," rather than a cause, "of the Spirits return unto him."

14. Milton, *The Reason of Church Government*, in *Works of John Milton* III, p. 276. In *Eikonoklastes*, *Works of John Milton* V, p. 257, Milton refers to the "strength of that *Nazarites* locks."

15. Arnobius, *Seven Books of Arnobius Against the Heathen*, in *The Ante-Nicene Fathers: Translations of the Writings of the Fathers down to A.D. 325*, ed. Rev. Alexander Roberts and James Donaldson (Grand Rapids, Mich., 1987), vol. VI, pp. 456, 457. See Terence Spencer and James Willis, "Milton and Arnobius," *N&Q* CXCVI (1951): 387.

16. J. B. Broadbent notes this parallel with Luke in *Milton: Comus and Samson Agonistes* (London, 1961), p. 42.

17. Margaret Cavendish, *Philosophical Letters: or, Modest Reflections Upon Some Opinions in Natural Philosophy by the Thrice Noble, Illustrious, and Excellent Princess, The Lady Marchioness of Newcastle* (London, 1664), p. 112. I develop the connection between Milton and Cavendish in *The Matter of Revolution: Science, Poetry, and Politics in the Age of Milton* (Ithaca, N.Y., 1996).

18. William Harvey, *De motu cordis* (London, 1628); quoted here from the first English translation, *The Anatomical Exercises of Dr. William Harvey* (London, 1653), pp. 93–94.

19. There may in fact be more physiological wisdom than theological despair behind Samson's strange invocation of vermicular perception: fearing he has become "Inferior to the vilest . . . / Of man or worm," he expresses in his blindness an envy of what Milton may well have believed to be the panorganismic perceptiveness of worms: "the vilest here excel me, / They creep, yet see" (73–75).

20. William Kerrigan offers a psychobiographical reading of the vision-endowed bodies of Milton's angels in *The Sacred Complex: On the Psychogenesis of "Paradise Lost"* (Cambridge, Mass., 1983), pp. 211–12.

21. It will be apparent in what follows that I have not fully assented to the argument for the non-Miltonic authorship of *Christian Doctrine* forwarded by William B. Hunter, in "The Provenance of the *Christian Doctrine*," with comments by Barbara Lewalski and John Shaw-cross, *SEL* XXXII (1992): 129–66.

22. Stephen M. Fallon, *Milton Among the Philosophers: Poetry and Materialism in Seventeenth Century England* (Ithaca, N.Y., 1991).

23. Consider, for example, Milton's unqualified denunciation, in *Christian Doctrine*, of the segregation of body from soul implied by *Samson*'s Chorus: "that the spirit of man should be separate from the body, so as to have a perfect and intelligent existence independently of it, is nowhere said in Scripture, and the doctrine is evidently at variance both with nature and reason" (XV, p. 43).

24. The central discussions of the Body without Organs appear in Gilles Deleuze and Félix Guattari, *Anti-Oedipus: Capitalism and Schizophrenia*, trans. Robert Hurley et al. (Minneapolis, 1983), pp. 9–16; and *A Thousand Plateaus: Capitalism and Schizophrenia*, trans. Brian Massumi (Minneapolis, 1987), pp. 149–66.

25. *A Thousand Plateaus*, pp. 150–51.

26. Ibid., pp. 158–59.

27. This conceptual interdependence of physiology and politics was felt perhaps most keenly by early modern Calvinists. According to the commentators in the Geneva *New Testament* (London, 1602), p. 85ᵛ, Paul in 1 Corinthians xii, 17, rejects the image of the Body without Organs in order to dissuade the Corinthians from the political belief that "all should be equall one to another": "And that no man might finde fault with this division as unequall, hee addeth that God himself hath coupled all these [separate bodily parts] together." I discuss some of the discursive ties binding natural and political philosophy in *Matter of Revolution*, pp. 1–16.

28. Christopher Hill, *Milton and the English Revolution* (Harmondsworth, 1977), pp. 317–33.

29. Albert C. Labriola discusses the divinity of the "rousing motions" in "Divine Urgency as a Motive for Conduct in *Samson Agonistes*," pp. 106–107. For a dialectical reading of motivation in *Samson*, see Edward Tayler, *Milton's Poetry: Its Development in Time* (Pittsburgh, 1979), pp. 105–22; and especially John Guillory, "The Father's House: *Samson Agonistes* in Its Historical Moment," in *Re-membering Milton: Essays on the Texts and Traditions*, ed. Mary Nyquist and Margaret W. Ferguson (New York, 1987), pp. 148–76.

30. Samuel Johnson, *Works of Samuel Johnson*, 10 vols, ed. H. W. Liebert et al. (New Haven, 1969), vol. IV, p. 379.

31. I defend the value of Satan's heresy in *Matter of Revolution*, pp. 122–29.

32. *The Riverside Shakespeare* (Boston, 1974), p. 1337.

SAMSON AGONISTES AND THE DRAMA OF DISSENT

Sharon Achinstein

I N 1662, THE Quaker Thomas Ellwood spent two months in a London prison without knowing the charge against him. He had been arrested soon after the great crackdown on religious nonconformists in August. At his appearance before the court, he was asked to take the oath of Allegiance to the restored Stuart monarchy and its episcopacy, a requirement newly enjoined by the Act of Uniformity. As a Quaker, Ellwood likely would resist taking the oath on grounds that he owed allegiance to Christ and not to the king. Ellwood did resist taking the oath on these grounds, but not before pursuing another line of argument. Rather, he insisted that his condition of being a prisoner prevented him from offering the oath freely. Here are his words: "I conceive this Court hath not power to tender that oath to me, in the condition wherein I stand." The court asked for clarification, inferring Ellwood was challenging their jurisdiction. Here is his reply:

"Not absolutely," answered I, "but conditionally, with respect to my present condition, and the circumstances I am now under."
"Why, what is your present condition?" said the Recorder.—"A prisoner," replied I.—"And what is that," said he, "to your taking or not taking the oath?"—"Enough," said I, "as I conceive, to exempt me from the tender thereof while I am under this condition."—"Pray, what is your reason for that?" said he—"This," said I, "that if I rightly understand the words of the statute, I am required to say that *I do take this oath freely and without constraint,* which I cannot say, because I am not a free man, but in bonds and under constraint. Wherefore I conceive that if you would tender that oath to me, ye ought first to set me free from my present imprisonment."[1]

Ellwood's response to his interrogators was to ask for the granting of his civil liberty so that the act of consent (or the withholding of consent) could be freely performed. He could not promise he would take the oath if he were freed, but, not being free, he was not able to take the oath: thus he challenged the conditions under which he was being asked to perform as a moral agent.

Ellwood, like Quakers and many others attempting to live conscien-

133

tious lives in the Restoration, spent a good deal of time in and out of prison, wrangling with civil authorities, and in fear of further punishment. Yet Ellwood's exchange with the state authorities highlights the degree to which those living under persecuting religious conditions were aware of the larger philosophic stakes of their assent or dissent. Ellwood's act went beyond the questions commonly asked by those opposing conformity, questions concerning allegiance to state authority, and inversely, grounds by which to justify resistance to that authority. Ellwood's story raises an important philosophic point: allegiance to the state, and the verbal act of consent by which allegiance is signified, must be offered from a position of freedom to act. As Ellwood asks that the guarantee of civil liberty precede his acts of consent he makes a striking challenge to the culture of oppression: a counterdiscourse of civil—not strictly religious—right.[2]

I begin with Milton's pupil Thomas Ellwood in order to summon the terms in which I read *Samson Agonistes,* not to claim that Milton is a Quaker, but to open our eyes to a Restoration context of religious persecution of dissent.[3] In that context, the play may be seen as an exploration of the nature of, and conditions under which, moral agents might perform acts of obligation. In Barbara Lewalski's elegant reading of this work, "the poem achieves . . . a brilliant mimesis of the confusions attending moments of political crisis and choice," yet I suggest that these are not just *any* moments of political crisis, but those supplied by a context of Restoration dissent, not solely by an abstract Christian paradigm, or by classical languages of tragedy. My terms are taken from Restoration discussions about obedience, compulsion, and coercion, and thus my critical emphasis turns away from the question of whether Samson can be considered a Christian hero, away from the critical debate over the nature of Samson's inspiration and regeneration. Samson, it is true, struggles for personal meaning over the course of the play, and the questions of inspiration and spiritual growth are vital to understanding the Christianity in the work; I hope to illuminate here obligations other than the spiritual ones Samson is also shown struggling to fulfill. Samson in the play seeks not to dishonor the following—"our God, our Law, my Nation, or myself" (1425): each element on this list of obligations counts. By immersing the play back into its Restoration context, where debates over toleration for dissenters focused precisely on these different realms of obligation, we shall see how this is so.[4]

Regardless of when the play was written, the fact remains that it was published in the autumn of 1670. What could the play have meant at that time? Historicist critics have looked to the author's biography to understand Milton's intentions—both to understand his choice of dramatic genre and his choice of topic. This historical approach has tended to allegorize the play either in terms of Milton's biography or in terms of the Puritan cause; Milton, like Samson, found himself blind, in prisons both literal and metaphoric during the Restoration; he, like Samson, was questioning his divine gifts: "What is strength, without a double share / Of wisdom" (53–54). Samson has been seen to represent the New Model Army, or the crushed Good Old Cause. *Samson Agonistes,* in this reading, is Milton's working out the meaning of that personal and national failure. Such a historical approach sees *Samson Agonistes* as Milton's way of writing a political tract for his times in poetry, a message for how one *ought* to behave by the exemplary (or negative exemplary) story of Samson's internal growth and final action, an action that resembles—or doesn't—that of the Christian paradigm of sacrifice.[5]

The historical questions I choose here, rather, are those raised by debates over Restoration religious dissent. During the winter and early spring of 1670, both houses of Parliament had discussed the merits of a bill against conventicles—an act that tightened persecution of dissenters when it went into effect. Following the passage of that bill in April, and with the adjournment of Parliament, there was a great crackdown on dissenters as well as civil unrest in London. That summer, during which Charles was pursing his secret treaty with France, *Samson Agonistes* made it to the licenser, and its publication virtually coincided with the reconvening of Parliament in the fall. That Parliament early set as its task the reconsideration of the conventicles bill. The year 1670 also saw the publication of Samuel Parker's antitolerationist *Discourse of Ecclesiastical Politie* (followed of course by Marvell's parody, *The Rehearsal Transpros'd,* in 1672), as well as other important rebuttals; but I am concerned about Milton's philosophy, not merely his polemic. I posit the contemporary debate over Restoration nonconformity as a lens through which to understand the purpose of Milton's work. By illuminating Milton's local historical context, I hope to draw Milton into that larger philosophic conversation known as the liberal tradition.[6]

In short, I see Milton's *Samson Agonistes* as political theory. In this reading, I do not emphasize the ending of the drama, that final vengeful violence as the action offered for imitation.[7] Focus on the ending has skewed our understanding of the philosophic richness of the text. Is it a coincidence that this notorious missing middle is blotted out by the conservative Tory Samuel Johnson? In my reading, I shift attention away from the ending of the play and attempt to restore something of that missing middle. The ending does not fully answer the dilemmas Samson faces, dilemmas that offer occasions for understanding moral action and political obligation, and whose resolution provides a context and ground for acting with responsibility to obligations. Barbara Lewalski has emphasized the imperfect and partial state of knowledge that attends Milton's moral choices, arguing that "the drama has demonstrated that political choices must be made and actions taken *in medias res*, in circumstances always characterized by imperfect knowledge and conflicting testimony. The thematics of true political experience in this work offers readers no definitive answers, but instead presents a process for making such choices in such circumstances."[8] By thinking about the persecuting conditions of Restoration Anglicanism, I see that the ending of *Samson Agonistes*—its final act of retributive violence—is not the only clue to its historical meaning. What would happen in the end was, for the dissenter, not the only problem; rather, what to do in the meantime was. How to define a conscientious life, how to live it, even under the yoke of arbitrary and cruel persecution, was the problem for dissenters. It is this context I see reflected in the play.

The middle of the play, as we shall see, does not satisfy readers with positive answers to difficult questions. Stanley Fish has powerfully argued that *Samson Agonistes* is an exploration of radical indeterminacy—it provokes our "interpretive lust," but its ultimate tease is in refusing to fulfill that lust with a climax of knowable meaning: "The only wisdom to be carried away from the play is that there is no wisdom to be carried away, and that we are alone, like Samson, and like the children of Israel of whom it is said in the last verse of Judges: 'and every man did that which was right in his own eyes'" (Judg. xxi, 25). What Fish manages to leave out is the verse immediately preceding this one: "In those days there was no king in Israel." He leaves out the fact that both verses have previously served as a refrain during the course of the Book of Judges; and that for those seeking to understand the nature of political sovereignty in seventeenth-century England, the Book of Judges provided many examples of righteous action—figures such as Ehud, Deborah, Jephthah, and even Samson—were favorites of those authors thinking about virtuous self-rule without kings—the republicans. Those lines that provide the compelling proof-text of radical indeterminacy for Fish also served as polemical ammunition in debates over toleration; for instance, the epigraph to Thomas Tomkyns's 1667 tract, *Inconveniencies of Toleration*, was "In those dayes there was no King in Israel, but every man did that which was right in his own eyes": the Judges passage was quoted in order to argue *against* toleration for dissenters. The plot thickens, as we locate Milton's words within the realm of the political, not just the personal or hermeneutical.[9]

I agree with Fish that *Samson Agonistes* raises many questions it cannot answer, but raising unanswerable questions is not the same matter as voicing hopelessness about arriving at meaning. Raising possibly unanswerable questions is in fact the essential art of political theory that takes asking questions seriously.[10] Milton's *Samson Agonistes* may be the most brilliant piece of political theory created in the seventeenth century if we think about political theory not only in terms of a discourse of abstraction, but also of contemplation, experience, and subjective experience. *Samson Agonistes* is all those—both humanistic and spiritual, secular and divine, philosophical and political; and it is very fine poetry. Contradictions and failures to arrive at meaning are its strengths, as it offers a political theory that leaves in the working-through of problems, links us to its hero, the individual struggling with questions fundamental to social existence. It is not a good book to turn to for answers, but it is one to turn to for questions. Those questions I see Milton asking belong to a long tradition of arguments over freedom and religious toleration, and ultimately concern citizenship, rights, and responsibilities. As political theory and not polemic, *Samson Agonistes* spurs us to thought—and for Milton, is not thought also a kind of action?

In what follows, I bring this dissenting context, where the nature and purview of the subject's rationality and freedom are central issues, to Samson's struggles to live under the external condition of enslavement. Samson strives against a regime that was compelling him to submit to its command to perform obedience, and he seeks to retain not only his dignity, but his obligations to his people and his God. In the middle sections of the play Samson examines the spheres of his obligation—to his father, his wife—but he also examines the nature of his own freedom to act. What we find is that freedom is not only an inner condition, but also a performance in the world. The focus here is on the final encounter in Samson's drama, the scene with the Public Officer, though further study can link the other scenes as well to a Restoration context. In the scene under scrutiny here, Samson performs a drama of dissent, specifically in the acts where he contemplates his obligations, examines the moral conditions under which obligations may be performed, and takes action. The drama of dissent, as we shall see, is a drama of a liberal political subject, both deliberating and acting in a civil sphere.

I began this essay with Ellwood, not to argue that Milton was writing a biography of his friend or that Milton was a Quaker, but to set the dissenting dilemma before us. That dissenting dilemma was not solely one of faith: Where is God and how could He have let me down? But it was also: How can I live under conditions of oppression, persecution, and compulsion—conditions very like those Samson faced in prison? Though I claimed I would avoid allegory, of course I am using allegory: rather than representing a particular historical character or event, Samson represents a "type" of moral agent. The dissenting dilemma is a dilemma of free moral action under conditions that allow little or no room for freedom of moral action.

With religious dissent a chief domestic problem of the Restoration governments, the Restoration Anglican Church put the problem of compulsion in sharp focus. The Restoration had left unsettled the dispute over the nature of the English church, a dispute that some historians blame as the cause of the English civil war. The Restoration resurgence of religious and political tensions was a complex dynamic, one of national and international dimensions, and not just a reversal of civil war projects. Although Charles II's return had brought hopes for wider latitude for religious practices, these were undermined by the Anglican Royalist Cavalier Parliament, which pursued instead a policy of religious persecution in order to secure the goal of uniformity of religious practices. A strict penal code was put into place beginning in 1662 with the Act of Uniformity, and with other legislation of increasing severity over the next decade. This code and these laws were not based on simple prejudice nor were they random, but they reflected thinking about what made for an orderly nation.[11]

The conditions of Restoration dissent give us a context in which to place the philosophic defense of nonconformity, with its preoccupations with questions of obedience, conscientious action, slavery, and resistance. After 24 August 1662, London lost one third of its ministers. At least two thousand ministers, clergy, and lecturers were forced from their livings between 1660 and 1662. Most of these were moderate Presbyterians, who would have supported a national church but were forced into separation by the requirements of the act. In one stroke, legislation created a class of dissenters. Historians estimate the number of dissenters after the Great Ejection to be well over one hundred thousand souls. The Act of Uniformity was followed by a series of intolerant legislation which reduced civil liberties and due process of law on a massive scale: nonconformists were prohibited from assembling and ministers were driven out of towns. These laws, collectively called the Clarendon Code, promised punishment by incrementally stiff fines, often steep to the point of ruin; nonconformists were also subject to searches of their homes without warrants and, in order to pay fines, to seizing of their property without trial: this often meant depriving a poor or middling sort of man with the tools of his trade. In the climate of suspicion regarding sedition, due process was invaded; those suspected of nonconformist activity could be arrested and found guilty on the basis of a reduced number of witnesses.[12]

Milton himself was intimately familiar with consequences of persecution of dissent. His own neighborhood, St. Giles Cripplegate, was an area of London nonconformist concentration, and there was controversy about its local church ministry through the early 1660s. Its nonconformist vicar, Dr. Annesley, was legally ejected and an Anglican royalist installed in his place.[13] Milton's neighbor and friend, the Quaker Isaac Pennington, was arrested in 1665 and his family turned out of their house; Mrs. Pennington took lodgings near Milton while her husband was in prison. And the prisoner Ellwood was Milton's pupil, asker of the famous question about the sequel to *Paradise Lost.*

This dissenting context intersects with *Samson Agonistes* in that key moment in the play where Samson is pressed to perform for the state an action we know offends his conscience. At this moment, he is asked to attend the Philistine feast; first he refuses, and then he assents. This sequence of events seems to be lifted out of the pages of the history of compulsion and finds meaning in dialogue with nonconformist deliberation—about freedom of performance of required acts. It raises, and works through, questions about the obedience a subject owes to a state authority, specifically with regard to religious compulsion. Critics have combed over this sequence in order to find out what changes inside Samson's heart in order to understand the nature of his regeneration.[14] Yet this history and this discourse also frame Milton's exploration of the nature of Samson's freedom—his freedom to perform acts, and thus his obligations, in the play. *Samson Agonistes* is not solely a drama of the awakening of conscience with regard to God; it is the awakening of a political conscience as well.

In the text, the Public Officer demands Samson's attendance at a public festival:

> This day to *Dagon* is a solemn Feast,
> With Sacrifices, Triumph, Pomp, and Games;
> Thy strength they know surpassing human rate,
> And now some public proof thereof require
> To honor this great Feast, and great Assembly;
> Rise therefore with all speed and come along.   (1311–16)

Rites, triumph, pomp: all these recall the familiar language of idolatry in Milton, with a distinct whiff of antiroyalism, as critics have amply shown. Yet this feast commanded in *Samson* and its relation to the discourses of iconoclasm and antipopery are not merely topical allusions, cheap asides attacking the restored Stuart monarch. This description of what goes on at the Philistine festival, and the invitation, especially with its language of "public proof," recall the specific context of Restoration Anglicanism. Much of the Clarendon Code enjoined compelling "public proof" of conformity, as authorities enforced allegiance by significant public performances. This act required all ministers and teachers to adopt the new prayer book and to mark their "unfeigned assent and consent to the use of all things contained and prescribed in and by . . . the Book of Common Prayer" by St. Bartholomew's Day or face ejection from their posts.[26] The act pertained not only to ministers, but to all manner of public speakers, including college students and schoolmasters.[15]

According to the act, it was not enough that ministers adopt the revised prayer book in their services; they also had to *perform,* as the words of the law require: to "openly and publicly before the congregation there assembled declare his unfeigned assent and consent" with words prescribed by the statute. The minister was required to use "these words and no other."[16] Failure to perform this public action, that of reading a set script, would lead to stripping of his office. Thus accordance to the get-tough religious regime required not only passive obedience—the adoption of liturgical conformity by using the new prayer book—but also active obedience—public, active assent to the adoption thereof. Both gestures of obedience were displayed in a public spectacle.

The experience of living under this harsh legislation was painful for those now labeled nonconformists, and their reaction, it is important to remember, was not uniform. The very difficult decisions—whether or not to wear the surplice, whether or not to take the oath, whether to attend a now illegal religious meeting: how to live conscientiously under such religious persecution—created daily choices for the nonconformist, and resistance to this policy was widespread. The Baptist John Bunyan went to prison for disobeying these laws, and prisons filled with a vast number of Quakers. Most nonconformists, however, inhabited the more complex middle ground between total obedience to the state and total obedience to God: perhaps God was working through the state, they considered.[17]

In their justifications of religious compulsion, Anglican Tories appealed to civil order, fear of sedition, and the threat of yet another civil war; and Anglican divines found scriptural precedent for their rigor. As Benjamin Laney, bishop of Lincoln, put it, in defending the Uniformity Act in a sermon preached before Charles in April 1663, *"That our Liturgie or Common Prayer is a true Sacrifice to God. . . . And to this I shall not beg the assent* of those that like it not, but *require* it." The key text authorizing such compulsion was the parable of Jesus' calling all to the feast (Luke xiv, 16–23). Samson's invitation to the feast honoring Dagon resonates with this situation. In Luke, chapter xiv, a lord bids a servant to invite others to come in for a supper, and when they do not come voluntarily, Jesus recounts that the lord says to the servant: "Go out into the highways and the hedges, and compel them to come in, that my house may be filled." Luke, chapter xiv, was thus a powerful symbol for those defending the policy of persecution. The archconservative Benjamin Laney used this text in a sermon preached before Charles in March 1664, "For our Saviour in the *Parable,* when the guests came not to the *banquet* at his invitation, commanded his servants to *compel them to come in"* (Luke xiv, 23;—glossed in margin). Compulsion to attend the "feast" here is thus a scriptural precedent that Milton must address. Milton's text asks us how such compulsion squares with freely given obedience.[18]

Against these defenses of compulsion came a range of responses, yet for nonconformists to question this policy was to consider the possibility of disobedience, and defenses of disobedience were dangerous to make in public, to say the least. Algernon Sidney was executed for making such a defense only in private. It is easy to understand why many nonconformists stayed far clear of defenses of resistance to the code. They spent their time, rather, portraying themselves as good subjects and citizens, simply following their consciences and asking to be let alone. These respondents worked out definitions of subjecthood that could include obedience to the crown but nonconformity in spiritual matters. John Owen, in a 1667 pamphlet, expressed allegiance to the king: "We own and acknowledge the power of the king or supreme magistrate in this nation . . . and are ready to defend and assist in the administration of the government in all causes, according unto the law of the land, with all other good protestant subjects of the kingdom."[19]

Yet High Church Anglicans liked to portray nonconformists either as noncitizens or as seditious. They saw nonconformist pleas for liberty of conscience as defenses of rebellion, as did the conservative Anglican apologist Samuel Parker: "These men are ever prepared for any mischief. . . . And there needs no other motive to engage their Zeal in any Seditious Attempt, than to instil into their minds the Necessity of a thorow Reformation. . . . And therefore, it concerns the Civil Magistrate to beware of this sort of People above all others, as a party, that is always ready form'd for any Publick Disturbance." The conservative Benjamin Laney, preaching to Charles at Whitehall in March 1661, argued that liberty of conscience was a dangerous thing for an orderly state: "If a man should be so unreasonable as to say, his conscience may be bound by himself, but not by any else . . . though the truth is, they bind none but themselves . . . and misleading the people into Faction, Sedition and Disobedience, to say no worse." Nonconformists sever the bonds of society and therefore cannot enjoy the privileges of freedom.[20]

In their own defense, however, nonconformists portrayed themselves as loyal citizens, struggling to maintain their livings, and they appealed, as Owen did, to charity. It was persecution, moreover, that might drive them to rebel. In contrast to Laney, the persecutor was made responsible for the breakdown of social ties. Nicholas Lockyer warned that "this unnatural severity tends either to deter from known duty (in attending the Worship of God according to his Word) or from the Extremity, to provoke to Sedition,

Tumult or Rebellion; necessitating thereby a falling either into the hands of
God or Man." John Locke, in his 1667 *Essay on Toleration*, also claimed that
nonconformity itself did not spawn disobedience; rather, harsh penalties
imposed by the state did: "for force and harsh usage will not only increase
the animosity but number of enemies. . . . if you persecute them you make
them all of one party and interest against you, tempt them to shake off your
yoke and venture for a new government." Rebellion, it was admitted, was a
possible consequence of nonconformity, in the conservative argument, because nonconformity *was* rebellion, or, in the protolerationist argument, because persecution created conditions where rebellion was likely—or even
was necessary—to occur.[21]

Yet what about the second part of the equation to consider, what powers or rights belonged to the subject? Thomas Ellwood's claims—that he
could not even offer consent while under the conditions of imprisonment—
lead in this direction. Milton, in *Samson Agonistes*, also offers an analysis
of the subject's obligations that sorts with the public discourse of political
argument during 1660s and 1670s. Milton directly engages with the philosophical discourse on toleration of nonconformity. Over the course of the
play, Samson has a chance to address several spheres of political and social
obligation, and in each encounter—with Manoa, Dalila, and Harapha—law
is evoked to consider and settle competing claims. But in his final encounter,
Samson considers the moral conditions that ground any attachment to law
and under which compliance to law is at all possible.[22] In the scene with the
Public Officer, Milton examines the meanings of compulsive state power
from the vantage point of a discourse of civil liberty. Divine injunction is
one, but not the only, source of political authority and knowledge in the
play. There is, as we shall see, a counterdiscourse of civil liberty, specifically
focusing on the liberty of the subject.

The discourse of slavery was used by seventeenth-century thinkers to
think through the nature of sovereign authority and of liberty from the vantage point of the subject. Over and over in Milton's prose and poetry we
find the author engaging with the topic of slavery—slavery, of course, was
not one thing to Milton. In his long career he opposed many different kinds
of slavery, from the spiritual tyranny of bishops, to the yoke of Presbyterian
prelacy over conscience, to the Charles I's suppression of his subjects, to
those who opposed liberty of conscience, to the self-enslavement of humans
to their lusts and passions, and the slavery of idolatry and popery.

Milton most often described the condition of people under the returning Charles II by drawing upon the story of Exodus: the Jews returning to
bondage in Egypt. That analogy worked in two ways: not only were the
English slaves, but they were also subjugated to a foreign power, with Egypt

overlord to Israel. Milton himself merges these two facets of slavery in his jeremiad, *The Ready and Easie Way;* returning to monarchy is comparable to accepting "forein or domestic slaveries."[23]

Milton returns to this theme in *Samson Agonistes,* where Samson accepts responsibility for his own self-enslavement. But the play also explores his duties as a literal slave to the Philistines when Samson resists attending the Feast of Dagon. The Public Officer asks him to examine his condition: "Regard thyself, this [refusal] will offend . . . highly" (1333), asking Samson to take stock of his condition: "Art thou our Slave, / Our Captive" (1392–93). Samson, therefore, has no liberty to refuse. But Samson chooses to redefine himself not by the external condition of slavery, but by the internal liberty by which he knows himself to be as fully human: "Myself?" he answers, "my conscience and internal peace" (1334). Samson here rejects the Public Officer's definition that he is a slave and therefore has no power to refuse.

Though he defines himself by his inner state, Samson still suffers under two kinds of slavery: self-enslavement of his submission to Dalila ("foul effeminacy held me yoked," 411); and slavery under the Philistine conquerers. Internal slavery is more disgraceful than the other kind, as Samson explains early on in the play when he laments his condition:

> This base degree to which I now am fall'n
> These rags, this grinding, is not yet so base
> As was my former servitude, ignoble,
> Unmanly, ignominious, infamous,
> True slavery. (414–18)

True slavery, as these remarks show, is to be complicit in one's own enslavement, freely and willingly to contribute to surrender of one's own freedom, a republican concept of dependence.

Yet Samson's personal enslavement is connected to his outward condition, and to the condition of his nation. As Samson remarks, again sounding a republican note:

> But what more oft in Nations grown corrupt,
> And by thir vices brought to servitude,
> Than to love Bondage more than Liberty,
> Bondage with ease than strenuous liberty. (268–71)

Samson invites comparison between his personal condition of self-enslavement and the national condition of Israelite subjection to Philistine rule.

The theme of self-enslavement was used often in the Restoration to describe English citizens' complicity in their loss of liberty under the re-

stored Stuart monarch, especially in republican writing. By welcoming back
the Stuart regime, English citizens were willingly reducing themselves to
the condition of slaves, as the republican Algernon Sidney wrote in the mid
1660s: "God hath deliver'd us from slavery, and shewd us that he would be
our King; and we recall from exile one of that detested race." In the last
lines of his eleventh-hour appeal to his nation to oppose the return of monarchy, Milton also, and once again, evokes the myth of Exodus in the closing
sentences of his *Ready and Easy Way* (1660), challenging his audience "to
become children of reviving libertie; and may reclaim, though they seem
now chusing them a captain back for *Egypt*" (YP VII, p. 463).[24]

Samson's story begins where *Ready and Easy Way* leaves off, with a
man reduced to slavery because of an act of his own free will. Though it is
important for the drama that Samson come to recognize his voluntary complicity in his own enslavement, the play also meditates on the consequences
of slavery, not merely its causes. What is to be done given conditions of
enslavement, once responsibility for that condition has been taken? That
outward condition of slavery poses new questions, questions that a traditional republicanism perhaps cannot answer. Instead, those who sought to
understand the rights of a slave or captive turned to other languages—those
of Christian charity, mercantilism, or natural rights theories.[25]

Writers opposing religious persecution in the 1660s confronted the situation of coercive state authority and religious persecution by likening it to
slavery. The Presbyterian Nicholas Lockyer, for example, likened the severity of the Anglican orthodoxy to "much at that rate as *Pharaoh* dealt with
the *Israelites*, when he required them to make Brick without Straw, and
beat them to if they brought not the full tare." John Locke also used the
metaphor of slavery to argue for a toleration for protestant dissenters in
1667: persecution will "bring this island to the condition of a galley where
the greater part shall be reduced to the condition of slaves, be forced with
blows to row the vessel, but share in none of the lading, nor have any privilege or protection." Those suffering under religious persecution, he argued,
were not only subject to force, but they were also denied their rightful en-
titlements as citizens, being denied the benefits of their lading, the "privilege or protection." Under such conditions, protection is not offered as a
reciprocal benefit of obedience: the essential social contract begins to tear.
Dependence alone did not define slavery in this analysis; since a slave was
denied reciprocal obligations of society, slavery put at stake a human's physical, moral, and civil status. Protection was not exchangeable for that kind
of obedience: against a Hobbesian argument, Locke suggests here, liberty
is not absolutely alienable.[26]

Compulsion and slavery were intolerable not only because of their physical consequences, but because of their assault on the will and on human rationality: the condition of compulsion denied the free operations of conscience and rationality that were necessary for faith to grow. As Charles Wolseley put it, "force upon men will never beget, or change Principles or Opinions. . . . When I have used rational su[i]table means to inform another, I ought to acquiesce . . . he that forceth me to a Religion, makes me hate it, and makes me think, there wants reason, and other evidence to evince it. Nature abhors compulsion in Religious things, as a spiritual rape upon the Conscience." A "spiritual rape" not only evokes the subjection to force, but performs a gender reversal as well: citizens become women victims. According to Wolseley, fear or slavish considerations cannot succeed in extracting a subject's accord; in fact, conversion under such compulsion is "an impossibility." As Quentin Skinner has argued, Hobbes in *Leviathan* sought to construct a polity in which coercion and liberty could be made consistent with one another. But in these attacks on compulsion, Wolseley and others denied that liberty and coercion could coexist. Hugo Grotius had attacked religious compulsion, and he put his finger on the same passage from the Bible, Luke, chapter xiv, offering a tolerationist interpretation: "as in that Parable the word *compel* argues nothing else but a vehement sollicitation." In opposing religious compulsion, Milton himself indirectly seems to reflect on the meaning of Luke xiv in his *Treatise of Civil Power* (1659): "We read not that Christ ever exercis'd force but once; and that was to drive prophane ones out of his temple, not to force them in" (YP VII, p. 268).[27]

As Samson ponders whether or not to attend the feast of Dagon, Milton explores active, voluntary compliance to obligations. Samson works through several thorny political questions as he settles his own inner peace specifically regarding the conditions under which moral action—whether compliance or disobedience—might take place. Samson first refuses the Public Officer's invitation to the Feast of Dagon, refusing on the grounds of Hebrew law, "our Law": "Thou knowest I am an *Ebrew*, therefore tell them, / Our Law forbids at thir Religious Rites / My presence; for that cause I cannot come" (1319–21). Note Samson's equation of "law" with "cause," an ambiguity we might well ponder. The adherence to Hebrew law is the reason Samson cannot come, that is, the explanation for his nonattendance. But Hebrew law is also a cause, perhaps like the Good Old Cause, in the sense of a prior political allegiance. His resistance to the Public Officer's message—and indeed to the state-authorized compulsion—is grounded in his self-definition, "I am an *Ebrew*," which signals two prior obligations: both his national allegiance to the Hebrew nation, and his allegiance to the law.[28]

I call attention to the collective ownership of this law; it is not "my vow"—his personal Nazarite commitment to God, broken and betrayed to

Dalila—but rather law shared by Samson and other humans. Samson draws a distinction between these two realms of obligation, vouching that he will do nothing that will "dishonour / Our Law, *or* stain my vow of Nazarite" (1385–86; italics mine). Samson acknowledges the presence of this collective law—"our law"—over and against his personal vow. This distinction indicates that his shared bonds with his people might present different kinds of obligations.[29]

What is Samson's relation to these obligations? The answer to this puzzle depends on a construal of how free he is to act. In his first response to the officer, Samson adheres to these named laws from necessity: "I cannot come." This begins his moral analysis. First of all, his physical impediments keep him from behaving as a moral agent: even Hobbes admitted that physical constraint or impediment of motion was unliberty (*Leviathan*, chap. 21). Yet as Samson reflects, he realizes that he "can" come—that is, he is physically able to come—and he then ponders the meaning of his action relative to the Philistine audience. What becomes clear to him is that the Philistines will look at his performance as "sport," like those "Wrestlers, Riders, Runners, / Jugglers and Dancers, Antics, Mummers, Mimics": as a performance, theatrical inauthenticity (1324–25). Darkly, he reasons that it might not be the content of his performance that counts; his powerlessness is itself a kind of entertainment. Perhaps the command merely stages his moral position as a slave and their own power as masters: "Do they not seek occasion of new quarrels / On my refusal to distress me more, / Or make a game of my calamities?" (1329–31). Such action must be resisted, not on grounds of necessity—for that would merely make him a "slave" to his own law—but by a positive choice.

By analogy, obedience to law based upon necessity—a "cannot"— denies freedom to choose to act. If he resists the invitation to become the Philistines' puppet only to become God's puppet, Samson has not done any better; in either case, Samson would merely be acting in a slavish and instrumental way: "he had bin else a meer artificiall *Adam,* such an *Adam* as he is in the motions" (YP II, p. 527). Freedom, it turns out, is power to *choose* to act in accordance with right. After considering this possible meaning of his performance he shifts the ground of his resistance from *necessary* obedience to Mosaic law to *voluntary* consent to that law. "I will not come," Samson repeats twice. In the interim, he has imagined what attendance at the spectacle means: it is not only to submit to being the object of sport, but also to willingly ratify the compulsive power of his oppressors. After these thoughts come his willed refusal, not a compelled one: "Return the way thou cam'st I will not come" (1332). In his move from "cannot come" to "will not come," Samson is growing to acknowledge the full responsibility of his own assent to higher law; and he is coming to act as a voluntary agent, not a slave, either to law itself or to the commands of an external captor. The language of necessity is transformed into a language of free choice.

Now armed with his voluntaristic sense of obedience, Samson asks whether he might then willingly obey the Philistine command. He could, perhaps, consent to the terms of his servitude:

> But who constrains me to the Temple of *Dagon*,
> Not dragging? The Philistian Lords command.
> Commands are no contraints. If I obey them,
> I do it freely; venturing to displease
> God for the fear of Man, and man prefer,
> Set God behind. (1370–75)

Samson's understanding that "commands are no constraints" mirrors his previous move from "I cannot come" to "I will not come"; that is, it reflects an understanding that compliance with the law is voluntary, a free action of the will, and under his own responsibility.[30] Samson has come to see that submission to law or to command involves freely entering into an agreement to obey, through an act of the will. By acknowledging the voluntary basis of his compliance with law, Samson is fully able to understand that consent is essential for moral action—the classic liberal starting point. I recall Ellwood's response to his captors: no freedom implies no capability to offer consent. Samson finds, however, in this case, that his free consent to the Philistine command might offend God.

At this point, when Samson owns up to the voluntary nature of his compliance—to the Philistine commands, to the common laws of the Hebrews, and to his own personal commitments—he begins "to feel / Some rousing motions" (1381–82). He has recovered not only his personal pride, his connection to law and community, but also his moral center as a free agent.

Behind the Philistine command, however, is the threat of force. Does force foster conditions under which consent is possible? The play considers this question by addressing Samson's options. The Public Officer threatens to compel Samson to come to the feast; if Samson resists, "we shall find such Engines to assail / And hamper thee, as thou shalt come of force" (1396–97). What room is left for Samson's humanity under such a command? Is there a possible free answer to this question? Since Samson has begun to recognize the full range of his obligations, he refuses now not on grounds of prior obligation, but on moral ones; he refuses to be reduced to the moral status of a beast: "They shall not trail me through thir streets / Like a wild Beast" (1402–03). Samson has complained about his slavish status as that of a beast early on in the play: "O glorious strength / Put to the labor of a Beast, debas't / Lower than a bondslave!" (36–38), but in that earlier case, beasthood was defined sheerly in terms of physical labor. To be a beast is to exert "strength without a double share / Of wisdom" (53–54), to lack rational powers.

Yet here, bestiality is also considered in light of its moral status. As Sir Charles Wolseley saw it, "Men are to be ruled over as Creatures, that have immortal souls to be chiefly cared for, and they are to be ruled over as such who have a special relation to God, and a homage to pay him, above all the rest of the world; a rule over men without some respect to this, would denominate Mankind into Brutes."[31] The difference between man and beasts is not sheerly human rationality, but also that "special relation to God"—a form of obligation.

The play asks, What are the moral conditions under which free consent may be offered? The Quaker Thomas Ellwood entertained this question in his own trial, resisting to perform the oath on the grounds that he could not freely and voluntarily be in a position to take a consenting action because he was in prison. I now take Ellwood's position in light of Samson's dilemma, when Samson ponders the topic of "absolute subjection": "Masters' commands come with a power resistless / To such as owe them absolute subjection" (1404–05). Samson considers not only what he "owes" masters, but the moral conditions under which obligation is exacted. The masters, by enslaving Samson, have taken away his condition of freedom to consent and allow him no room for action according to free will. By removing occasions for Samson to exert his free will, the oppressors have denied him a fundamental right to be recognized as a human being and instead have reduced him to the moral status of a beast.

When Samson assents, "I am content to go" (1403), however, he signals his acceptance of responsibility for his actions to the officer and his friends, and confirms that he will perform as a morally free agent and not as a beast. The last episodes of the play show that the conscience must not only be free from self-enslavement, but also that action not derive from external compulsion. Rather, action must be self-motivated and "owned" in order for Samson to be open to contact with God. The law can never compel without removing human freedom; it merely offers occasion for accord and compliance.

Performing freely is not just thinking freely, and it is performance that is at the center of Milton's notion of consent. Dissent was a drama, in which preserving the inner realm of conscience alone was not enough to define human freedom; actions in public mattered, for there was a link between opinion and action in nonconformist thought. In *Truth and Innocence Vindicated,* John Owen remarked that liberty of conscience was not only an inner freedom: "if conscience to God be confined to thoughts, and opinions, and speculation about the general notions and notices of things, about true and false and unto the liberty of judging and determining what they are or no, the whole nature and being of conscience, and that to the reason, sense, and experience of every man is utterly overthrown. . . . Conscience . . . obligeth men to act or forbear accordingly" (Owen, *Works* 13: 442).

Conscience acts in the world. In nonconformist defenses of freedom of religion, because conscience involves both the inner and the outer moral life, external religious ritual must be undertaken with extreme attention to the ways it might bind conscience. As John Owen argued against the imposition of liturgies in 1662, "It is not about stinted forms of prayer in the worship and service of God, by those who, *of their own accord,* do make use of that kind of assistance, judging that course to be better than any thing they can do themselves in the discharge of the work of the ministry, but of the imposition of forms on others."[33] Occasional conformity—the practice of performing Anglican ritual yet withholding conscience's assent from the performance thereof—would not do in this scheme. Moral performance is freely consensual performance that reflects an internal obedience, "of their own accord." The word *accord* has at its root the word *heart:* "joining heart with." According is the action of joining the heart—inner—with an external performance.

What is the connection between the inner and the outer realms of action? External compulsion in religious matters mistook the outer for the inner, according to Wolseley: "this is as much to say, 'You may as well cure a man of the Cholick by brushing his Coat, or fill a mans belly with a Syllogysme' " (*Liberty,* p. 38). Earlier in Milton's career, it seemed that preserving the inner realm of freedom was sufficient for virtue: in the masque *Comus,* the Lady's defense against compulsion was to assert against her captor, "thou canst not touch the freedom of my minde" (663). Yet in *Samson,* inner and outer are closer together, as we see when the Chorus asks Samson why he resists attending the feast when he does not mind performing physical labor for his oppressors. Samson answers the Chorus that his resistance to attending the feast of Dagon is not in contradiction to his compliance to perform other acts for the state. His response upholds a distinction between civil and religious spheres of obligation: "Not in ther Idol-Worship, but by labor / Honest and lawful to deserve my food / Of those who have me in thir civil power" (1365–67). These lines reveal the conditions under which performance of his slave-labor is consensual: to earn his food, and to submit to conquest, to exchange protection for obedience. Idol worship is different, as there are no reciprocal obligations owed to the state in the case of religious worship.

The Chorus proposes, however, that Samson ignore the conditions of consent, and it suggests that Samson offers external compliance to the state's compulsion in religious worship—occasional conformity. He could do this without surrendering inner compliance, "where the heart joins not, outward acts defile not" (1368). This line echoes *Areopagitica*'s defense of freedom in defending publication of books: "to the pure all things are pure." But Samson rejects that inner and outer performances are so distinct: "where outward force constrains," he says back, "the sentence holds" (1369). By this statement, Samson seems to contradict the doctrine of inner purity that is the reserve of individual conscience, as sufficient to ground a moral life. And so, he rejects the Chorus' pleas for "occasional conformity." This seems to turn back from Milton's earlier positions concerning inner freedom as represented in *Comus* and *Areopagitica*. External action, how one "performs" in the world, matters. Samson's final action then is taken in this spirit of the only freedom left to him—willing compliance to God's laws, and as the voluntary exercise of his human power, "Of mine own accord."

When Samson finally consents to go to the feast, then, he is in a position to own his voluntary obligations. He claims that he will not do dishonor to "our God, our Law, my Nation, or myself" (1425). This list stands as a kind of declaration of obligation, in which each element establishes a realm of responsibility and a context for liberty. And these lines—the last Samson utters—establish an order in obligations one owes, starting from the most general to the most specific.[34] To John Selden's list of laws adumbrated at the opening of his great text, *Uxor Hebraica*—natural or divine law; Law of Nations, civil law—Milton adds a last sphere of obligation: "myself." Each term in this list is important, and the addition of the last term unequivocally posits a sphere of personal liberty and responsibility. This declaration of obligations signals that personal regeneration is predicated on, and *inseparable from* social regeneration, national regeneration, and political regeneration. Authentic performance encompasses all these spheres of moral obligation: Samson finally "owns" his actions, as he has owned up to his full morally free nature, as he has owned up to the need for a consensual basis for a moral political society. With these recognitions, Samson has *chosen* to act like Samson; Samson himself is defined in relation to these realms of obligation: "*Samson* hath quit himself / Like *Samson*" (1709–10).

External slavery poses challenges for the oppressed, offering a range of responses from violent rage to despair. A possible consequence of slavery is hopelessness, and I do not mean to undermine the importance of the psychological resources the play seeks to draw upon. Despair is eased, however, by Samson's reuniting with his community, by his movement away from self—whether self-absorption or self-accusation—and toward fulfilling the social obligations that make Samson a member of the Israelite community. He is able finally to act on behalf of that larger community, once he has understood himself to be a fully free moral agent.

What kind of action, then, is the play offering for readers? Despite Milton's profound humanism in this work, there is also the apocalyptic and spiritual element—the matter of that violent ending, to say nothing of the companion piece, *Paradise Regained*. And yet I wish to gesture at some possible reconciliation between what has been largely a secular or civil discourse, and what is incontrovertibly a providential or even millenarian ending of the play, and that reconciliation takes place in a discussion of genre. Though the action of the play is clearly mental action, it is cast as dramatic action, specifically as tragedy. Greek tragedy in democratic Athens, it has been argued, was specifically a site for the exploration of the most important questions of political philosophy, and Milton allies himself with that tradition, despite important reservations. This drama is not intended for the stage, but it is not only mental action, action taking place within Samson's inscrutable mind. It is a series of choices taking place in a public forum, not only as Samson deliberates before a chorus of friends, but dialogically, as Milton's text unfolds before the audience of the play, an audience of separated, silent readers. Samson's final action can only take place after he considers, addresses, and fulfills all his obligations, and I find it crucial that he does so before others to whom he is bound by those obligations.[35]

Michael Walzer has suggested that "oppressed individuals rarely experience their oppression as individuals. Their suffering is shared, and they come to know one another in a special way. . . . From this understanding obligations follow."[36] In *Samson Agonistes*, Samson does not suffer alone. His entire nation, on whose behalf his final actions are taken, is also suffering. Samson has justified his earlier resistance to the Philistine lords by claiming it was action taken, with divine command, on behalf of his people: "I was no private but a person rais'd. . . . I was to do my part from Heav'n assign'd" (1211–17). The play leaves readers to contemplate the meaning of action so that their freedom is not lost. Only when Samson has recovered his full freedom is he capable of "acting" according to God's agency.

Milton has chosen the genre of drama and has represented Samson's obligations to his nation as a "part" assign'd from heaven. It is significant that Samson's obligations are acknowledged, voiced by him publicly, and worked through to their bloody conclusion before an audience—first of the Chorus and second of the community of readers. The Chorus serves to place

Samson in a social context, even if he feels isolated. The Chorus watches his drama, offers remedies and suggestions, takes his side, suffers with Samson, experiences *com-passion.*

Co-suffering was the reason many nonconformists took up pens. The experience of ten years in prison was depicted by John Bunyan in *Grace Abounding to the Chief of Sinners* (1666) as a physical condition that offered the occasion for spiritual examination. But prison sitting also gave Bunyan a novel occasion for performing his duty to his people, by giving him the conditions necessary to write. As Bunyan claimed God told him, "I have something more than ordinary for thee to do." His writing was a form of living out that divine injunction, that his "imprisonment might be an awakening to the saints in the country." Suffering may have made him feel isolated, but Bunyan used it as an opportunity to unite with others.[37]

Samson's actions are his "own," in the sense that he has taken full responsibility for them, and yet they are enacted on behalf of his people, to whom he is connected by a common condition of suffering. The consequences of his final act are liberatory for others: "To *Israel* / Honor hath left, and freedom" (1714–15), Manoa rejoices, adding, "let but them / Find courage to lay hold on this occasion" (1715–16). Samson's final act is linguistically represented, it has been noted, in a bounty of metaphor and symbol: he is the thunderstorm, the evening dragon, the eagle, the phoenix (1691–1706). The symbols work to help the survivors explain and understand the power and thus appreciate the mystery of Samson's final act. They help to tell the story, since mimetic language itself cannot represent the mystery of Samson's action. The attempts by those left behind to seal meaning, however, are not futile. Rather, they represent an important aspect of public, or community obligation: finding stories and apt symbols through which to express, and to experience, collective identities. The messenger, Manoa, the Chorus, and the Semichorus all contribute to the telling, this accumulation of symbols and meanings and narratives. It is now up to the Israelites to "lay hold on this occasion" and perform acts of their own. Manoa's storytelling is one such act, and another is his sending for all his kindred to attend a funeral train, something that might have been forbidden before, but now, "*Gaza* is not in plight to say us nay" (1729). Telling the story itself, performing the play as a drama of the mind, is itself an action of suffering, of passion, of active memory. These actions are not a release from obligations, but rather an invitation to be obliged. Critics have argued that the ending of the play is a catharsis that serves as a moderation, tempering, or even removal of passions.[38] I am not sure about this quietistic understanding of catharsis. Samson confronts his obligations in a drama played out before the Chorus, his father, and an unseen community of readers. Milton throughout his late writing appealed to that unseen community, that "fit audience . . . though few." As a drama "never intended" for the stage, *Samson Agonistes* works to release "God's servants" from their bondage. Is Samson's final violence supposed to leech away their passion for freedom by moderating or lessening their love of it?

In my reading, Milton's voice in the debate over toleration was not merely consoling those under persecution that God would finally look after them by sending a deliverer, if they accepted responsibility for their previous failures. *Samson Agonistes* addresses problems dissent posed in the public sphere, problems that included such fundamental questions concerning liberty of consent as Ellwood was asking his interrogators. I do not agree with Samuel Johnson that the play has a beginning and an end, but no middle. My analysis looks at the middle as very important: it is, in fact, what is in the middle that matters. In that middle, the play investigates spheres of obligation and contributes to the Restoration conversation about political obligation, not only as an abstract philosophic discourse, comparable to theorizing by John Locke or Algernon Sidney, but as a matter to be worked through, performed.

If performance was part of Milton's intention, then, how are we to understand the catharsis at the end of the play? The protolerationist Robert Ferguson describes freedom not as an emptying out, but a filling up: "when the *Saints* arrive at consummated purity, and are actually stated in glory, [do they] remain in a dubious suspension between Good and Evil, or in an equal propension to both? No! But though the liberty of our Souls be then dilated to its utmost dimensions, yet we shall from an eternal Principle steadily adhere to God." Freedom, and the condition in which humans might find grace, is not a moderate entity: "If the Essential *idea* of humane Freedom were an *aequilibrious* Disposition of the mind, then by how much holier a man becomes, by so much the less Free he is."[39] Could this conception of freedom help us to understand the combustion of civil and spiritual discourses? When passions are spent in *Samson Agonistes*, following this conception of freedom, I take it to mean that the full measure of liberty is felt, and with that, suffering, and the full scope of obligations. That is the position from which action may be taken. Samson has not *erased* his passion, but has allowed himself and his cosufferers to feel the full measure of it and thus to experience the extent of their liberty. Passion here I take not in the sense of immoderate emotions, but in the Greek sense of suffering. Suffering, understanding the moral consequences of the deprivation of external liberty as well as taking responsibility for self-enslavement, could be the precondition for a new moral awareness for those who choose to *suffer with*, to experience compassion. That catharsis is not an emptying out of passion, but an invitation for readers to attend to their own condition of persecution with courage, and to remember not to surrender even further their liberty.

Henry David Thoreau, in prison for refusing to pay his taxes, greeted his friend Emerson who was visiting him. With the famous question, Thoreau asked, "what are you doing out there?" *Samson Agonistes*, by asking its Restoration readers to witness the drama of deliberation, the sorting-out of personal and social obligation, challenges its readers to consider the conditions under which actions for liberty might be taken. It asks, "what are you doing out there?" It is the power of this text to provoke a robust response to that question.

Northwestern University

NOTES

I wish to express my appreciation to the Northeast Milton Seminar, and especially to Albert Labriola, for inviting me to present an earlier version of this paper, as well as to the University of Chicago Renaissance Seminar. Thanks also to Steven Pincus, David Loewenstein, and Lawrence Lipking for engaged readings of earlier drafts.

1. Thomas Ellwood, *The History of Thomas Ellwood* (London, 1885), pp. 157–58.

2. See Michael Walzer, *Obligations: Essays on Disobedience, War, and Citizenship* (Cambridge, Mass., 1970), p. xiv: "it is not enough, however, that particularly striking acts of consent be free; the whole of our moral lives must be free, so that we can freely prepare to consent." See also Don Herzog, *Happy Slaves: A Critique of Consent Theory* (Chicago, 1989), pp. 182–93.

3. A pre-Restoration date for the composition of *Samson Agonistes* is posited by W. R. Parker, "The Date of *Samson Agonistes* Again," in *Calm of Mind: Tercentary Essays on "Paradise Regained" and "Samson Agonistes*," ed. Joseph Anthony Wittreich (Cleveland, 1971), pp. 163–74. Restoration topical allusions have been analyzed by Christopher Hill, *The Experience of Defeat: Milton and Some Contemporaries* (New York, 1984), pp. 310–19; Blair Worden, "Milton, *Samson Agonistes*, and the Restoration," in *Literature and Society in the Stuart Restoration: Literature, Drama, History*, ed. Gerald Maclean (Cambridge, 1995), pp. 111–36; Nicholas Jose, *Ideas of the Restoration in English Literature, 1660–1671* (Cambridge, Mass., 1984), pp. 142–63; and Laura Knoppers, *Historicizing Milton: Spectacle, Power, and Poetry in Restoration England* (Athens, Ga., 1994). Other treatments of a Restoration *Samson* that bear on my own reading include David Loewenstein, "The Kingdom Within: Radical Religious Culture and the Politics of *Paradise Regained*," *Literature and History* III, no. 2 (1994): 82–83. On the interpretive issues concerning chronology, see Jonathan Goldberg, "Dating Milton," in *Soliciting Interpretation*, ed. Kathy Maus and Elizabeth Harvey (Chicago, 1990), pp. 199–222.

4. Barbara Kiefer Lewalski, "Milton's *Samson* and the 'New Acquist of True [Political] Experience,' " in *Milton Studies* XXIV, ed. James D. Simmonds (Pittsburgh, 1988), pp. 233–51. Joseph Wittreich reads *Samson Agonistes* as one of those "how-*not*-to live poems" in *Interpret-*

ing *Samson Agonistes* (Princeton, 1986), p. 379. On tragedy, see Anthony Low, *The Blaze of Noon: A Reading of "Samson Agonistes"* (New York, 1974). David Loewenstein's essay in this volume explores Samson's spiritual obligations.

5. All citations to *Samson Agonistes* are from Merritt Y. Hughes, *John Milton: Complete Poems and Major Prose* (Indianapolis, 1957). All subsequent references to the play are from this edition and will be cited by line numbers in the text. On representations of Samson, see Christopher Hill, *Milton and the English Revolution* (London, 1977), pp. 435, 437, 441; Jackie DiSalvo, " 'The Lord's Battels': *Samson Agonistes* and the Puritan Revolution," in *Milton Studies* IV, ed. James D. Simmonds (Pittsburgh, 1972), pp. 39–62; Mary Ann Radzinowicz, *Towards "Samson Agonistes": The Growth of Milton's Mind* (Princeton, 1978), p. 178.

6. On the bill against conventicles, see John Spurr, *The Restoration Church of England, 1646–1689* (New Haven, 1991), pp. 57–61; *Journals of the House of Commons* IX; *Journals of the House of Lords* XII; *Cobbett's Parliamentary History of England* (London, 1808), vol. IV, pp. 444–47. On civil unrest, see Richard L. Greaves, *Enemies Under His Feet: Radicals and Nonconformists in Britain, 1664–1677* (Stanford, Calif., 1990), pp. 154–59. David Masson, *The Life of John Milton* (London, 1880), vol. VI, p. 651, notes the play was licensed on 21 July but not entered into the stationers' registers until 20 September 1670. Parliament went into session on 24 October 1670; one of its topics was to establish a committee to inspect the April law against conventicles. See *The Parliamentary Diary of Sir Edward Dering, 1670–1673*, ed. Basil Duke Henning (New Haven, 1940), p. 7.

7. Hill, *Milton*, p. 446; likewise, Loewenstein, "The Kingdom Within," p. 83, argues that the 1671 volume lets the reader "decide which kind of revolutionary response—verbal duelling [*Paradise Regained*] or iconoclastic violence [*Samson Agonistes*] is more appropriate in an age of Royalist ascendancy." My rejoinder to Loewenstein is that by looking not only at the ending, we might find a third option: political theory.

8. Lewalski, "Milton's *Samson*," pp. 236, 248.

9. Stanley Fish, "Spectacle and Evidence in *Samson Agonistes*," *Critical Inquiry* XV, no. 3 (1989): 586. On the book of Judges, see Christopher Hill, *The English Bible and the Seventeenth-Century Revolution* (New York 1993). Note that Tomkyns was the censor who balked at the "eclipse" passage of *Paradise Lost* and who approved the *Samson* volume for publication in the summer of 1670.

10. I am influenced by Richard Ashcraft, *Revolutionary Politics and Locke's "Two Treatises of Government"* (Princeton, 1986), esp. pp. ix–xi, which defends analyzing historical conditions as a way to understand political theory. In reaction against current "Cambridge school" methodology, see Joyce Appleby, "Ideology and the History of Political Thought," in *Liberalism and Republicanism in the Historical Imagination* (Cambridge, 1992), pp. 124–39.

11. On compulsion, see B. Worden, "Toleration and the Cromwellian Protectorate," *Studies in Church History* XXI (1984): 199–233. See also Nicholas Tyacke, "The 'Rise of Puritanism' and the Legalizing of Dissent, 1571–1719," in *From Persecution to Toleration: The Glorious Revolution and Religion in England*, ed. Ole Peter Grell, Jonathan I. Israel and Nicholas Tyacke (Oxford, 1991), pp. 17–49; and Gordon Schochet, "From 'Persecution' to 'Toleration,' " in *Liberty Secured? Britain Before and After 1688*, ed. J. R. Jones (Stanford, 1992), pp. 122–57; and John Spurr, *The Restoration Church*. On religious and political tensions, see Tim Harris, "Introduction: Revising the Restoration" in *The Politics of Religion in Restoration England*, ed. Tim Harris, Paul Seaward and Mark Goldie (Oxford, 1990), p. 10. On the Act of Uniformity, see Alan Craig Houston, *Algernon Sidney and the Republican Heritage in England and America* (Princeton, 1991), p. 122.

12. On moderate Presbyterians, see Tim Harris, *London Crowds in the Reign of Charles II: Propaganda and Politics from the Restoration Until the Exclusion Crisis* (Cambridge, 1987),

p. 63; Michael R. Watts, *The Dissenters: From the Reformation to the French Revolution* (Oxford, 1978), pp. 219, 227–38; Greaves, *Enemies Under His Feet*, p. 1. See also Richard L. Greaves, *Deliver Us from Evil: The Radical Underground in Britain, 1660–1663* (New York, 1986); N. H. Keeble, *The Literary Culture of Nonconformity in Later Seventeenth-Century England* (Leicester, Eng., 1987).

13. Harris, *London Crowds*, pp. 59, 66, 222. Masson perhaps misses the real attractions this dissenting climate may have had for Milton, and explains that Milton moved to Giles Cripplegate in order to seek quieter quarters (*Life* VI, p. 406).

14. Fish, "Spectacle and Evidence," p. 575, claims Samson's movement from "I cannot come" to "I will not come" is a backward movement toward the self-imprisonment of his own quest for certainty. My reading is much closer to that of Joan Bennett, *Reviving Liberty: Radical Christian Humanism in Milton's Great Poems* (Cambridge, Mass., 1989), pp. 134–37, who explores Samson's fulfillment of his different obligations in terms of rational faith.

15. On antiroyalism, see Knoppers, *Historicizing Milton*, p. 43; Worden, "Milton, *Samson Agonistes* and the Restoration," an important essay that places the drama next to radical republicans Edmund Ludlow and Algernon Sidney; and David Loewenstein, *Milton and the Drama of History: Historical Vision, Iconoclasm, and the Literary Imagination* (Cambridge, 1990), which examines such rites in considering the theme of anti-idolatry in Milton. Quote from John Kenyon, *The Stuart Constitution, 1603–1688*, 2nd. ed. (Cambridge, 1986), pp. 353–56; see also Harris, *London Crowds*, pp. 62–95; a standard account is Gerald R. Cragg, *Puritanism in the Period of the Great Persecution, 1660–1688* (Cambridge, 1957).

16. Kenyon, *Stuart Constitution*, p. 355.

17. See Harris, *London Crowds*, pp. 65–71, for reaction of nonconformists. See also John Owen, *A Discourse Concerning Liturgies, and Their Imposition* (London, 1662).

18. Benjamin Laney, *Five Sermons* (London, 1669), pp. 14, 85. For the importance of the citation from Luke, and the uses made of it by Anglican royalists defending intolerance, see Mark Goldie, "The Theory of Religious Intolerance in Restoration England," in *From Persecution to Toleration*, pp. 331–68.

19. John Owen, *The Grounds and Reasons on Which Protestant Dissenters Desire Their Liberty* (1667), in *The Works of John Owen*, 16 vols. (New York, 1850–1853), vol. XIII, p. 578. Owen also pursues the "good citizens" argument in *A Few Sober Queries Upon the Late Proclamation for Enforcing the Laws Against Conventicles* (1668), p. 10.

20. Samuel Parker, *A Discourse of Ecclesiastical Politie* (London, 1670), p. liii. See also Roger L'Estrange, *Toleration Discuss'd* (London, 1663); Laney, *Five Sermons*, p. 31.

21. Nicholas Lockyer, *Some Seasonable and Serious Queries Upon the Late Act Against Conventicles* (London, 1670), p. 16; John Locke, *Essay Concerning Toleration* (1667), in *Political Writings of John Locke*, ed. David Wootton (New York, 1993), p. 207.

22. On Milton and Mosaic law, see Jason Rosenblatt, *Torah and Law in "Paradise Lost"* (Princeton, 1994); and Joan Bennett, *Reviving Liberty*, pp. 119–60, for detailed examination of the kinds of laws—Mosaic, Pauline, natural—that Milton adopts in *Samson Agonistes*.

23. *Complete Prose Works of John Milton*, 8 vols., ed. Don M. Wolfe et al. (New Haven, 1953–82), vol. VII, p. 462, hereafter cited in the text as YP.

24. On the discourse of slavery and republicanism, see Houston, *Algernon Sidney and the Republican Heritage*, chap. 3. On Milton and republicanism, see Nicholas von Maltzahn, *Milton's "History of Britain": Republican Historiography and the English Revolution* (Oxford, 1991); Blair Worden, "Milton's Republicanism and the Tyranny of Heaven," in *Machiavelli and Republicanism*, ed. Gisela Bok, Quentin Skinner, and Maurizio Viroli (Cambridge, 1990), pp. 225–46. Sidney, *Court Maxims* (1665–66), p. 203, cited in Jonathan Scott, *Algernon Sidney and the English Republic, 1623–1677* (Cambridge, 1988), p. 186.

25. Languages not found in J. G. A. Pocock, *Politics, Language, and Time: Essays on Political Thought and History* (Chicago, 1989), and *The Machiavellian Moment: Florentine Political Thought and the Atlantic Republican Tradition* (Princeton, 1975), which emphasizes historical precedent, law, and the principle of custom over natural rights in the early modern period. Richard Tuck discusses the radical appeal against slavery on grounds of inalienable rights in *Natural Rights Theories: Their Origin and Development* (Cambridge, 1993), p. 147.

26. Lockyer, *Some Seasonable*, p. 26; John Locke, *Essay Concerning Toleration* (1667) in *Political Writings*, p. 205; See also James Tully, *An Approach to Political Philosophy: Locke in Context* (Cambridge, 1993), pp. 287–91.

27. Sir Charles Wolseley, *Liberty of Conscience Upon Its True and Proper Grounds Asserted and Vindicated* (London, 1668), p. 29. See also Robert Ferguson, *A Sober Enquiry Into the Nature, Measure, and Principles of Moral Virtue* (1673), who stressed that compulsion removed a man's rational capacity (p. 175). See also Greaves, *Enemies*, p. 124. Quentin Skinner, "Thomas Hobbes and the Anti-Liberal Theory of Liberty," paper delivered to the Center for the Humanities, Northwestern University, April 1995. Compare Gordon Schochet, "Intending (Political) Obligation: Hobbes and the Voluntary Basis of Society," in *Thomas Hobbes and Political Theory*, ed. Mary G. Dietz (Lawrence, Kans., 1990), pp. 55–73. Hugo Grotius, *The Most Excellent Hugo Grotius His Three Books Treating the Rights of War and Peace*, trans. William Evats (London, 1682), p. 390.

28. See Rosenblatt, *Torah and Law*, pp. 87, 125, which stresses Milton's reliance on John Selden. However, the Law of Nations was not necessarily identical to Jewish law, according to Selden: "The Law of Nations is what was . . . enjoined by God either on the remainder of mankind [after creation], at the same time as the Hebrews, or on some of mankind. . . . The Civil Law is that which was, or at least that which was held to be, the law for that particular Church or commonwealth of the Jews," in *John Selden on Jewish Marriage Law: the "Uxor Hebraica,"* trans. Jonathan R. Ziskind (New York, 1991), p. 33.

29. Grotius, *Rights of War and Peace*, p. 172, too, draws a distinction between "oath" and "vow"; a vow is a type of oath, "being made to God."

30. Such an understanding does not by necessity invoke antinomianism; it could, on the contrary, mirror an argument for occasional conformity; that is, the opportunistic conformity with Anglican ritual. Samson, unlike many nonconformists, rejects this logic, too, arguing like his contemporaries that he owed his allegiance to God, not to man's laws. See Thomas Corns, *Regaining Paradise Lost* (New York, 1994), 131.

31. Wolseley, *Liberty of Conscience*, p. 24.

32. On opinion and action, see Ashcraft, *Revolutionary Politics*, p. 65. *Truth and Innocence* in Owen, *Works*, vol. XIII, p. 442.

33. John Owen, *A Discourse Concerning Liturgies, and their Imposition* (1662), in *Works*, vol. XV, p. 21 (italics mine).

34. Irene Samuel, "*Samson Agonistes* as Tragedy," in *Calm of Mind*, p. 246, sees these lines as Samson's tragic monomania, his fatal flaw, yet the notion of a fatal flaw seems to negate a premise of free will. Hugh MacCallum, "*Samson Agonistes*: The Deliverer as Judge," in *Milton Studies* XXIII, ed. James D. Simmonds (Pittsburgh, 1987), p. 279, reduces the emphasis on these lines to two terms: self and God.

35. Mary Ann Radzinowicz, "The Distinctive Tragedy of *Samson Agonistes*," in *Milton Studies* XVII, ed. James D. Simmonds (Pittsburgh, 1983), pp. 249–80, sees the play as a "philosophical tragedy" that replaces the drama of action, with its dramatic suspense, with intellectual conflict. See J. Peter Euben, "Introduction," *Greek Tragedy and Political Theory* (Berkeley, 1986), pp. 1–42.

36. Walzer, *Obligations*, pp. 51–52.

37. Christopher Hill, *A Tinker and a Poor Man: John Bunyan and his Church, 1628–1688* (New York, 1989), p. 107. John Bunyan, *Grace Abounding to the Chief of Sinners* (London, 1987), pp. 1, 94.

38. John M. Steadman, " 'Passions Well Imitated': Rhetoric and Poetics in the Preface to *Samson Agonistes*," in *Calm of Mind*, p. 187; Sherman Hawkins, "Samson's Catharsis," in *Milton Studies* II, ed. James D. Simmonds (Pittsburgh, 1970), pp. 211–30; and Radzinowicz, *Toward "Samson Agonistes*," pp. 105–07.

39. Ferguson, *A Sober Enquiry*, pp. 275–78.

THE REVENGE OF THE SAINT:
RADICAL RELIGION AND POLITICS
IN *SAMSON AGONISTES*

David Loewenstein

J UST A YEAR after Milton published his dramatic poem based on
Judges, the Quaker Francis Howgill compared one of the most fiery and
prophetic early Quakers, Edward Burrough, to Samson. Burrough was
"very dreadful to the Enemies of the Lord," Howgill observed in his testimony concerning the life, trials, and labors of "That True Prophet, and
Faithful Servant of God"; and he went on to marvel: "how great an Alarum
didst thou give in thy day, that made the Host of the Uncircumcised greatly
distressed!" Howgill paid testimony to the powerful Quaker writer and
charismatic political leader by representing him in militant biblical terms
and as one of "the Valiants of *Israel,*" Burrough had resembled not only the
champion David—"how have I seen thee with thy Sling and thy Stone . . .
wound the Mighty!"—but the mighty combatant from Judges who slew the
uncircumcised and carried out other "great exploits" (*SA* 32): "with [the
Jaw-bone of an Ass] thou hast slain the *Philistines* Heaps upon Heaps, as
Sampson." As Howgill's testimony suggests, the militant and faithful Samson
who represents the godly saint actively at war with the world could have
great potency for radical religious culture and writing—even after the Restoration.[1]

As a biblical model intended to represent a version of the radical saint
in a state of crisis, the Miltonic Samson is intensely inward looking, suffers
acutely from a sense of failed vocation, and yet rouses himself once more as
he is prompted by "the inward perswasive motions of [the] spirit" to engage
in decisive violent action. Although it is difficult to date *Samson Agonistes*
precisely, its publication in 1671 does indeed invite us to construe its implications in relation to the Restoration, as well as to the turbulent years of the
English Revolution: it is a work that looks painfully back to the past, registers the sharp disruption between the glorious past and the tragic present,
and depicts a militant saint who, moved by the Spirit, acts "of [his] own
accord" (1643) in response to the present moment of political bondage and
idolatry. My aim is to consider its radical spiritual dimensions, apocalyp-

159

ticism, and politics in relation to a wide range of radical religious writings from the 1640s, 1650s, and thereafter. Such works from the Revolution and its aftermath help to illuminate the radical spiritual and political implications of Milton's *Samson Agonistes,* the texture of its dramatic writing and its raw emotional power, as well as the poet's distinctive handling of the Samson story from Judges. Nevertheless, my aim is not to align *Samson Agonistes* with any one particular group of radical religious writers (since Milton himself, after all, cannot be thoroughly aligned with any one radical religious movement or sect) or even with one contemporary historical event—readers of Milton's Old Testament drama, I believe, need not make such connections too literally or narrowly. Rather, the drama remains highly suggestive: its radical spiritual and political themes evoke the religious politics of the Revolution as well as the Restoration—a critical moment when God's saints, many of them "prisoner[s] chained" (7), were subject to "the unjust tribunals, under change of times" (695) and yet still might be represented in a radical Protestant poem as "very dreadful to the Enemies of the Lord," to use the words of the Quaker prophet Francis Howgill.[2]

Milton's is an unsettling drama, I will argue, about the mightiness of the Spirit of God which comes upon the militant saint yet once more and prompts him to commit an act of "horrid" destruction (1542)—one whose apocalyptic and dreadful character can be closely aligned with the fiery radical religious discourse of the Revolution and its aftermath. To state the point another way, Milton's daring treatment of the Samson story enabled him to dramatize, and at times complicate, some major concerns of religious radicalism and its politics. His drama registers the intense inwardness of radical religious culture, its emphasis on the Spirit's motions and the saint's waiting upon God, its concern with the inscrutable actings of Providence, and, among more militant visionaries, its concern with terrifying apocalyptic vengeance. In its own way, then, *Samson Agonistes* powerfully dramatizes the interaction of politics and radical religion in Milton's age—an age when religious ferment had often fueled revolution.[3]

Radical Religion and the Spirit of the Lord

The Samson story allowed Milton to write a drama of the inward Spirit of God which, one last time, comes mightily upon the militant saint (the Spirit of the Lord moving Samson is emphasized in Judges xiii, 25; xiv, 6, 19; xv, 14). Milton's radical Protestant drama of the Spirit's workings is of course much more interior than the story narrated in the Book of Judges, and his imaginative handling of the motif owes much to radical religious ideology which flourished during the Revolution and continued, despite fierce persecution of the saints, into the Restoration. Like other religious radicals, Milton had stressed in his controversial and theological prose that one should follow the Spirit within rather than any law of humankind (see, for example, *Civil Power,* YP VII, p. 242; *De doctrina,* YP VI, pp. 527, 531). A wide spectrum of revolutionary Puritans, from Cromwell to the Seeker William Erbery to the early Quakers, waited for the Spirit to take them out of Babylon and to lead them in the wilderness of the world. Milton's tutor, the Smectymnuan Thomas Young, while never as radical as Milton became in the Revolution, observed, moreover, that *"Gods Spirit strengthens* all such as waite upon the Lord." *Samson Agonistes* illustrates this observation in a particularly daring fashion, as his intensely inward-looking and anguished Samson, prompted by the Spirit's inward persuasive motions, finds the strength at the end to commit his final act of catastrophic devastation against the lordly idolaters of Dagon.[4]

While encouraging saints to wait upon the Lord for an intimate impulse and to be guided by his power, however, revolutionary Puritan writers stressed that saints should never murmur against God despite their acute sufferings, persecutions, anxieties, and feelings of rage. "Whatsoever your condition is, murmur not at it, but waite," Gerrard Winstanley observed to the oppressed saints in the midst of one of his most potent visions of apocalyptic crisis. "Why," asked Edward Burrough as he addressed the saints in the year of the Restoration, "should *we murmure* against God? or say, Why has thou *done it?* But let *us* travel in *Patience* through all the *Oppressions.*" Furthermore, Thomas Young, who in 1644 singled out Samson as a saint for his valiance in waiting upon the Lord, also warned the faithful in Parliament of the dangers of murmuring against God in moments of great spiritual crisis: "If it bee one propertie of Gods people to waite on the Lord in all their troubles, then such as are so farre from waiting on God in the day of their troubles that they dare murmure, fret and rage against the Lord."[5]

Samson Agonistes, however, was written by a poet who at moments of spiritual crisis could indeed record his own "restless thoughts" (19) and feel the powerful temptation to murmur against God (as in the famous sonnet on his blindness, where Patience checks his "murmur"); his poem thus dramatizes the urge to murmur against Providence rather than quietly wait for the Lord's next command. Milton's drama, in other words, offers a more probing treatment of this issue than the Puritan sermon by Young who had singled out Samson as one of the faithful saints: the dramatic poet does not retreat from representing the disturbing implications of an anguished saint who feels such a profound sense of "shame and sorrow" (457) and thus passionately murmurs against God. Rather, Milton dares to highlight that anxious murmuring—the urge to "quarrel with the will / Of highest dispensation" (60–61)—in his radical Protestant work about the apparently failed career of God's valiant saint who, plagued by a sense of his uselessness and "heaven's desertion," has become "the scorn and gaze" of ungodly "cruel enemies" who despise him (632, 34, 642). "Ask for this great deliverer now, and find him / Eyeless in Gaza at the mill with slaves, / Himself in bonds under Philistian yoke," murmurs the blind, embittered Samson in the "day of his troubles" before checking this powerful urge and sharply blaming himself: "Yet stay, let me not rashly call in doubt / Divine prediction" (40–44; compare 373–80). The tormented Samson, who is nearly ready to mutiny against Providence, wrestles with his own powerful urge to murmur against God—an urge augmented by the profound humiliation of his blindness and slavish imprisonment which expose him "to daily fraud, contempt, abuse and wrong" (76). By dramatizing at first a despairing Samson who must restrain his urge to "fret and rage against the Lord" and who finds that he is far from waiting patiently upon God in the midst of all his troubles, Milton represents the acute agony of an inward-looking radical Puritan saint who truly believes that the days of his divine impulses are over.

Samson Agonistes, as some of its most provocative commentators have recently shown, is an unsettling drama that raises profound questions and doubts in the troubled minds of its characters and readers struggling to interpret the meaning of Samson's shocking tragedy.[6] Nevertheless, there is no need to turn Samson Agonistes into a drama of indeterminacy where all meanings—especially in relation to Samson's ruptured and painful career, as well as his last divine prompting—are simply ambiguous and doubtful. The context of radical Puritanism enables us to recognize the disturbing features of Milton's drama as essential to its daring treatment of radical religious concerns. But we need not adopt a position of extreme skepticism that prompts us to doubt the profound source of Samson's "rousing motions"—the inward persuasive motions of the Spirit which guide this Hebrew champion in matters of war and politics and which identify Samson with the saints of radical religion in Milton's age. In his De doctrina Christiana, the heretical Milton had considered the Spirit preeminent, even in relation to scriptural authority, stressing as well how it superseded all human laws and should therefore be followed by faithful saints before them—no matter how inscrutable the workings of the inward Spirit and God's providence might appear to human commentators and understanding.[7]

The scene where Samson follows the leadings and "motions" of the Spirit as he is commanded to appear before the Philistine spectacle thus evokes the concerns of radical religion and its saints with the inner work of the Spirit and its impulses to act and engage with worldly powers. The Quaker prophet and leader George Fox, for example, recounts in his famous

Journal how "several times" while suffering imprisonment he "had motions from the Lord" to go out and confront the priests, justices, and people committed to the world who were often "in great rage" against him.[8] Physical imprisonment of the sort Samson suffers or Fox frequently endured could not stop the inward motions of the Spirit: fervently rejecting fixed forms in matters of religion, Milton considered one of the "two most unimprisonable things" "that Divine Spirit of utterance that moves" our prayers (YP III, p. 505), and *Samson Agonistes* dramatizes how "the quickning power of the *Spirit*" (*Of Reformation*, YP I, p. 522) has its own secret motions not stifled by outward prison chains any more than it could be by carnal forms in religion or by an oppressing civil power. Furthermore, in radical religious culture, as one of its major historians has shown, this emphasis on the immediate movings of the Lord's Spirit within the saint had little to do with human reason or rational faith.[9] Milton's radical Protestant drama, much more than the original story in Judges, highlights the impromptu workings of the Spirit in the tense episode where a scornful Samson, recalling his holy commitments as a Nazarite, at first refuses to perform in Dagon's idolatrous temple and submit himself to the contempt and derision of his foes ("to be their fool or jester") and then concedes finally to go along (1319–89). It is "that spirit that first rushed on [him] / In the camp of Dan" (1435–36) that returns yet once more to the warrior saint, inwardly prompting him to go off to the heathen temple and act.

We have seen already how Milton's drama of the anguished saint complicates the radical Puritan emphasis on the virtue of waiting patiently and obediently upon the Lord for the divine impulse—an issue Milton richly explores in *Paradise Regained* where the inward-looking Jesus embodies the perfect saint who waits with a spirit of meekness and patience. Thus the Quakers, who were constantly warring against worldly institutions and anti-Christian powers, particularly emphasized how their saints waited patiently while suffering great reproaches and persecution during the Interregnum and Restoration. In *Samson Agonistes* the Chorus extols "patience" as "more oft the exercise / Of saints" (1287–88) and it is toward the end of Milton's radical Puritan drama that the blind Samson finally demonstrates his own particular kind of saintly patience when, having responded to the promptings of the rousing motions within, he is first displayed in the great Philistine spectacle: as the Messenger relates, Milton's saintly Samson was "patient but undaunted where they led him" (1623). In *Samson Agonistes* Milton has presented an anguished saint who is afflicted by his enemies, and then, during the last hour of his career, waits patiently in a fearless manner; like a radical saint who remains firm in the midst of worldly adversaries, he waits for the Spirit of the Lord to move him to commit one final, terrifying act of apocalyptic force. "Patient but undaunted" at the very end of his spiritual and physical trials, the Miltonic Samson illustrates dramatically what the fiercely religious and fearless republican Edmund Ludlow called "the howre of the Saints' patience" as they wait for the moment when the "Lord's wrath" will strike, thereby "vindicating of his honour and great name, so much reproached"; his stance likewise illustrates what the visionary Digger Winstanley, who addressed the saints in an age when priestly and kingly powers continued to oppress them, called waiting for "the breakings forth of the powerfull day of the Lord."[10]

For radical religious writers, Samson being moved by the Lord's Spirit could signal the operation of an awesome conquering power of divine origin, as it did for the Independent minister and Fifth Monarchist preacher John Canne, a writer whose own justification of the Revolution closely resembled Milton's in *The Tenure of Kings and Magistrates*. Milton's Old Testament champion roused by the Spirit becomes, in Canne's words, one of God's mighty warrior saints who "shall have God's presence so . . . powerfully with them, that the enemies, through a dreadful fear, shall not know what to do for their own safety, nor how to oppose the work of God in the hands of his mighty ones. As it is said of *Barak, Gideon, Samson* . . . that *the Spirit of the Lord came upon them,* and in that Spirit they went forth, conquering and to conquer." And so once its militant saint feels the urging of his inward rousing motions, *Samson Agonistes* becomes a drama about the work of the Spirit and its conquering power that gives poetic vision to the notion voiced by the regicide and Anabaptist William Goffe during the famous Putney Debates of 1647: "Now the work of the Spirit is, that we do pull down all works [that are not] of the Spirit whatsoever."[11]

"Unsearchable" Providence

Samson Agonistes is nevertheless a radical religious drama that suggests that the Spirit's power and providence can operate in mysterious and profoundly unsettling ways. The issue of providentialism, which I want to address in this section, was crucial to radical Puritan culture. But while Providence was often invoked by Milton's revolutionary Puritan contemporaries to explain extraordinary political and military events—including Cromwell's great military successes in the 1640s and early 1650s—"the secret and unsearchable Mysteries of high Providence," to use Milton's words (YP III, p. 564), could indeed seem inscrutable, while its actings could seem unexpected.[12] Cromwell, who himself believed in the power of the Spirit, likewise fervently believed with many other revolutionary Puritans in a wondrous providential design at work in the civil wars and the traumatic political events of the Revolution, which swept away the bishops, the monarchy, and the House of Lords; but he also observed "those strange windings and turnings of Providence; those very great appearances of God, in crossing and thwarting the purposes of men."[13] In its own way, *Samson Agonistes,* a work deeply concerned with "the mystery of God" (378), dramatizes how truly unexpected and confounding the "turnings" of Providence can be with its great alterations.

In the past, Samson's glorious career as a militant deliverer under God's "special eye" seemed to confirm a sense of marvelous providential triumphs—those "wondrous actions" and "high exploits by him achieved" when his locks contained the strength "of a nation armed" and Israel's Lord "wrought things . . . incredible / For his people of old" (636, 1440, 1492–94, 1532–33). In those days, the "strange windings" of providence included prompting the saintly deliverer, by means of an "intimate impulse" (223; compare 421–22), to marry women of the enemy tribe. To the Israelites who visit the dejected Samson of the present, however, God's providential ways—"the unsearchable dispose / Of highest wisdom" (1746–47)—remain not only mysterious, but seem, as the deeply perplexed Chorus reveal in their agonized responses, utterly confounding and contradictory, especially toward one of his solemnly elected champions:

> God of our fathers, what is man!
> That thou towards him with hand so various,
> Or I might say contrarious,
> Temper'st thy providence through his short course,
> Not evenly. (667–71)

Having just heard Samson's highly graphic lament over his acute mental torment and "sense of heaven's desertion," the Chorus grope, like bewildered characters out of a Greek tragedy, for some comprehensible meaning to what appears as God's unfathomable and mutable providence, which has brought about this "change beyond report, thought, or belief" (117). The Danites remain confounded too at the crucial moment in the drama when Samson, prompted by the inward motions of faith, agrees to accompany the Philistine officer to the temple of Dagon: "How thou wilt here come off surmounts my reach" (1380).

As revolutionary Puritan writers noted, that sense of uncertainty or the unknown was itself part of the saint's trials as he was guided by the Spirit and served as an instrument of Providence. Thus John Owen, the apocalyptic Independent preacher of the Commonwealth, stressed the inscrutability of God's providences, noting that God keeps men in

darknesse and obscurity, whereby he holds the minds of men in uncertainty, and suspense, for his own glorious ends. . . . he brings not forth his work all at once, but by degrees, and sometimes sets it backward, and leads it up and down, as he did his people of old in the wildernesse. . . . When God is doing great things, he delights . . . to keep the minds of men in uncertainties, that he may . . . try them to the utmost.

In Owen's terms, Milton's Samson as an instrument of God's providence has indeed been set "backward" as God keeps both his saint, who is tried to the utmost in this drama, and his Hebrew compatriots in a state of profound "uncertainty," as well as "suspense." The "actings of God's providence," as Owen stressed elsewhere, are "exceedingly unsuited to the Reasonings and Expectations of the most of the Sonnes of men": Milton's dramatization of the Chorus' baffled responses to the torment and inward griefs of God's former champion would seem to confirm such a view of mysterious providential workings which altogether defy human "Reasonings and Expectations."[14] Owen's comments about the enigmatic providence by which the Lord works his "glorious ends" and does "great things" also convey in contemporary terms something of the Chorus' final sense, expressed after Samson has desolated the Philistine temple and lords, that

> Oft [God] seems to hide his face,
> But unexpectedly returns
> And to his faithful champion hath in place
> Bore witness gloriously.   (1749–52)

But Owen's statements attempting to explain the inscrutability of Providence do not fully convey, as Milton's drama so powerfully does, the sense of profound spiritual and mental agony felt by the suffering, humiliated, and imprisoned saint whose unassuaged griefs "ferment and rage" internally as "a lingering disease" (617–19); and by those Israelites who desperately attempt to comprehend the mysterious—and seemingly contradictory— turnings of Providence after having observed the depth of his suffering and tragic condition. *Samson Agonistes* dramatizes, as one revolutionary commentator on the paradoxes of Providence observed, how the "Saints extremities are Gods opportunities."[15] Milton's drama of this blind and tormented saint, whose shattered career seems like a painful enigma, is thus among the most daring and disturbing literary treatments of the paradoxes and ambiguities of Puritan providentialism that we have.

In *Samson Agonistes* the obscure workings of Providence and the Spirit are conveyed through Samson's own tentative, unspecific language as he prepares himself for and begins to speak about his last (but in his mind uncertain) performance before the Philistines: in response to the Chorus, Samson refers to God dispensing with him "in temples at idolatrous rites / For *some* important cause" as he feels "*some* rousing motions in [him] which dispose / To *something* extraordinary [his] thoughts" (1378–79, 1382–83; emphasis added). And as he leaves with the Public Officer, there remains a sense of mystery about Samson's assertion that "this day will be remarkable in [his] life / By *some* great act" (1388–89; emphasis added). Nor is that sense of mystery dispelled when the Messenger describes Samson, situated between the pillars, revolving in his mind "*some* great matter" (1638; emphasis added). As the drama suggests, the Spirit or the "motions" Samson feels inwardly may lead toward an unknown or uncertain end, though not necessarily a disreputable one: "Happen what may, of me expect to hear / Nothing dishonourable, impure, unworthy / Our God, our Law, my nation, or myself, / The last of me or no I cannot warrant" (1423–26). In effect, when Samson agrees to enter the temple of Dagon, a "place abominable" (1359) to a Nazarite, he submits to the providence of God, much as a godly and religious soldier like Cromwell often claimed to be doing: and Samson does so even when it appears to be an inscrutable authority. Thomas Young wrote, in a work that emphasizes the Spirit guiding the saints (including Samson) that "*Hee* can bring the [saints'] wayes to passe though *they* see not how"—a perspective that applies to Milton's Samson, especially when Young adds that such saints "grow courageous, because *Gods Spirit strengthens* all such as wait upon the Lord." That is indeed what happens to Milton's Samson, who finds new resolve as he follows the motions of the Spirit, even as an element of uncertainty remains about what will transpire in Dagon's temple. Toward the end of the Interregnum, the Quaker prophet Francis Howgill wrote that "as the day of the Lord is a mysterie, the spirit of the Lord is the onely discoverer of it": the unexpected cataclysmic destruction at the end of *Samson Agonistes*—that "some great act" Samson commits after he has felt his rousing motions within—does indeed suggest that the mighty day of the Lord is a mystery and that the Spirit is the "discoverer of it."[16]

Some radical Puritans, moreover, highlighted the relation between God's mysterious providences and unsettling acts of apocalyptic destruction and overturning in their age. Revolutionary Puritans did not see terrifying shakings and unexpected acts of destruction as arbitrary or capricious events; rather, they saw them as acts designed by Providence itself. John Canne, for example, registered that sense of a surprising, disorienting Providence when he wrote in a tract addressed to Cromwell and Milton's friend Robert Overton (the army radical and Fifth Monarchist warmly praised in the *Defensio Secunda*) that "these latter times will be accompanied with such great destractions, confusions, divisions, as people will be at a losse, and so in darknesse, that they will not know what to doe, which way to take, nor how to dispose of themselves. . . . Gods marvelous work now in the world, will move so contrary to mens expectations." Similarly, another commentator on the inscrutable and mighty ways of God's providence observed that when God "shall come" and "overturn" and "throw down the mighty, lay waste and make desolate strong Cities, fortified Nations, and the greatest Monarchies," this may be "unexpected by us" and "unlooked for." Indeed, by operating mysteriously or secretively, God would confound his enemies all the more effectively: the radical minister Thomas Brooks, exulting in the Revolution just after Pride's Purge and commenting on "strange providences," observed that "God . . . will save his people, and ruine their enemies by very darke, and mysterious wayes . . . and unlikely meanes" so "that their enemies may be the more dreadfully ashamed, and confounded." And so it happens in the horrid catastrophe of *Samson Agonistes*. Like these revolutionary Puritan writers, Milton himself powerfully conveys a sense of mysterious, "unlooked for" destruction and God's participation in it as Providence "unexpectedly returns" at the end of the drama: thus the Philistine lords and nobility are "distracted" and struck "with amaze" (1286, 1645) by Samson's great act and the power of "Gods marvelous work in the world." To quote Milton's *De doctrina*, the catastrophic devastation wrought by Samson the militant saint and the wonder it evokes dramatically illustrate that "the extraordinary providence of God is that by which he produces some effect outside the normal order of nature or gives to some chosen person the power of producing this effect" (YP VI, p. 341).[17]

"DEARLY-BOUGHT REVENGE"

Radical religious writers who violently denounced ungodly earthly powers and authorities during the revolutionary years and the Restoration could emphasize a powerful ethic of apocalyptic and Old Testament vengeance wrought by a mighty God of hatred and fury against his idolatrous and profane enemies. This is an important contemporary context that illuminates the apocalyptic fury of Milton's own terrifying God in *Samson Agonistes*, as well as the "dreadful way" (1591) that the militant Samson, capable of "sudden rage" (953), takes his revenge on the idolatrous and uncircumcised Philistines. Milton's work, in other words, is a poetic dramatization of divine vengeance potently expressed in the more vehement and apocalyptically threatening radical religious discourse of the Interregnum and its aftermath. "A day of vengeance is coming upon you all; that the Lord will be recompensed upon you all his adversaries," George Fox prophesied to the ungodly ones of his age (echoing Isa. xxxiv, 8 and xxxv, 4) as he evoked a sense of terror and warned that the dreadful day of the Lord's wrath was near at hand. And in the year of the Restoration, Milton's student and Quaker friend Thomas Ellwood prophesied that God's "indignation and fury [would] break out upon" the priests of the nation and "utterly consume [them] from off the earth," while another Quaker prophet in 1666 envisioned "times of horror and amazement . . . amongst those that have withstood him," since God's appearance would "be fierce and terrible; even so terrible, as who shall abide his coming? for the Lord will work both secretly and openly." In a similar fashion, Milton's Old Testament drama shows the awesomeness of Israel's God of power who works "both secretly and openly" to destroy his enemies, the aristocracy and priesthood of the Philistines, thereby creating a scene of "horror and amazement."[18]

Revolutionary Puritans could compare Samson's act of destruction against the Philistines to the Lord's desolation of worldly powers in their own age. As John Owen observed in a sermon preached before the House of Commons during the new Commonwealth,

Now as *Sampson,* intending the destruction of the Princes, Lords, and residue of the Philistines, who were gathered together in their Idoll temple, he effected it by pulling away the pillars whereby the building was supported; whereupon the whole frame topled to the ground: So the Lord intending the ruine of that mighty power, whose top seems to reach to heaven, will do it by pulling away the pillars and supporters of it, after which it cannot stand one moment. Now what are the Pillars of that fatall Building? are they not the powers of the world as presently stated and framed?[19]

The "Idoll temple" of Dagon in *Samson Agonistes*—with its "great feast" and "great pomp," its "illustrious lords," its "idolatrous rites" (1315, 436, 1318, 1378) and superstitious ceremonies—does indeed represent such worldly powers; and its destruction "with burst of thunder" (1651) enables Milton to imagine a horrid scene in which the powers of the world "cannot stand one moment," as the Lord demonstrates his dreadful power. The last great act of Milton's Samson thus embodies the impulse of apocalyptic revolutionaries to pull down mighty worldly powers so that only the Lord himself is exalted: militant revolutionaries in Parliament's army had considered that one of the chief aims of the civil wars was "the pulling down of Babylon," and Cromwell himself observed after one of his great military victories that "wherever anything in this world is exalted, or exalts itself, God will pull it down, for this is the day wherein He alone will be exalted."[20]

Radical religious writers in the Revolution and Restoration frequently envisioned that the mighty day of the Lord's wrath and desolation would come unexpectedly and suddenly upon the ungodly. Gerrard Winstanley suggested that the destruction of Babylon, when it came, would indeed be quick—"The Lord will do this work speedily, *Babylon* shall fall in one hour"—while Francis Howgill envisioned desolation and "great slaughter" coming upon the ungodly when they are unaware. Moreover, the Quaker Dorothy White, claiming that the Spirit of the Lord was upon her and warning the nation with fierce prophecies just before the Restoration, envisioned "that the Approach of the *Great* and *Terrible Day* cometh, and that very swiftly." And in verses dating from 1662, Thomas Ellwood prophesied "that speedy vengeance He will take on all / Who persecute His saints and them enthrall," while elsewhere he envisioned that "day of sad calamity" and "utter desolation" which would "speedily overtake" the ungodly priests of his nation and the sons of Belial. Such swift, unexpected vengeance against those Philistine lords and priests who persecute and enthrall God's saint does indeed occur in *Samson Agonistes;* as the Chorus observe about the mighty deliverer, anticipating the final catastrophe: "Swift as the lightning glance he executes / His errand on the wicked" (1284–85). Moreover, God himself assists the apocalyptic catastrophe by sending "a spirit of frenzy" among the idolatrous and drunken Philistines, urging "them on with mad desire / To call in haste for their destroyer"; thus "insensate left" and struck "with blindness internal," they "unweetingly importuned / Their own destruction to come speedy upon them" (1675–78, 1685–86, 1680–81). In Milton's drama, the destruction and slaughter suffered by the Philistines who have "fallen into wrath divine" are both great and sudden: "Gaza yet stands," reports the Messenger, "but all her sons are fall'n, / All in a moment overwhelmed and fall'n" (1683, 1558–59).[21]

Milton himself had urged the speedy destruction of Babylon in his own fiery polemical writings. Recognizing that reformation was often slow-moving and long work in his tumultuous age, he nevertheless reminded his fellow citizens that such good kings of Judah as Asa, Hezekiah, and Josiah had effected reformations, including the destruction of idols and idolatrous priests, which were "speedy and vehement" (*Of Reformation,* YP I, p. 602); and as early as *The Reason of Church-Government* he was warning that the miseries of papist Ireland, where his Protestant countrymen had been recently slaughtered and martyred, were "urgent of a speedy redresse" (YP I, p. 799). Consequently reformation, he suggested, needed to be pushed forward "with all possible diligence and speed" (p. 800). In its own way, Milton's drama envisions such a "speedy redresse," as God and his militant saint speedily enact a terrifying vengeance against the ungodly Philistines who have "fallen into wrath divine."

In 1660 the Quaker Ellwood prophesied, moreover, that "the Lord is arisen to fight for Sion" and that the fall of Babylon "shall make a great noise" (as in Jer. l, 46) and that "the sound . . . shal strike terror to all those who admire and love her beauty: fear, amazement, [and] astonishment" would seize upon all who worship her. Though it is not mentioned in

Judges, such a "great noise" of desolation and ruin capable of striking terror is indeed heard in *Samson Agonistes:* there the fall of Dagon is described as a "hideous noise . . . / Horribly loud," a

> universal groan
> As if the whole inhabitation perished,
> Blood, death, and deathful deeds are in that noise,
> Ruin, destruction at the utmost point.   (1509–14)

As Samson is about to wreak his act of terrible destruction, he prophesies that the spectacular performance of his strength "with amaze shall strike all who behold" (1645), a line evoking a sense of wonder at the great power of this God of terror and his militant saint, and a line recalling the Chorus' earlier observation that those ungodly who are struck swiftly "lose their defence distracted and amazed" (1286): so God confounds and destroys idol worshippers whose temple collapses "with burst of thunder." Milton's *Samson Agonistes* is thus the product of a turbulent age when radical spiritualist writers still believed, as the prophet George Fox did for example, that "the power of the Lord was so strong as it struck a mighty dread amongst the people" so that "they were in an amazement."[22]

Like Fox's dreadful God who threatened to execute vengeance during the years of revolutionary Quakerism, Milton's in *Samson Agonistes* is also a God of "dread" (1673) and terror—a God who is awesome in his power and who will prove terrifying to his idolatrous, heathenish enemies. "Dreadful is the Lord . . . and terrible to the wicked," Fox announced in one of his most fiery prophetic tracts from the Interregnum, *Newes Coming Up Out of the North*, where he envisioned that "the terrible One is coming with his power, to shake terribly the earth" and astonish the heathen and profane. And the Quaker prophet Edward Burrough who could make "the Host of the Uncircumcised greatly distressed," as Howgill put it, had himself warned that "the day of the Lord is powerful and dreadful, that shall come upon the Heathen" and be avenged upon them. Radical religious writers envisioned their own tumultuous age of revolution and upheaval in terms of an apocalyptic theomachia, a mighty "contest . . . / 'Twixt God and Dagon" (461–62); yet the "power of Israel's God" (1150) was so great and dreadful that it could not be resisted by the uncircumcised: "who is there amongst all the mighty Host of the Uncircumcised," asked one bellicose Quaker prophet at the time of the Restoration, "that shal lift a hand *against the Sword of the Lord, and of Gideon, and prosper?*" And so when Samson, that "dreadful enemy" of "the uncircumcised," goes off to perform in the temple of Dagon, he serves God's "glory best, and spread[s] his name / Great among the heathen round" by showing "whose God is strongest" (1622, 640, 1429–

30, 1155) and astonishing them with his final, terrifying performance of the Lord's vengeance.[23]

Like the threatening God of religious radical writing, Milton's God of awesome power in *Samson Agonistes* is likewise a mighty leveler—leveling in a moment Dagon's theater and temple and decimating the "choice nobility and flower" (1654) of the Philistines. To be sure, Milton's God of power differs in one sense from the leveling God of such mid–seventeenth-century radical spiritualists as Abiezer Coppe, George Foster, Winstanley, or Fox himself: unlike them, Milton does not depict a mighty Lord who, in the day of his dreadful appearance, will furiously level the economic and social order. Nevertheless, *Samson Agonistes* gave Milton one last opportunity to represent in a poetic drama the Lord as an apocalyptic leveler—a depiction that resonates with enthusiastic visions of revolutionary leveling in the 1640s and 1650s, while highlighting the horrid consequences of the destruction and slaughter. Coppe, for example, depicted the Lord of Hosts as "a mighty Leveller" who would rise "to shake terribly the earth" and "utterly abolish" the idols, while the New Model Army chaplain and Seeker William Erbery observed that when "the Spirit and power of the Lord appear[s] in [the saints], all the powers of men, and mighty things, Kingdomes and Cities shall fall down before them, and be levelled at their feet." Moreover, the apocalyptic revolutionary Cromwell, who emphasized waiting on the Spirit and the Lord, could envision a terrifying God who "breaks the enemies of His Church in pieces." In the turbulent Old Testament world of *Samson Agonistes*, we find such a powerful God of leveling and desolation—a Lord who brings earthly powers to nothing and transforms an idolatrous place of worship into a "place of horror" (1550).[24]

The language of militant religious radicalism could stress as well that the warrior Lord of awesome power would manifest himself in the saint who battles against the ungodly and profane world. As the Quaker prophet Edward Burrough told the saints, "the Lord is with you as a mighty terrible one." So the "terrible" Lord is with Milton's Samson during the final catastrophe—we have seen how he contributes to it by sending a "spirit of frenzy" among the Philistines. Moreover, the radical religious saint—a "single combatant" (344) accompanied by this "mighty terrible one"—could assume a Samson-like power, reminding us of the Old Testament warrior capable of conquering a thousand Philistines: "in the battle," Burrough went on to envision, "shall you obtain the conquest, and all your enemies shall be put to flight, and one of you shall chase a thousand, for he is with you who hath all power in his hand . . . therefore be not discouraged at the raging and swelling words of your Adversaries . . . Ye are my fellow Souldiers." Nor is the Miltonic Samson, when he aligns himself yet once more with "the power of Israel's God" (1150), discouraged by the raging words of his adversaries: in his confrontation with Harapha, a trial scene Milton has added to the Judges story, Samson himself is not discouraged by the verbal "indignities" of his giant adversary who calls him "a murderer, a revolter, and a robber" (1168, 1180); Milton's saint not only mocks this adversary and his "glorious arms," as well as the "honourable lords" of the Philistines, but no longer despairing of the Lord's "final pardon" and faithfully trusting "in the living God" (1130, 1108, 1171, 1140), he is soon moved inwardly by the Spirit to go off and commit another hostile act against the Lord's enemies. "Nothing but . . . the mighty power of God in men," William Erbery wrote using scriptural and militant language in the midst of the traumatic over-turnings of the Revolution, "could in so short a time cast down so many strong Holds, conquer so many . . . Armies": this "appearance of God in the saints" had brought about "the greatest destruction in the Land."[25] When Milton's Samson casts down the stronghold of the Philistine temple, bring-ing desolation to a hostile city, he too has become a warrior saint who, "with inward eyes illuminated" (1689) and accompanied by the Lord's Spirit, has once again internalized and manifested the power of "the mighty terrible one" to become "the dread of Israel's foes" (342).[26]

Moreover, it is notable that in his portrait of Samson as radical saint moved by the Spirit to enact the dreadful vengeance of the Lord, Milton has significantly suppressed the implications of Judges xvi, 30: "And Samson said, Let me die with the Philistines." Milton, in other words, has carefully chosen not to portray Samson as a radical saint on a suicide mission of de-struction. In the argument to his drama, Milton notes that the destruction Samson brought to the Philistines he did "by accident to himself"; and the subsequent passages in the drama make it clear just how much Milton wishes to dissociate his inward-looking saintly hero from the traditional ac-cusation of suicide and "self-violence": Samson with the Philistines "in-mixed, inevitable / Pulled down the same destruction on himself" (1584, 1657–58; compare 1586–87), the Messenger reports, and he was "self-killed / Not willingly, but tangled in the fold, / Of dire necessity" (1664–66), the Chorus observe. Manoa, moreover, describes Samson's violent death as "noble" (1724)—a characterization that modern critics may feel uncomfort-able with because of the militant nature of Samson's life and final act, though one that corresponds with Milton's suppression of the issue of suicide.[27] The Miltonic Samson is a saint moved one last time by the Spirit to commit an act of revenge and destruction, but willful self-destruction is not part of that horrid act in which he fulfills his vocation "gloriously"; in the words of the Protestant commentator Peter Martyr (whose commentary on Judges Milton admired), "Neyther can it be properlye sayde that Samson kylled himselfe.

He dyed in deede, but he prescribed not unto hymself his ende, namely to dye. [He] sought vengeance of hys enemies, whych he understoode woulde by this meanes ensue." By suppressing the implications of suicide, Milton has by no means lessened the horrifying nature of Samson's great act—a revenge "dearly-bought" which results in "heaps of slaughtered" enemies whose blood soaks his own dead body and covers it with "clotted gore" (1660, 1530, 1725–26, 1728). But Milton also makes it more possible for the radical godly reader—a reader less likely to be morally repulsed by the drama's apocalyptic violence—to perceive the vengeful Samson as a valiant saint moved by the Spirit to carry out God's militant work against idolatrous and uncircumcised enemies who are, in the words of the fiery Quaker Francis Howgill, "to be slain heaps upon heaps."[28]

Milton's drama does indeed highlight the motivation of dreadful revenge: in his act of terrifying destruction, Samson "hath quit himself / Like Samson" and "fully revenged" himself upon Israel's enemies, leaving "them years of mourning" (1709–12). The authority of the biblical story itself lies behind an emphasis on vengeance when Samson prays, just before destroying the Philistine temple, "O God, that I may be at once avenged of the Philistines for my two eyes" (Judg. xvi, 28). The crucial difference is that *Samson Agonistes* presents the spectacular vengeance as more cosmic and apocalyptic—not as Samson's private revenge taken on the Philistines for the loss of his two eyes.[29] Milton's handling of the motif of divine vengeance, furthermore, is consistent with his political and theological writings where he could justify it as fervently as some radical Puritan contemporaries did, especially upon enemies of God or of the church; and it evokes comparisons, as I have been arguing in this essay, with radical religious writers who either encouraged militant activism or used bellicose language to further what they perceived to be the will of the Lord and to highlight their warfare with an ungodly world.[30] In one political sermon, for example, John Owen justified the wrathful Lord of power taking "great revenges" on his enemies by referring to Psalm cx, 6, a militant passage close to the vengeful spirit dramatized in *Samson Agonistes* and one Milton cited in his *De doctrina* to emphasize God's judgment upon the Gentiles: the Lord "shall judge among the heathen, he shall fill the places with the dead bodies" (YP VI, p. 624). Moreover, Milton's immediate contemporary, the radical poet-prophet and pamphleteer George Wither, described in 1660 the "Lord of Hosts" as a "General of a two-fold *Militia*, furnished with distinct weapons according to the several services whereby they are to glorifie him; the one *Natural*, and the other *Spiritual*; and that he makes use of both to . . . destroy the *Enemies* of his *Kingdom*." Milton's Samson could well be aligned with the first group of Wither's radical saints who, as executioners of God's judgments, resort to more militant actions: they are employed by the Lord "in shedding the blood of his *malicious opposers* . . . sometimes, with hazzard or loss of their own." In another text, written close to the Restoration, Wither compared himself to Samson as a saint who is roused up to execute divine vengeance: "as heretofore befel *Sampson*, (and hath oft befallen many of *Gods* servants in their *Frailties*) with the *Philistines*, he must have first have occasion given, by an outward injury, before he could be rowzed up to execute *GOD's* Vengeance upon the Enemies of his *Country*." Milton's radical Protestant drama does indeed highlight Samson's frailties (he is not the "perfect man" of *Paradise Regained*), as well as his inward griefs and "outward injury"; but it also presents his horrid act of revenge as an act of God's apocalyptic vengeance appropriate for one of God's saints roused by the motions of the Spirit within.[31]

As Samson executes divine vengeance and pulls down the temple and theater of Dagon "with horrible convulsion to and fro" (1649), he acts with the power of a tempest that has been internalized and unleashed: thus, when situated between the temple's "massy pillars," he strains "all his nerves" and bows "as with the force of winds and waters pent, / When mountains tremble" (1646–48; compare 963–64). The Messenger's description high-lights the awesome power contained and released, as though pent-up spiri-tual forces were being violently released through Samson's horrid act bringing down the temple pillars "with burst of thunder." In his revolution-ary apocalyptic writing, the Independent minister Peter Sterry envisioned that the Lord of awesome power would manifest himself "in a *tempest* of a *whirlwind*," as he comes "to shake dreadfully the whole Earth." Moreover, the vision of trembling mountains itself had apocalyptic resonance in the revolutionary years, especially for radical prophetic writers warning of the Lord's wrath and judgment: thus in *The Trumpet of the Lord Sounded* (1654), George Fox warned with prophetic fervor (echoing such scriptural passages as Isaiah v, 25, Jeremiah v, 24, and Habakkuk iii, 10), "Tremble, ye mountains and hills, before the Lord: for out of Sion doth the Lord utter his voice. Wo, wo to all you who inhabit the earth: you will be scattered as the wind scatters the chaff; you will be consumed as the fire consumes the stubble: for the mighty day of the Lord is coming." The sense of cataclysmic destruction that accompanies the coming of the mighty day of the Lord and consumes the ungodly is likewise conveyed through the forceful language of *Samson Agonistes* and its vision of horrifying destruction meted out to the heathenish worshippers of Dagon.[32]

Milton, furthermore, dramatizes at the end of *Samson Agonistes* the crucial activism of the vengeful godly saint whose destructive agency is in-terwoven with powerful divine forces. Providentialism itself could encourage a distrust of human agency and a dependence upon the divine; one revolutionary Puritan, for example, suggested that Providence was responsible for all human actions and that men were nothing but "secondary causes" in the process and instruments of its work: "all men good and bad are but Instruments in God's hand, secondary causes, and can do nothing but what God by Providence leads them to do, or permits to be done to effect his own purpose and secret decree, ordering all and every Action thereunto."[33] But in *Samson Agonistes* Milton has complicated this view by dramatizing the mutual interaction of Providence's mysterious designs and Samson's own agency as a warrior saint. As he asserts toward the drama's end when he chooses to obey the Philistine order and go to the temple of Dagon, "Commands are no constraints. If I obey them, / I do it freely" (1372–73). The conscience and faith of this radical Old Testament saint are neither constrained nor compelled so that he remains a free agent to respond to providential promptings and the leadings of the Spirit. Moreover, when Samson observes that "masters' commands come with a power resistless / To such as owe them absolute subjection" (1404–05), his ambiguous lines, addressed to the Public Officer, refer to two "masters"—the Philistines, who command that he appear before their feast in honor of Dagon, and the Lord himself, to whose will Samson is in the process of submitting. Much like a revolutionary Puritan saint, then, Samson shows disciplined submission in service of his demanding God, while also exercising his own agency. Thomas Young had urged the saints to wait upon the Lord—as Samson had—and yet to be active: "let . . . your hands [be] active with all faithfulnesse to fulfill what is required of you in your Sphere."[34] In Milton's drama, Samson, having obeyed the Philistine commands, "hast fulfilled / The work" (1661–63) required of him in his sphere when at the end he performs of "[his] own accord" and displays another act of his awesome strength and God's awesome power: the horrid retribution in which he slaughters more foes in number "than all [his] life had slain before" (1668) is both an expression of divine and human agency. Exercising his own agency one last time "with eyes inward illuminated," Samson the militant and faithful champion of God embodies Milton's unsettling dramatic vision of a radical saint "dreadful to the Enemies of the Lord."

University of Wisconsin, Madison

NOTES

1. See Francis Howgill's testimony prefacing Edward Burrough, *The Memorable Works of a Son of Thunder and Consolation: Namely, That True Prophet, and Faithful Servant of God*

. . . *Edward Burroughs* (London, 1672); Howgill echoes Judges xv, 16. Quotations from *Samson Agonistes* are taken from *John Milton: Complete Shorter Poems*, ed. John Carey (London: Longman, 1971), and noted parenthetically in my text.

2. "Inward perswasive" from *A Treatise of Civil Power*, in *Complete Prose Works of John Milton*, 8 vols., ed. Don M. Wolfe et al. (New Haven, 1953–82), vol. VII, p. 261; subsequent references to Milton's prose are taken from this edition and noted parenthetically in my text as YP. *Paradise Regained* represents another version of the radical religious saint, though I cannot pursue this matter here: see David Loewenstein, "The Kingdom Within: *Paradise Regained* and the Politics of Radical Religious Culture," *Literature and History*, 3rd ser., III, no. 2 (1994): 63–89. On dating *Samson Agonistes*, see especially the review of evidence in Anthony Low, *The Blaze of Noon: A Reading of Samson Agonistes* (New York, 1974), pp. 222–27 (emphasizing correspondences between *De doctrina* and the play); Mary Ann Radzinowicz, *Toward "Samson Agonistes"* (Princeton, 1978), pp. 387–407; and Christopher Hill, *Milton and the English Revolution* (1977; Harmondsworth, 1979), pp. 481–86. I am inclined to agree that the dramatic poem was completed after the Restoration. On the difficulty of identifying Milton, Cromwell, and many others with any one sect or "way," see J. C. Davis, "Cromwell's Religion," in *Oliver Cromwell and the English Revolution*, ed. John Morrill (London, 1990), pp. 184–85, 207. For various discussions of Milton's work in relation to the Restoration, see Sharon Achinstein, "*Samson Agonistes* and the Drama of Dissent," in this volume, as well as the following studies: Nicholas Jose, *Ideas of the Restoration in English Literature* (Cambridge, Mass., 1984), pp. 142–63; Laura L. Knoppers, *Historicizing Milton: Spectacle, Power, and Poetry in Restoration England* (Athens, Ga., 1994), chaps. 2 and 6; and especially the richly textured study by Blair Worden, who considers the context of the trials of regicides in 1662, in "Milton, *Samson Agonistes*, and the Restoration," in *Culture and Society in the Stuart Restoration: Literature, Drama, and History*, ed. Gerald MacLean (Cambridge, 1994), pp. 111–36.

3. On radical religion in Milton's age, see Michael A. Mullett, *Radical Religious Movements in Early Modern Europe* (London, 1980); *Radical Religion in the English Revolution*, ed. J. F. McGregor and B. Reay (Oxford, 1984); Geoffrey Nuttall, *The Holy Spirit in Puritan Faith and Experience* (Oxford, 1947) and *Visible Saints: The Congregational Way, 1640–1660* (Oxford, 1957); Nigel Smith, *Perfection Proclaimed: Language and Literature in English Radical Religion, 1640–1660* (Oxford, 1989); Michael Watts, *The Dissenters: From the Reformation to the French Revolution* (Oxford, 1978), chaps. 1–3. On radical religion and revolution, see esp. B. Reay, "Radicalism and Religion in the English Revolution: An Introduction," in *Radical Religion in the English Revolution*, pp. 1–21. See also the radical chaplain Hugh Peter's comments in the Whitehall Debates: *Puritanism and Liberty: Being the Army Debates (1647–49) from the Clarke Manuscripts*, ed. A. S. P. Woodhouse (London, 1938), p. 138.

4. Davis, "Cromwell's Religion," pp. 188, 199; Nuttall, *The Holy Spirit;* Thomas Young, *Hopes Incouragement* (London, 1644), p. 17. This sermon was delivered before the House of Commons.

5. Gerrard Winstanley, *Fire in the Bush* (1650), in *The Works of Gerrard Winstanley*, ed. George Sabine (Ithaca, N.Y., 1941), p. 488. Compare his advice to the saints to wait with "quietnesse of spirit under all temptations" (p. 178). Edward Burrough, *General Epistle to All the Saints* (London, 1660), p. 14. Young, *Hopes Incouragement*, p. 20; on Samson as a valiant saint who grew strong in waiting upon God, see p. 15.

6. See, for example, Stanley Fish, "Spectacle and Evidence in *Samson Agonistes*," *Critical Inquiry* XV, no. 3 (1989): 556–86; and esp. Joseph Wittreich, *Interpreting Samson Agonistes* (Princeton, 1986).

7. See, for example, YP VI, pp. 587, 589, as well as 490–91. For a valuable perspective on this topic, see the essay by Norman T. Burns, " 'Then Stood Up Phinehas': Milton's Antinomianism, and Samson's" in this volume.

8. *The Journal of George Fox,* ed. John N. Nickalls (London, 1975), pp. 53, 57, 108, 179. On the motions of the Spirit in radical religion, see Hugh Barbour, *The Quakers in Puritan England* (New Haven, 1964), pp. 25–28.

9. See Nuttall, *The Holy Spirit,* chap. 2. Compare the recent discussion of Milton's drama by Joan S. Bennett, *Reviving Liberty: Radical Christian Humanism in Milton's Great Poems* (Cambridge, Mass., 1989), chap. 5, esp. pp. 129, 132, 137, 140, 150; and Radzinowicz, *Toward "Samson Agonistes."* For a critique of scholars who have overstressed the role of reason in Milton's drama, see William Kerrigan, "The Irrational Coherence of *Samson Agonistes,"* in *Milton Studies* XXII, ed. James D. Simmonds (Pittsburgh, 1987), pp. 217–32.

10. On Jesus as perfect saint, see Loewenstein, "The Kingdom Within," 76–82. See Fox, *Journal,* pp. 277, 353, 381, on Quakers who for years underwent great sufferings with patience and meekness. Edmund Ludlow, *A Voyce from the Watch Tower,* 1660–1662, ed. A. B. Worden (London, 1978), pp. 240, 115; Winstanley, *Works,* p. 391. On Ludlow in relation to Milton and the Restoration, see Worden, "Milton, *Samson Agonistes,* and the Restoration," passim.

11. John Canne, *The Time of the End* (London, 1657), p. 22. For the influence of *The Tenure* on Canne's revolutionary writing, see *The Golden Rule, Or, Justice Advanced* (London, 1649). Goffe, in *Puritanism and Liberty,* p. 41.

12. Cromwell, for example, wrote of "an unexpected providence" in bringing judgment on Drogheda and Wexford: *The Writings and Speeches of Oliver Cromwell,* 4 vols., ed. W. C. Abbott (Cambridge, Mass., 1937–47), vol. II, p. 142. See also the work of the Fifth Monarchist John Cardell, *Gods Wisdom Justified, and Mans Folly Condemned* (London, 1649), p. 37.

13. I quote from Cromwell's speech of July 4, 1653, to the nominated (Barebones) Parliament: *The Writings and Speeches of Oliver Cromwell,* vol. III, p. 53. The theme of God's providence is pervasive in Cromwell's writings: see the same speech where he observes that "in taking off the King, the House of Peers, the pulling down of the Bishops, changing the government, . . . there is a remarkable print of Providence set upon it" (p. 54; compare vol. II, p. 186). The radical minister William Dell, *The City-Ministers Unmasked* (London, 1649), p. 25, agreed; compare Milton's *A Defence,* YP IV, p. 499, on "the wonder-working hand of God." For a wide-ranging discussion of the issue of Providence in this age, see Blair Worden, "Providence and Politics in Cromwellian England," *Past and Present* CIX (1985): 55–99.

14. John Owen, *A Sermon Preached to the Parliament* (Oxford, 1652), p. 25 (misnumbered 17); Owen, *The Advantage of the Kingdome of Christ in the Shaking of the Kingdoms of the World* (Oxford, 1651), p. 8. Compare the Chorus of *Samson Agonistes* on "vain reasonings," lines 322–25.

15. Cardell, *Gods Wisdom Justified,* p. 9.

16. On Cromwell submitting to providence, see, for example, *Writings and Speeches of Oliver Cromwell,* vol. II, p. 9. On submitting to the divine even when it was inscrutable, see J. C. Davis, "Religion and the Struggle for Freedom in the English Revolution," *The Historical Journal* XXXV, no. 3 (1992): 523. Young, *Hopes Incouragement,* p. 17; compare p. 19, where he refers to Isaiah xi, 31: "they that waite upon the Lord shall renew their strength." Francis Howgill, *Some of the Misteries of Gods Kingdome Declared, as They Have Been Revealed by the Spirit Through Faith* (London, 1658), p. 10.

17. John Canne, *A Voice from the Temple to the Higher Powers* (London, 1653), p. 10. On God's "secret Providence" and his permitting "something contrary extraordinarily to be done," see also Theodore Haak's commentary on Judges xiv, 3, in *The Dutch Annotations Upon the Whole Bible . . . Now Faithfully Communicated to the Use of Great Britain, in English* (London, 1657). "Throw down the mighty" from George Smith, *Gods Unchangeableness: Or Gods Continued Providence* (London, 1655), p. 7. Compare Burrough, *Works,* pp. 592, 612, on the hand of the Lord in wondrous "Overturnings" and "overthrowings." Thomas Brooks, *Gods*

Delight in the Progresse of the Upright (London, 1649), p. 46. Compare Thomas Banaster, *An Alarm to the World, of the Appearing of Sions King* (London, 1649), p. 5.

18. George Fox, *Newes Coming Up Out of the North, Sounding Towards the South* (London, 1654), p. 32; compare pp. 9, 10, 12, 21, 34. Ellwood, *An Alarm to the Priests; or, a Message from Heaven* (London, 1660), p. 7; Stephen Crisp, *An Epistle to Friends, Concerning the Present and Succeeding Times* (London, 1666), p. 13. The emphasis on the fierceness of the day of God's wrath and vengeance which threatens the ungodly runs throughout early Quaker discourse: see, for example, James Nayler, *A Discovery of the First Wisdom from Beneath, and the Second Wisdom from Above* (London, 1656), p. 24; and the fiery Interregnum prophecies by William Dewsbury.

19. John Owen, *The Shaking and Translating of Heaven and Earth* (London, 1649), p. 27; compare Banaster, *An Alarm to the World*, p. 5.

20. See [Robert Ram], *The Soldiers Catechisme* (London, 1644), p. 9, and Cromwell's letter to William Lenthall after the battle of Preston (20 August 1648), in *Writings and Speeches of Oliver Cromwell*, vol. I, p. 638.

21. Winstanley, *The New Law of Righteousness*, in *Works*, p. 186; Francis Howgill, *A Woe Against the Magistrates, Priests, and People of Kendall* (London, 1654), p. 1. Compare Mary Cary, *A Word in Season to the Kingdom of England* (London, 1647), p. 5, on the sudden ruin of Antichrist. Dorothy White, *A Lamentation Unto this Nation* (London, 1660), p. 5; her prophecy was delivered in March. Ellwood quotations from "Speculum Seculi: or, A Looking-Glass for the Times," in *The History of the Life of Thomas Ellwood*, ed. C. G. Crump (London, 1900), p. 120; *An Alarm to the Priests*, pp. 6, 3. On the day of the Lord as sudden and unexpected, compare Abiezer Coppe, *Some Sweet Sips, of Some Spirituall Wine* (1649), in *A Collection of Ranter Writings from the Seventeenth Century*, ed. Nigel Smith (London, 1983), p. 53. Compare *De Doctrina* on the workings of Providence: "Even in sin, then, we see God's providence at work, not only in permitting it or withdrawing his grace, but often in inciting sinners to commit sin, hardening their hearts and blinding them" (YP VI, p. 331).

22. Ellwood, *An Alarm to the Priests*, p. 3; Fox, *Journal of George Fox*, p. 74.

23. For the fullest exploration of the God of dread in *Samson Agonistes*, especially from a biblical perspective, see Michael Lieb, " 'Our Living Dread': The God of *Samson Agonistes*," in this volume. Fox, *Newes Coming up out of the North*, pp. 13, 20; compare pp. 7, 18, 25. See also Fox's prophetic tract, *A Voice of the Lord to the Heathen* (London, 1656), which warns of a God of dread shaking terribly the earth; and George Fox, the younger, *The Dread of Gods Power* (London, [1660]). But the notion of "the terror of the Lord" confounding "His enemies, as in that day" was by no means confined to the most radical of the period's religious writers: see Cromwell, *Writings and Speeches of Oliver Cromwell*, vol. I, p. 619. Burrough, *A Warning from the Lord to the Inhabitants of Underbarrow* (1654), in *Works*, pp. 3, 5. "Who is there" quote from John Anderdon, *Against Babylon and Her Merchants in England* (London, 1660), p. 7; compare Humphrey Smith, *The Sounding Voice of the Dread of Gods Mighty Power* (London, 1658), p. 5, and the "matchless Gideon" of Milton's drama, lines 277–89.

24. Coppe, *A Fiery Flying Roll*, in *Ranter Writings*, p. 87; Erbery, *The Armies Defence, or, God Guarding the Camp of the Saints* (London, 1648), p. 20; compare George Foster, *The Sounding of the Last Trumpet* (London, 1650), passim. *Writings and Speeches of Oliver Cromwell*, vol. II, p. 174; compare Erbery, *The Armies Defence*, p. 15.

25. Burrough, *A Warning from the Lord*, in *Works*, p. 13. Erbery, *The Armies Defence*, p. 14; see also pp. 8–9. The casting down of worldly strongholds echoes such scriptural passages as Micah v, 11, Isaiah xxxii, 11, 2 Corinthians x, 4.

26. Compare Burrough, *General Epistle to All the Saints*, pp. 4–5.

27. On Milton's suppression of the traditional theme of suicide, see also the valuable

comments by John Steadman, "Efficient Causality and Catastrophe in *Samson Agonistes*," in *Milton Studies* XXVIII, ed. Wendy Furman, Christopher Grose and William Shullenberger (Pittsburgh, 1992), pp. 219–20. Compare Wittreich, *Interpreting Samson Agonistes*, who sees Samson's final action "as a foolhardy embracing of self-destruction" (p. 231).

28. Peter Martyr, *A Commentary Upon the Booke of Judges* in *Most fruitfull & learned commentaries of Doctor Peter Martir* (London, 1564), fol. 236ʳ. For Milton's familiarity with Martyr's commentary, see the Commonplace Book in YP I, pp. 455–56; Milton considers Martyr "a Divine of formost rank" in *The Tenure*, YP III, p. 221. Howgill, *A Woe Against the Magistrates*, p. 5. Some modern readers have clearly been repulsed by Samson's vengeful act: John Carey, *Milton: Complete Shorter Poems*, p. 333, for example, considers the catastrophe "morally disgusting." See also Irene Samuel, "*Samson Agonistes* as Tragedy," in *Calm of Mind: Tercentenary Essays on "Paradise Regained" and "Samson Agonistes,"* ed. Joseph Wittreich (Cleveland, 1971), pp. 235–57; and Wittreich, *Interpreting Samson Agonistes*, passim. More persuasive in my view is Michael Lieb's discussion of *Samson Agonistes* as a work that extols violence; see his *Milton and the Culture of Violence* (Ithaca, N.Y., 1994), pp. 226–63.

29. Compare Wittreich, *Interpreting Samson Agonistes*, for the contrary argument that Samson's horrifying act is one of private revenge, shameful violence, and dubious heroism. But Wittreich also notes, quite rightly, that Miltonists have tended to discount revenge as a motive in the drama (p. 46).

30. See *De Doctrina*, YP VI, pp. 743, 755–56; compare pp. 346, 604. For Milton's justification of divine revenge or vengeance, especially against haughty prelates and tyrannical kings or rulers, see, for example, *Church-Government*, YP I, pp. 793, 861, and *A Defence*, YP IV, p. 352; on divine vengeance on Salmasius and other false prophets, see *A Defence*, pp. 431, 499; on vengeance overdue in regard to the dismemberment of the tyrant Domitian, see *A Defence*, p. 446; on divine vengeance on Alexander More's unclean head, see *Second Defence*, YP IV, pp. 599, 631.

31. Owen, *The Advantage of the Kingdome of Christ*, p. 13. George Wither, *Fides-Anglicana* (London, 1660), p. 25. Compare Erbery, *The Armies Defence*, p. 15. George Wither, *Epistolium-Vagum-Prosa-Metricum: or, An Epistle at Randome, in PROSE and METRE* (London, 1659), p. 27.

32. Peter Sterry, *England's Deliverance from the Northern Presbytery* (London, 1652), p. 29. George Fox, *The Trumpet of the Lord Sounded, and His Sword Drawn* (London, 1654), p. 9. On Fox's fiery writing of the Revolution, see David Loewenstein, "The War of the Lamb: George Fox and the Apocalyptic Discourse of Revolutionary Quakerism," in *The Emergence of Quaker Writing: Dissenting Literature in Seventeenth-Century England*, ed. Thomas N. Corns and David Loewenstein (London, 1995), pp. 25–41; the essay also appears in a special issue of *Prose Studies: History, Theory, Criticism* XVII, no. 3 (Dec. 1994).

33. Smith, *Gods Unchangeableness*, p. 11.

34. On the issue of submission and liberty in radical religious culture, see Davis, "Religion and the Struggle for Freedom," 518, 521, 523. Young, *Hopes Incouragement*, p. 38.

MISREADING MILTON

John T. Shawcross

T O S U G G E S T T H A T an author and creative work are misread is certainly presumptuous. The arrogance in the idea of anyone's finding any misreading of a piece of creative literature can set up antagonisms toward the alleged "true" readings that are put forward and toward the generator of those "true" readings. For words in themselves raise various meanings and meanings frequently change in different contexts. How can we know that one reading is better than another, that any reading is what the author's reading would be? Well, we don't. Yet John Milton has been one of the authors most frequently involved in critical wars that have propounded readings of his works, particularly *Paradise Lost* and *Samson Agonistes,* offering exclusionary interpretations. Such delimited reading can cast a pall over opposed readings as "misreadings." But are we misreading Milton when, for example, we see Satan as hero of *Paradise Lost* or Dalila as a "serpent" (as the Chorus calls her in *Samson Agonistes*) and as the cause of Samson's fall from strength and vocation? I reject those readings, myself, but I still ask, are they misreadings of Milton? The two works present differing answers to the question of misreading, while nonetheless rejecting the concept. The epic, as in the identification of its hero, sets up for the reader an interpretation of Satan as hero, among other candidates, but also nullifies that identification for the astute, close reader. However, that nullification should not label the view of Satan as hero as a misreading. On the other hand, the dramatic poem, throughout, is so ambiguous in characters, actions, "meanings," that, for instance, to label Dalila a serpent and relegate Samson's fall as being entirely her fault is unjustified. While that reading can be derived from the text, and seems to be the most common attitude on the part of critics, still the astute, close reader comes to recognize such uncertainties in the poem that Dalila is and is not a serpent. The close reader is aware that the "standard" view of the poem is far from adequate or all-encompassing. Unlike *Paradise Lost* the poem does not offer clear clues to direct us to reject either reading of Dalila as not representing Milton's reading. Dalila is a function of the reader's attitude, and in turn so are the other characters and the action. The dramatic poem does not sustain misreading even when one interpretation is privileged over another on the basis of a specific context or angle of vision: there are other contexts and other angles of vision provided by the poem.

Although I shall deal with *Samson Agonistes* in this essay, it will be significant to understand the complexities of misreading that a topic like the hero of *Paradise Lost* raises. The question of the hero has had a long history, and although I have expressed what I believe to be the "correct" answer elsewhere, the question does not dissolve. John Dryden was the first in print to propose Satan as hero, and this provoked contentions that the Son was the hero and then that Adam and Eve constituted the hero. Charles Batteux in the mid eighteenth century and William Godwin later in the century restated the identification, and Mary Shelley (Godwin's and Mary Wollstonecraft's daughter) wrote *Frankenstein* with a Monster who is a kind of Satan figure to Dr. Frankenstein's God the Father figure, and who, like Adam, queries that he had not asked to be born.[1] What we might label the "Satan interpretation" of *Paradise Lost* impugns God as not playing fair, as loading the dice against Satan and us, as exerting his omnipotence to the point of tyranny, such as Satan accuses him of. With Satan in such a central position the reader sympathizes with him and understands his desire for revenge, agreeing that the political situation that Satan presents should be upended. We should have some kind of democracy, not tyranny; we should not be led to expect one thing and then on a whim have everything changed as it was for Satan when the Father begot the Son, his only begotten Son. After all, as Satan says, we are all sons of God. Within the poem we have those glorious and rousing speeches of Satan: anyone oppressed will surely agree that it is better to reign in hell than serve in heaven, if heaven is controlled by a Charles I or a Louis XIII or mad King George the Third. Satan, democratically, in Book II lets the fallen angels debate what course they will take: Moloch, Belial, Mammon, and Beelzebub offer a range of solutions, with Beelzebub's proposal that which "would surpass / Common revenge" (II, 370–71), calling for an agent who will undertake the mission of determining the "advantagious act" (II, 363) that will annihilate or corrupt God's whole creation. "The perilous attempt," its pondered "danger," its "hazard" "thir matchless Chief," "arm'd with power," accepts. Satan's acceptance as agent evokes ideas of heroism by taking on odds against God and venturing into the unknown, offering himself for the good of his fellow diminished stars. Satan as hero is clear, so clear that William Blake, as we know, pondered whether Milton were not of the Devil's party without knowing it.[2] Though well aware of God's omniscience and omnipresence, as earlier remarks make clear, the fallen angels ignore those attributes in their zeal for revenge and seem to accept that the mission can "seek / Deliverance for [them] all" (II, 464–65). But, of course, only revenge is reached, through seduction to their party (II, 368).

To call this interpretation "misreading" is to forget that Milton is the author of all those signs of hero and heroism, and that he gave Satan all those glorious and rousing speeches. Satan does decline in splendor as the poem proceeds—in Book IV, where he is likened to a cormorant and a toad, and where he backs down when confronted by Gabriel, Zephon, and Ithuriel, and in Book X, where his exaltation over his achievement on earth is greeted by hisses as the fallen angels turn into various kinds of serpents and the apples they engorge turn to ashes. But Satan is an articulate leader in the war in heaven in Books V and VI; he accomplishes his goal, even if by guile, in Book IX, when he convinces Eve that a serpent can speak and that abrogating God's prohibition of eating of the Tree of Good and Evil will bring godliness and wisdom. If Milton did not want Satan to be considered the hero and one to be emulated, then he surely misdirected his potential reader.

Perhaps Milton foresaw the way that he could be misread in this instance, assuming that he did not approve of Satan as exemplary hero in his poem. That is, the perceptive author realized that such human issues as right or wrong, good or bad, moral suasion or license depend, for their understanding, upon specific contexts, upon people's specific circumstances at the time the question arises, upon their inner selves, and thus that the reader could misread if that reading were partial or biased or based on personal evaluations of self and the self's world. Milton's presentation of Satan and his party thus was conscious; he was aware of the risk of misreading and we might see his making Satan and his "heroism" very attractive as a way of forcing the reader to look more deeply into the character Satan and his motives. In the proem to Book VII, we recall, Milton wrote of hoping to find a "fit audience . . . though few." That points to another audience of the majority who, "unfit," are unable to separate the right from the wrong, the good from the bad, the moral from the unrighteous, liberty from license because of personal motives and experience. It does not mean that Milton was of that "unfit" audience, unaware of the effect that his Satan would create. What appears, when we read Satan as potentially glorious leader against oppression, is a veneer of what could be right action, credited when one reads under a feeling of oppression or when one does not read deeply enough through the poem's subtle hints of language and concept. Some of what has just been noted has been examined before; I offer one further example of how Milton in *Paradise Lost* provides for a reading that becomes "misreading" when clues are recognized by the fit reader.

Early in the poem Satan boasts that the fallen angels have God's "utmost power with adverse power oppos'd / In dubious Battel on the Plains of Heav'n, / And shook his throne" (I, 103–05). Three points should jump out for the reader, though they may not. First, the adverse power was *not* opposed by God's utmost power on days one and two, leading to a stalemate where the faithful angels under Michael seem to win and then where the rebellious angels, having discovered gunpowder and cannon, seem to win. Had God sent the two-thirds of the faithful angels remaining (though still not his "utmost power") to counter the rebels on the first day, logic suggests that Satan and his cohorts would have been vanquished and the battle would have been ended. On the third day God sends his Son, showing thus his utmost power, to confront them "alone . . . since by strength / They measure all" and "they astonisht all resistance lost, / All courage; down thir idle weapons drop'd" (VI, 820–21 and 838–39). Self-aggrandizement rather than fact clearly permeates Satan's boast. Second, the word *dubious* provides various meanings: from Satan's point of view it implies that he and the fallen angels did not know what the outcome of the battle would be; from God's point of view it indicates that a full and real battle could not emerge because of his omnipotence; and from the reader's point of view it becomes a sham battle, although that will not be described until Book VI. The sham battle has caused one critic to talk about tin soldiers, and others to object to the humor in some of its descriptions, and yet another to point out the phallic and testicular dimensions of Satan's deployment of cannon, quashing what might have been a serious war scene.[3] Clues that the heroism in Satan's language depends on angle of vision and experiential frustration with power are there for the fit reader.

The third point that should be clear is that Satan did not shake God's throne, although the reader here in Book I, looking at it from Satan's point of view, infers that any resistance to power might cause "shaking." The reader has been set up to misread here and in the second day of battle in Book VI to label it victory for the rebellious angels. However, on the third day when the Son has ascended in the Chariot of Paternal Deity with Victory sitting eagle-winged at his right hand and the Ensign of Messiah blazing above, the rebellious angels rally "thir Powers / Insensate, hope conceiving from despair. / . . . To final Battel [draw], disdaining flight, / Or faint retreat," until the Son speaks:

> That they may have thir wish, to trie with mee
> In Battel which the stronger proves, they all,
> Or I alone against them, since by strength
> They measure all, of other excellence

Not emulous, nor care who them excells;
Nor other strife with them do I voutsafe.

(VI, 786–87, 798–99, 818–23)

The Son then "on his impious Foes right onward drove . . . [and] in his right hand / Grasping ten thousand Thunders, which he sent / Before him . . . they astonisht all resistance list, / All courage; down thir idle weapons drop'd" (VI, 831, 835–39). Specifically we are told that "under his burning Wheels / The stedfast Empyrean shook throughout, / All but the Throne it self of God" (VI, 832–34). In Book VI, if we remember that earlier boast and the alleged "half" of heaven in resistance (rather than the doctrinal third of Revelation xii, 4, and cited by Death in Book II and corroborated by Raphael in Book V), we can misread the seeming stalemate of days one and two of the war and consign some kind of shaking to day two. But the fit reader, who rereads and rethinks as reading of the poem proceeds, learns that the Son's action shook heaven, not Satan's action, and that the throne of God did not shake, even so. Satan has arrogated the shaking of the heavens in another example of self-aggrandizement and self-deception, hardly attributes that one would credit to a heroic leader.[4]

Once Milton has his readers believing in the gloriousness of Satan (this cannot be "misreading"), they accept Satan's words without thinking about them, and if one has any kind of equatable feeling of unfairness and forced inferiority (that is, if a person feels that unfairness or forced inferiority has been directed toward that person, and that feeling equates with what Satan has described), his words strike significant chords. The "misreading" of Milton may arise from thinking that Milton did not know what he was doing (for example, in including Books XI and XII which have frequently been cast as excrescences on the poem), but largely, I would suggest, it arises from not reading the text closely enough. Clues in language and character delineation have been missed, and the overwhelming rhetoric and presence of Satan have aided in separating the fit from the unfit audience whose reaction has often been colored by experience and feelings of oppression and unfairness. We have been set up to misread, and behind that presumption on Milton's part is an elitist position, an intellectualization that appears as well in the "indolent rabble" cited in *Ad Patrem* and the "insolent speech of the multitude and . . . the vicious throng of readers" dismissed in *Ad Joannem Roüsium*, and, I add, the lack of discernment and the show of sentimental conventionality by Manoa and the Chorus as *Samson Agonistes* ends. It would be nice if Milton had the sense of equality that many today give lip service to, if he were totally politically correct, but he does not fit that mold any more than most people today do despite their protests.

Unlike *Paradise Lost,* the dramatic poem is a most uncertain text; ambiguity appears in characters, actions, language, even generic and prosodic concerns. It is a dramatic poem fraught with opportunities for misreading, that is, for creating differing views of the characters and the actions which this critic or that critic, in disagreement, might label "misreading." Comparison with *Paradise Lost* suggests that the epic provides clues, such as we have looked at briefly, to counter a reading that an unfit audience might derive from it; however, *Samson Agonistes* remains uncertain because we do not know where irony ends and "truth" takes over, the "clues" being double-edged. Contributing to the uncertainty of the dramatic poem, particularly in comparison with the epic, is the fact that God does not appear: the absence of godhead, indeed, raises a basic question. While we may discover in *Paradise Lost* a revolutionary and antimonarchical Milton who nonetheless rejects action against God because God is God and could not possibly be God and a tyrant too, in the dramatic poem we come to understand that a basic question is Whose god is God? and What is his nature? even though we know that the god of the Old Testament Israelites is Milton's God. Manoa shows no real faith in that God and casts him as an almost petty, vengeful god:

> Alas methinks whom God hath chosen once
> To worthiest deeds, if he through frailty err,
> He should not so o'rewhelm, and as a thrall
> Subject him to so foul indignities,
> Be it but for honours sake of former deeds.　　　　(368–72)

Just a little later he talks of "God, / Besides whom is no God" (440–41) but then of God who

> 　　　　　　　　　will not long defer
> To vindicate the glory of his name
> Against all competition, nor will long
> Endure it, doubtful whether God be Lord,
> Or *Dagon.*　　　　　　　　　　　　　　(474–78)

Samson, whose "trust is in the living God" (1140), echoes the question, though we know what his answer would be, when he tells Manoa early on,

> 　　　all the contest is now
> Twixt God and *Dagon; Dagon* hath presum'd,
> Me overthrown, to enter lists with God,
> His Deity comparing and preferring
> Before the God of *Abraham*　　　　　　(461–65)

and again when in meeting Harapha's challenge he says,

> In confidence whereof I once again
> Defie thee to the trial of mortal fight,
> By combat to decide whose god is God,
> Thine or whom I with *Israel*'s Sons adore.   (1174–77)

And, of course, Dalila argues that her act of seducing Samson and determining the source of his strength was committed for "all the bonds of civil Duty / And of Religion" (853–54); her

> Priest
> Was not behind, but ever at [her] ear,
> Preaching how meritorious with the gods
> It would be to ensnare an irreligious
> Dishonourer of *Dagon*.   (857–61)

Perhaps this is "feign'd Religion, smooth hypocrisie" (872) as Samson labels it, but over the whole of the poem is the question of Whose god is God? The reader will not misread this question and will conclude that, for Milton and the poem, Samson's god is God, not Dagon, a fish-god, being derived from the diminutive of the Hebrew for fish, whose worshipers, an "Idolatrous rout amidst thir wine," engage in "Great Pomp, and Sacrifice, and Praises loud" at their festivals (443, 436). These descriptions do not apply to Samson's God or to Milton's God especially; they suggest idolatry and superstition and immorality. Yet the question remains, for within the interpretation of Manoa and the Chorus rises a question of the nature of their god: their god does not square with Samson's (Milton's) God. What Manoa proposes, what action Dalila defends, what trial Harapha offers allow for a most different kind of god from that of Milton, but so does the god of the *kommos* and *exodus* expressed by Manoa and the Chorus, if we recognize the irony of the ending.

The question goes to the heart of the political dimension of the poem. Dalila has specifically coupled the political with the religious, and the history of Milton's mid-seventeenth-century England specifically couples political position with religious beliefs. Samson, as representative of Milton's political and religious beliefs, opposes the Philistines as representatives of a monarchic and different religious belief. The people for whom Samson is to be the great deliverer—the Danites—would seem not to be worthy, however, if Manoa and the Chorus represent seventeenth-century republicans and "Puritans." The poem seeks to find or at least to reassert who is the true God. It questions thus Milton's alleged fellow believers whose sense of God is inadequate if not wrong, whose pusillanimity shunts off responsibility and action. A simple either/or between the god of the Israelites and the god of the Philistines is superficial. The god who oversees and is the object of the actions of the "government" condoned by Samson or that condoned by the Philistines may be the true God or not: politically there are Parliamentarian and Independent versus Royalist and proto-Catholic. But the Danites, like Milton's supposed allies, do not act, do not set up resistance to their over-lords, are resigned to accept what has become custom and (like Manoa in offering to bribe the Philistine officers) to adjust even with lack of morality to live as best they can. That god, who certainly is not Dagon, is still not the same as the God who emerges through the character and action of Samson. The God and the politics he can be seen to represent are not the same for all Parliamentarians, or rather for some so-called Parliamentarians. The na-ture of that god is not the nature of Samson's God, and the seventeenth-century supposed adherents of Milton's God and political world in like fash-ion follow a different religio-political practice that separates the false from the true follower.

Even in a simple either/or consideration, can Samson's god be the true God if he allows such hard life for his true servants? Is not the Philistines' god one to be better trusted and believed in through his efficacy? In view of Samson's and the Danites' lot—and the position of the Parliamentarians whether in the 1640s or the 1660s—can the people be sure that their god is the true God? The outcome of the dramatic poem, thus, poses the uncer-tainty of whether Samson's God has aided his champion and achieved at least positive example for others to act upon or whether the Philistines' god has shown the upper hand in removing this former and now again potential enemy to Dagon, despite the loss of Philistines. The dilemma and its pos-sible answer suggest the same kind of thinking that revisionist Jews have pondered in trying to come to grips with the Holocaust.

The nature of God is significant in separating the true from the false follower of God. Does the Chorus rightly represent him as one who "Oft . . . seems to hide his face" (1749), implying a not very helpful god at times when need exists but one who allows direful things to occur, yet who "unex-pectedly returns" (1750) to bear witness gloriously to his faithful champions, implying now that not only does God not appear and aid those who are *not* his faithful champions, but that the faithful need not worry about what straits they get into because God will intervene at the right moment and save them without any act by them? Is not Milton setting his reader up to join the Chorus in their sentimental justification for doing nothing to flee the Philistian yoke? This cannot be what he wants his reader to take away from reading the poem. Rather, the reader is to ponder whether the god who is advanced as God would leave the chosen people still in servitude to the Philistines, or leave the English people under the yoke of monarchy (whether in the 1640s or the 1660s). Is such a god God? He is, instead, Milton may be read as positing, the great taskmaster who will guide and aid the gracious believer who acts, not to maintain custom and ease, but to assert freedom even if with direful action. If a reader reads one answer or if another reader reads another answer, has either "misread" the text?

The Chorus' phrase "Oft he seems to hide his face," however, poses further ambiguities. It has been commonplace to cite Psalm xxvii, 9, "Hide not thy face far from me," and Psalm lxxxviii, 14, "Lord, why castest thou off my soul? why hidest thou thy face from me?" The first psalm of David acknowledges that the Lord is his light and salvation, a context that points to Samson's acknowledgment of the "true" God of the Bible; its next line is thus appropriate also: "put not thy servant away in anger." The second psalm is a prayer for deliverance from death for the sons of Korah, again appropriate for Samson here. The biblical intertexts thus emphasize that his god is God, that he has learned that it is only through the persistent acknowledgment of God's presence that salvation may come, and that only God can deliver one from death through his omnipotence. But this is not the only way to read the line intertextually as one would expect in this very uncertain poem. The Chorus' line raises the specter of those who do not abide by the Law, this having been Samson in his bravado of the past and the Danites in their obeisance to their captors and, at least indirectly, their captors' god. The reference is to Deuteronomy xxxi, 16–18:

> And the Lord said unto Moses, Behold, though shalt sleep with thy fathers; and this people will rise up, and go a whoring after the gods of the strangers of the land, whither they go to be among them, and will forsake me, and break my covenant which I have made with them.
>
> Then my anger shall be kindled against them in that day, and I will forsake them, and I will hide my face from them, and they shall be devoured, and many evils and troubles shall befall them; so that they will say in that day, Are not these evils come upon us, because our God is not among us?
>
> And I will surely hide my face in that day for all the evils which they shall have wrought, in that they are turned unto other gods.

(In the discussion of divine decree in *De doctrina Christiana*,[5] Milton cites the same texts as proof that God foreknew the lapse of the Israelites from their own accord—a significant word used by Samson [1643] as he employed his strength to demolish the Philistian temple—and own impulses—another significant word used by Samson [223] to justify his marrying the woman of Timna.) The text in Deuteronomy is followed by the composing of the Song of Moses, which will thenceforth be "a witness for [God] against the children of Israel" (19). While the song makes clear whose god is God and the nature of God, the children of Israel in alien lands will nonetheless often place strange gods before them, and the Chorus of Danites in the dramatic poem, if they do not truly receive "new acquist / Of true experience from this great event" (1755–56), will be no different. Politically the contemporary counterparts of the Danites are admonished that the Civil Wars and the Interregnum, as great events, should yield (or should have yielded) "new acquist," but they have not: there have only been "calm of mind" and "all passion spent."

The beginning of the dramatic poem offers a Samson being led from dark steps to a bank that has choice of sun or shade as day-spring is born, and he remarks that this particular day will see a solemn feast held to Dagon. (The imagery immediately sets up what the outcome of the day may be, positive or negative, God-filled or not.) The story of Samson's feats of strength, his enticement by Delilah, and his subsequent loss of strength through the cutting of his hair and his blinding—all occurring before the poem opens—was known to Milton's readers, and they also were aware that he would exert his strength yet once more to pull down the pillars of the Philistian temple where the feast was held and thus would kill many of his nation's enemies as well as himself. That anticipation at the beginning of *Samson Agonistes* sets the stage for dramatic irony as the reader proceeds through Miltons filling in the gaps on that particular day. The poem, of course, is not a retelling of a biblical episode but an imaginative enactment of what might have gone on that day, with the single event of the destruction of the temple in Judges xvi, 25–30. The Chorus acknowledges the fulfillment of that expectation when they react to the Messenger's words:

> O dearly-bought revenge, yet glorious!
> Living or dying thou hast fulfill'd
> The work for which thou wast foretold
> To *Israel*, and now ly'st victorious
> Among thy slain self-kill'd
> Not willingly, but tangl'd in the fold
> Of dire necessity, whose law in death conjoin'd
> Thee with thy slaughter'd foes in number more
> Then all thy life had slain before.   (1660–68)

We should pause over these remarks; they are not so simple as at first they seem. The Chorus emphasizes "revenge" and then assigns that to Samson's prophesied work: the ideas are hardly compatible. But it was the biblical Samson who called for revenge: "O Lord God, remember me, I pray thee, and strengthen me, I pray thee, only this once, O God, that I may be at once avenged of the Philistines for my two eyes" (Judg. xvi, 28). He is victorious in their view because he has "slaughter'd" more than he had slain altogether heretofore (which quotes xvi, 30): but this is not meaningful if changes are not effected by such loss of life to bring delivery. It is rather empty gloating, as well as inhumane. And does it imply that Samson had not done a very good job in the past when he had his strength, if killing off Philistines is commendable? The biblical text is not a good gauge for heroism or delivery from servitude, and Milton, understanding biblist views, has produced a poem to question the whole point of the Samson story and, accordingly, to question the revolutionary action of his co-"republicans." Samson's death, for the Chorus, is the result of dire necessity in order to achieve this slaughtering. The sparagmatic Milton that Michael Lieb has described[6] might argue on the side of such human destruction but always in a justified cause leading to improved political life. The "justified cause" of delivery is almost forgotten and the improvement to which it should lead is ignored. The biblical text is again being interrogated for the astute reader: "And Samson said, Let me die with the Philistines. And he bowed himself with all his might; and the house fell upon the lords, and upon all the people that were therein" (xvi, 30). The Chorus and Manoa in his response are not explicit about this statement of desired suicide, but readers of Milton's poem have not been blind to this action which was not accomplished because of "justified cause" but for "avengement" according to the Bible, the Chorus, and Manoa ("A dreadful way thou took'st to thy revenge," 1591), and with suicidal wish according to the Bible and implied by Manoa's "Self-violence? what cause / Brought him so soon at variance with himself / Among his foes?" (1584–86). Reactions may agree with the biblical account, but they are not only not commendable, they reject a god who renovates a sinner and who guides his true servants to moral action. The problem in reading *Samson Agonistes* is exacerbated by not recognizing that the poem may be interrogating the Bible, not accepting such concepts as revenge and suicide, although the Chorus and Manoa do. Yet, on the other hand, both revenge and suicide have not been ruled out by the text, particularly if one accepts the words of the Chorus and Manoa as representing Milton's belief.

The Messenger iterates the sun imagery of the beginning in lines 1596–99:

> Occasions drew me early to this City,
> And as the gates I enter'd with Sun-rise,
> The morning Trumpets Festival proclaim'd
> Through each high street,

and remarks that "The Feast and noon grew high" (1612). The fit reader will recognize that a hint may be here that God is shining his light on the situation, that the outcome will have God's approval and indeed his help, and even further that Samson, a traditional sun god, his hair now apparently grown and perhaps streaming like the rays of the sun (although this is not explicitly indicated), will have *his* high noon. The imagery of light that appears throughout the *prologos*, and now here again at the end, is likewise implied in the eyes within that are illuminated (if the Chorus' words are to be credited): the irradiation of God throughout Samson's body, the "wisdom" that light metaphorizes now that he is about to act. (Milton is amplifying the biblical text "O Lord God, remember me, I pray thee, and strengthen me, I pray thee, only this once." The words "remember me" suggest that Samson had thought of himself as forgotten by God in his imprisonment.) We may assume that the face of God has not become hidden again during the afternoon that follows and that John xii, 35, is pertinent: "Yet a little while is the light with you. Walk while ye have the light, lest darkness come upon you." Yet we have no hint that the Danites stirred before darkness came upon them again.

What the above imagery poses is that Samson and God worked together to bring about this destruction of their foes. That is one possible reading, positive though negative in further action. That the Danites might have followed through without resistance seems to be implied in Manoa's remark about a more limited action, the acquisition of Samson's body, "*Gaza* is not in plight to say us nay" (1729). But is it misreading to understand that Samson has acted entirely alone; that he simply did something without much thought or reason; that suicide became an answer out of his miseries instead of defeat by return to his father's house or by forgiveness of his wife and nurturing by her? Do we have Samson the Great Deliverer finally or only an enactment of the unwise, bullish, conceited strong man such as Joseph Wittreich has uncovered in much of the religious (particularly sermon) literature of the period?[7] The Bible surely allows for a vengeful and escapist Samson; Milton complicates the situation and person, however, and thereby lies the difficulty in reading this text, setting up this misreading or that.

While Samson may have been a foolish, carnal, bragging strongman in the past, Milton's poem has frequently been read as developing his regeneration (and has as frequently been denied such development). A more accurate term would be *renovation*, for what seems to happen to Samson articulates with the discussion in *De doctrina christiana*, chapter 17:

It is by MAN'S RENOVATION that he is BROUGHT TO A STATE OF GRACE AFTER BEING CURSED AND SUBJECT TO GOD'S ANGER. . . . Renovation takes place either naturally or supernaturally. . . . VOCATION is that natural method of renovation by which GOD THE FATHER, ACCORDING TO HIS PRECON-CEIVED PURPOSE IN CHRIST, INVITES FALLEN MEN TO A KNOWL-EDGE OF THE WAY TO PLACATE AND WORSHIP HIS GODHEAD AND, OUT OF GRATUITOUS KINDNESS, INVITES BELIEVERS TO SALVATION SO THAT THOSE WHO DO NOT BELIEVE ARE DEPRIVED OF ALL EX-CUSE. . . . Special vocation means that God, whenever he chooses, invites selected individuals, either from the so-called elect or from the reprobate, more clearly and more insistently than is normal. . . . The change in man which follows his vocation is that whereby the mind and will of the natural man are partially renewed and are divinely moved towards knowledge of God, and undergo a change for the better, at any rate for the time being.

Since this change comes from God it is called *light* and *the gift of will*. . . . What can this mean but that God gives us the power to act freely, which we have not been able to do since the fall unless called and restored? We cannot be given the gift of will unless we are also given freedom of action, because that is what free will means. . . . The kind of faith which corresponds to penitence is a submission, itself natural, to the divine call. It is accompanied by a confidence also natural and often mistaken.[8]

Samson in Milton's poem, though not really the Samson of the Bible, is presented both by himself and by the Chorus as fulfilling renovation with such words as "I begin to feel / Some rouzing motions in me which dispose / To something extraordinary my thoughts" (1381–83) and "What if his eye-sight (for to *Israels* God / Nothing is hard) by miracle restor'd / . . . With inward eyes illuminated / His fierie vertue rouz'd" (1527–28, 1689–90). "Vertue" implies both "power" and "righteousness"; "rouzing/rouz'd" work together to make his "motions" come from within, through inward light, with "power" and "righteousness," and to assert that his "vertue" has only been dormant, not extirpated—that it "oft seems to hide its face but unex-pectedly returns" (1749–50). If we accept that this "light" and its implied power ("vertue") have returned with God's miraculous action, then it is logi-cal that the previous episodes of the dramatic poem have been developing Samson in such a way as to make him again worthy in God's eyes.[9] The poem becomes the development of Samson's vocation to be followed (ac-cording to the concepts of *De doctrina christiana*) by a change which renews mind and will, through God's "light," and is defined by "submission" and "confidence." While he first asserts a trifold "I will not come," he differenti-ates between being constrained to come and going of his own free will, as others have remarked.[10] With the rousing motions he affirms, "I with this Messenger will go along" and "I am content to go."

A rather standard view is that "*Samson Agonistes* can be read either as a closed affirmation of Christian providence, or as an interrogative text which calls in question the benevolence of 'highest wisdom'."[11] According to that statement the text can be read as a positive thesis of God's presence and omnipotence or as a questioning uncertainty that God's omniscience is ultimately wise or at least ultimately successful. The most significant uncertainty for the text would seem instead to be viewing it as either/or rather than "this and that": a disjunctive reading should, rather, be replaced by a reading that holds the multiple readings of the text in mind conjunctively, opposed though they may seem to be. The text certainly affirms Christian providence but does not necessitate Providence as humankind would like to interpret it.[12] It demands more than only belief in God's providence; it demands the "grace" that Milton talked of in *Sonnet VII,* which would be employed under the great taskmaster's overview. Humankind must act, not just sit back and let God do it. The text also does not question the benevolence of "highest wisdom"; it questions human understanding of that wisdom and of the demands put upon humankind to uphold its covenant with its god. The text does not put into question Milton's belief in God; it renders negative the thinking of humankind exploiting its own desires, its customs, its pleasure principle and ease, its misplaced allegiances, and its obsequious inaction. Indeed, it represents Milton's dejection with humankind who are too much the rabble, too little the fit few. The answers to the questions that impinge upon the text are not simple ones of believing this or doing that, and are repeatedly limited by contexts, the reader's especially. "Misreading Milton" in the case of *Samson Agonistes* may be more accurately stated as reading the cross-signals in the overwhelming uncertainties of the characters, their actions, the language, the allusions. Milton may be discouraged and disillusioned by the ignorance of his compatriots in matters political and religious (and we can observe this condition in Manoa and the Chorus in the *exodos*), but is he still hopeful that some in a position of doing will act to oust the religio-political world of Charles I or Charles II? An underlying definition of hero and heroism permeates the poem and its political application, with its sharp contrast to Satan.

Manoa and the Chorus think only of such crassness as building Samson a monument, hanging up his trophies, having virgins bring flowers to adorn his tomb, or of God's working miracles; there is nothing contemplated to aid deliverance through their action. There is no readiness here to allow "Time [to] run back, and fetch the age of gold" (Nativity ode, 135). But the fit reader has such readiness, having anticipated that the dramatic poem will lead to the means to have "choice of [metaphoric] Sun or shade," for oneself, if not as leader of others. It will allow not only Samson to "respire" (again breathe as free person and again hope [from *re* and *spiro* > *spero*]), but the reader too. It will demonstrate that indeed "light is in the Soul, She all in every part" and thus not abrogated by the loss of one part (the eye). The dramatic poem, in this way of thinking, evidences the ravages of time and defeat, experience and human indulgence, but it also implies an ideal to be sought, politically, religiously, personally.

The ending of the poem presents attitudes on the part of Manoa that oppose Samson's action and on the part of the Chorus attitudes that echo people in general, those whose anticipation would seem to be fulfilled.[13] Samson has quit himself like Samson, he has had revenge on his enemies and mutilators, he will become a hero for the women to commemorate with flowers, he will become an example for the men to engage in valorous and high adventures, he will be given a recognition worthy of Willy Loman with a monument and laurels and palms and trophies. The outward show and ostentation of public acclaim, for Manoa and the Chorus, make Samson's life and now death meaningful. The bathetic lucky words wished for by the uncouth swain of *Lycidas* will appear "In copious Legend, or sweet Lyric Song" (1737). So viewed, Samson is but a mere idol, not a great deliverer. The reactions of Manoa and the Chorus suggest that for them there has been no renovation of Samson, only, beneath his final words though unacknowledged, what would be a continued braggadocio:

> Happ'n what may, of me expect to hear
> Nothing dishonourable, impure, unworthy
> Our God, Our Law, my Nation, or my self,
> The last of me or no I cannot warrant. (1423–26)

The reputed republicans of the 1640s or the 1660s only vaunt the Good Old Cause and its principles and temporary ascent; they do not act for its maintenance, for its currency. Memory of what has been achieved is enough for these "stalwart" interpreters of God's wisdom. We can understand why *the Chorus* says that there is "calm of mind all passion spent"; but the uncertainty of the poem and of its ending asks whether indeed there can be any calm of mind in these circumstances.

From a reading of Samson as renovated arises a quite different interpretation of the above lines. Rather than the vengeful person of the Bible, rather than the suicide of the Bible, the Samson of Milton's dramatic poem has accepted the uncertainty of outcome since he has given himself up to God's guidance ("Happ'n what may"), but with the inherent being of God's presence within, which all humankind may enjoy, there can be "nothing dishonourable, impure, unworthy" originating with him. The structure of significance from high to lower dictates line 1425: God/Law/Nation/self. Reprobate Samson's action in the past had reversed that structure. The verb of the next line ("The last of me or no I cannot warrant") is especially telling. Offhand it says simply that he cannot prophesy with any assurance; it also says that he just doesn't know what he can assure his audience of as a result of what he will do or what the Philistines will do. With their potential exasperation at the sight of him, as the previous lines imply, the Philistines may do something to make this his last day (cause his death or execute his death), but whether it will be through something he does that "authorizes" such action, he cannot say. Yet we read the line ironically because we know that his action will bring his death without any action by the Philistines. Will his action thus "warrant" his death with his own "authorization"? Milton would not allow his interrogation of the Bible to deny the biblical account—thus the continued possibility of revenge and suicide, but analysis of this confused and often redacted biblical text, at the same time, makes possible the reading that his action is as Great Deliverer, truly guided by the Holy One of Israel, and his death as "authorized" to manifest what may be involved in executing God's commission.

The heroism which the renovated Samson exhibits, strongly contrasting with the alleged heroism of the past which dealt only with destruction for the sake of destruction, with its accompanying egotism, parallels the heroic action of the Son in the companion poem *Paradise Regain'd.* True heroism in God's people requires faith in God through a unity of person and God, and obedience to the godhead against all seemingly opposed demands and against all self-serving urges. Samson has altered in the course of the poem from one who has not shown faith in God, one who has acted on his own (despite rationalizations of "divine impulsion"), one who has acted in presumption. He has been a "hero" to the general populace of Dan in the superficial way that military heroes have been, a view of the heroic that Milton rejects in the proem to Book IX of *Paradise Lost.* That kind of hero in certain ways is also represented by Satan, who supposedly fights against injustice and oppression. Samson's defiance and ranting pride of the past place him in that camp, and that is the version of this strong man that was disowned by some of the sermonists of the seventeenth century, in distinction from the culture hero of the Puritan revolution waging a holy war which was also current. In *Areopagitica* Milton employed the figure of Samson as a strong man rousing from sleep and shaking invincible locks to figure England as a noble and puissant nation on the verge of great achievement (YP II, p. 558). In the dramatic poem, aware of the false heroism possible and of the obsequious inaction of some, Milton gives us both Samsons, but unfortunately the renovated Samson as exemplary hero exhibiting exemplary heroism is not understod by Manoa or the Chorus, representative of the "people." The renovation that takes place through the encounters in which he participates has been recognized before, predicating a human similarity to the figure of the Son (though he should not be viewed as a Christ). Yet the earlier Samson breaks through from time to time and the final scene of the dramatic poem can easily lead the reader not to delve into Samson's action any more deeply than Manoa and the Chorus do. God has reappeared as he always does in the nick of time, and Samson has quit himself like Samson. In reading thus we may not be reading Milton's "message," but we are not misreading either. Unlike the clues that lead the fit reader to recognize Satan in his true colors from the very beginning of the epic (not only as he seems to lose luster later on), the clues to Samson are ambiguous. There is still some boastfulness in "I could be well content to try thir Art, / Which to no few of them would prove pernicious" (1399–1400); there is a hint of acedia and of despair in "And for a life who will not change his purpose?" (1406). If Aristotelian resolution of tragedy is to be read from "calm of mind all passion spent," then perhaps the attitude of the Chorus is proper and they are "dismist" "With peace and consolation" (1758, 1757).

The reading I propose for the ending, different from many other interpretations, focuses upon Samson, and thus focuses upon him within the whole poem, not upon one of his dialogists and not upon one of the episodes only. Most prominently the episode with Dalila has been wrenched from its component position in much recent criticism, as if the work were almost totally summed up there and as if, regardless of how it is read, Dalila were the focal character. As Merritt Y. Hughes remarked, "Today it may seem inevitable that a scene with Dalila, the Philistine who betrayed her lover to save her country, should be the keystone of any Samson drama. . . . In the seventeenth century it was not clear that in a classical tragedy whose action occurred on the last day of the hero's life she had a proper place."[14] First, however, we should glance at the "misreadings" that the episode permits. Is Dalila lying and showing hypocrisy when she asks forgiveness and says she did what she did out of political loyalty to her people who had been harassed by Samson and out of religious belief in her god, Dagon? or should we read her as being sincere? The standard reading is the first; only a few people (usually to disbelief and strong denial) have allowed the second.

Problems exist in accepting Dalila as false. This is a dramatic work, demanding verisimilar characters who act within their own integrity in that work. For Dalila to be insincere, she must have a purpose in coming to Samson which accords with that insincerity. Critics have not posited a psychologically or strategically valid reason for such falseness: there is nothing to be gained by the Philistines in having Samson—a blind man, even if his strength is returning—repair to his wife's home; and there is no picture of a Dalila vaunting her former "achievement" prior to Samson's rebuff. What she can learn from her interview with Samson that will be helpful to her people is unclear. The reading of a false Dalila seems to be borne out, for some, by her entry decked out like a ship of Tarsus with all her finery—a common symbol then of the prostitute—and by having the Chorus call her a serpent finally revealed. Yet such dress may simply be what a Philistian woman, particularly a celebrity, might wear on occasion, especially on an important festival occasion as this day was for Dagon. Her dress may be seductive, and worn for that reason, but Samson, after all, is blind. The perfume that precedes her might have seductive effect, but it is also what any woman dressed in her best finery might have put on. Further, she seems at first a matron to the Chorus, hardly a seductive type, one would think. Have these "clues" of occasion and matronly appearance simply been missed by those viewing Dalila as insincere? Or has Milton purposely allowed his readers to envision the Delilah of the story preceding the beginning of the dramatic poem as continued in the Dalila of the poem? The Chorus' almost pornographicly confused "She's gone, a manifest Serpent by her sting / Discover'd in the end, till now conceal'd" (997–98) comments upon her seeming abjection and sympathy in the beginning of the dialogue and her boastful lashing out once insulted and rejected toward the end of the interview. Does this make her a serpent through the full episode—evil, insincere, a temptress only? Or has Milton again interrogated the Bible and its popular interpretation?

The Bible says that she was charged by the Philistian lords to entice him to learn the source of his strength so that they could bind him and afflict him after he had been so long destructive of their people and, significantly, after he had tricked the Gazites who wanted to kill him, following a previous night with one of their harlots. Delilah's reward was to be eleven hundred pieces of silver from every one of them, a very large sum. (Her name means "weakness," as Michael Lieb has demonstrated.)[15] Perhaps Milton would not question the validity of such a reason for a prostitute, but making her Samson's wife would tend to reject that reason and allow for an interesting, though misread, position on marriage as convenant—misread because it is Samson who raises the issue now though his former actions belie concern with the marriage covenant.

The "sincere" Dalila offers reasons for her act that may have a relationship with William Riley Parker's discussion of Euripides' *Troades* as background for the dramatic poem.[16] To Menelaus, Helen, also dressed in finery, defends her elopement with Paris as patriotic to save Greece and then as the will of the gods, finally asking to be pardoned for her offense. That intertext puts a strong sense of falsity and treason on Dalila's argument; nevertheless, we would expect Milton to honor sincere devotion to one's political and religious beliefs even if such devotion abrogates personal relationships and commitments. A telling criticism of so-called adherents of liberty in *The Tenure of Kings and Magistrates* is their drawing back from action against the monarchic leaders because of personal concerns and desires:

If men within themselves would be govern'd by reason, and not generally give up thir understanding to a double tyrannie, of Custom from without, and blind affections within, they would discerne better, what it is to favour and uphold the Tyrant of a Nation. But being slaves within doors, no wonder that they strive so much to have the public State conformably govern'd to the inward vitious rule, by which they govern themselves. For indeed none can love freedom heartilie, but good men; the rest love not freedom, but license. . . . Consequentlie neither doe bad men hate Tyrants, but have been alwayes readiest with the falsifi'd names of *Loyalty*, and *Obedience*, to colour over thir base compliances. And although sometimes for shame, and when it comes to thir owne grievances, of purse especially, they would seeme good Patriots, and side with the better cause, yet when others for the deliverance of thir Countrie, endu'd with fortitude and Heroick vertue to feare nothing but the curse writt'n against those *That doe the worke of the Lord negligently*, would goe on to remove, not only the calamities and thraldoms of a People, but the roots and causes whence they spring, streight these men, and sure helpers at need, as if they hated only the miseries but not the mischiefs . . . not only turne revolters from those principles, which only could at first move them, but lay the staine of disloyaltie, and worse, on those proceedings, which are the necessary consequences of their own former actions. (1–2)

Dalila may be one of the "bad men" who cry loyalty and obedience for the wrong "Tyrant," for a false god, yet she does not, like the "bad men," turn revolter from those principles because of some other, more personal covenant: she cannot be counted disloyal to her people and her god by now offering aid to her incapacitated husband. Milton has presented a Dalila who may be read as sincere though wrong, wrong because the object of her sincerity is a false god: again it is the question of Whose god is God? Were Dagon true god, we certainly would expect Milton to champion Dalila and her abrogation of the marriage covenant. The episode is part of the dramatic poem not only because Samson's giving in to temptation in the past has to be reversed before renovation can take place, but because it raises, for the reader, the whole issue of true or false nation and god. As a verisimilar character in a drama, Dalila should be looked at from her individual person, and one of the pictures we derive from this is someone who has done what she thought was right, who has come to reevaluate her action in terms of wedlock vows, and who repents the dire consequences that have resulted.

The question of marriage vows is significant for the poem and has been a catalyst for seeing Samson as Milton and impugning Milton as misogynist. None of those who have argued this question has pointed out that Samson raises such a covenant only now after the fact; that he himself kept to no such covenant in the past; that he, both in the Bible and in the poem, married out of carnal desire only. This lack of issue for Samson occurs with the Woman of Timna, also presented as "wife," as well as Delilah, and makes it important for Milton to have altered the biblical tradition (although it occurs rarely in some exegeses) of Delilah as concubine. Samson is entreated four times by Delilah to tell the secret of his strength, and three times he lies to her. He has shown no adherence to the marriage covenant he now tries to make so much of in transferring blame to Dalila: the husband should trust the wife. As masculinist (perhaps as misogynist), Samson (not Milton) shows an attitude that the husband can break marriage vows but the wife cannot. He has not only not treated Delilah as wife, he has not awakened to her treachery on three occasions without, apparently, recourse to raising the issue of wedlock vows.

Unfortunately, even some feminist critics have fallen into the masculinist view that woman is always seductress, untrustworthy, deceitful, self-concerned, and the cause of all man's woes. The insincere Dalila may offer that reading on Milton's part, but the sincere Dalila offers a different reading that takes man to task: "In argument with men a woman ever / Goes by the worse, whatever be her cause" (903–04), and that accuses Samson of not, in the past, living up to his position as Great Deliverer, true servant of God, coauthor with his God of worthy achievement. The task that Milton placed before himself in his revision and interrogation of the biblical story, which depicts an ambiguous Samson as "good man" and champion of God and as "bad man" strutting around "like a petty God" "swoll'n with pride" (529, 532), a destroyer and slayer of many, predicated obverse readings. Milton's solution was to acknowledge Samson's failings, which takes on more significance by assigning to Dalila a character that is not simply venal, and to have Samson transcend himself, both what he was and what remained of his past self. This is achieved by Samson's renovation, but that renovation must occur in stages, moving the self-absorbed and still proud and recriminatory defeated blind man into one who gives himself up fully to guidance and selflessness and action.

The dramatic poem is not built on plot: there is Samson and then three personifications of issues that confront him, preceded by community and followed by forces outside community. It is not a "play" with interconnected actions and truly "real" characters: Manoa, Dalila, and Harapha stand for issues that raise the bases for Samson's failure as prophesied Great Deliverer. These are issues with which he as individual must wrestle in order to take up the challenge of demonstrating to outsiders (though misread by his countrymen, as evidenced by Manoa and the Chorus) whose god is God and the nature of that God and how that God operates. The message to Milton's co-republicans fell on deaf ears, it seems, as well as those who "misread" the poem by giving independent weight to the extrabiblical episodes that Milton constructs.

University of Kentucky

NOTES

1. John Dryden, "Dedication of the *Aeneis*," in *The Works of Virgil* (London, 1697), p. 154; Charles Batteux, *Principes de la littérature* (Paris, 1764), vol. II, pp. 207–08; William Godwin, *An Enquiry Concerning Political Justice* (Dublin, 1793), vol. I, pp. 241–42; Mary Shelley, *Frankenstein, or the Modern Prometheus* (London, 1818); and John T. Shawcross, *With Mortal Voice: The Creation of "Paradise Lost"* (Lexington, 1982), Chap. 4, "The Hero," pp. 33–41. Quotations of Milton's poems are from *The Complete Poetry of John Milton*, ed. John T. Shawcross (Garden City, 1971); those of the prose are from *Complete Prose Works of John Milton*, 8 vols., ed. Don M. Wolfe et al. (New Haven, 1953–82), hereafter cited as YP in the text. "Dalila" refers to the character in Milton's dramatic poem; "Delilah," to the character in Judges, entering discussion of the poem in the substance of the biblical text occurring before the action of the poem begins, being only reported or implied.

2. See William Blake, *The Marriage of Heaven and Hell* (1790–93), plate 6.

3. See Marjorie Hope Nicolson, *John Milton: A Reader's Guide to His Poetry* (New York, 1963), p. 257; for one example, see Arnold Stein, *Answerable Style: Essays on Paradise Lost* (Minneapolis, 1953), "The War in Heaven": "The laughter is symbolic action, but there is also real action that produces real laughter by the participants, besides the action that is intended to induce laughter in the reader" (p. 22); and Michael Lieb, *The Dialectics of Creation: Patterns of Birth and Regeneration in "Paradise Lost"* (Amherst, 1970), pp. 117–21. David Norbrook has demonstrated (in an unpublished talk) that this parodic war in heaven derives from Lucan's *Pharsalia* and its ridiculing depiction of war.

4. It has not previously been pointed out that Milton in the war in heaven is echoing and implying Isaiah's oracle concerning Babylon in chapter xiii, specifically in these lines and following (emphasis added):

Lift ye up a banner upon the high mountain, exalt the voice unto them . . . The noise of a multitude in the mountains, . . . a tumultuous noise of the kingdoms of nations gathered together; the Lord of hosts mustereth the host of the battle. They come from a far country, from the end of heaven, even the Lord, and the weapons of his indignation, to destroy the whole land. Howl ye; for the day of the Lord is at hand; it shall come as a destruction from the Almighty. Therefore shall all hands be faint, and every man's heart shall melt: and they shall be afraid: pangs and sorrows shall take hold of them. . . . Behold, the day of the Lord cometh, cruel both with wrath and fierce anger, to lay the land desolate: and he shall destroy the sinners thereof out of it. . . . And I will punish the world for their evil, and the wicked for their iniquity; and I will cause the arrogancy of the proud to cease, and will lay low the haughtiness of the terrible. I will make a man more precious than fine gold. . . . *Therefore I will shake the heavens*, and the earth shall remove out of her place, in the wrath of the Lord of hosts, and in the day of his fierce anger.

This prophecy of the coming of Christ and his destruction of the proud and sinful by the shaking of the heavens recurs in the Gospels (although no scholarship has offered it as an intertext to Book VI), along with other prominent images; see Matthew xxiv, 29; Mark, chapter xiii; Luke, chapter xxi.

5. Book I, chapter 3, where verses 16 and 18 are cited in Latin and with "&c." following the partial quotation of 16. Thus the specific words "hide my face" are not given, but the full biblical passage and its use in this discussion of decree are significant for us to recall in reading the dramatic poem. See *The Works of John Milton*, ed. Frank Allen Patterson et al. (New York, 1931–38), vol. XIV, p. 87, where the fuller text is given in the translation; YP VI, pp. 65–66, gives a literal translation of the Latin, omitting, therefore, the important phrase in v, 18.

6. Michael Lieb, *Milton and the Culture of Violence* (Ithaca, N.Y., 1994).

7. Joseph Wittreich, *Interpreting Samson Agonistes* (Princeton, 1986). Wittreich's detailed discussion of the different Samsons available in the mid seventeenth century goes to the heart of the uncertainties of text with which I am here concerned. In relation to Samson's final act and its interpretations, for example, Wittreich refers to Heinrich Bullinger and writes, " 'bending the pillars of the theatre,' Samson, blindly led by self-love, is 'himself slain with the fall of the palace,' " but also to William Carter's view that Samson brought down "the whole structure of the Romish Babel" and to Nathaniel Fiennes's remark that it was the whole structure of the English church government (pp. 185 and 195n41). References are to *The Decades*, trans. H. I., ed. Thomas Hardy (Cambridge, 1849–52), vol. III, pp. 209–10; *Israels Peace with God, Beniamines Overthrow* (London, 1642), p. 43; and *Private Papers of State*, in *Historical Collections*, ed. John Rushworth (London: 1721), vol. IV, p. 180.

8. *Of Christian Doctrine*, trans. John Carey, *Complete Prose Works of John Milton*, ed. Maurice Kelley (New Haven, 1973), vol. VI, pp. 453–59. The argument that Milton was not the author of *De doctrina christiana* is not only not proved, it does not engage such statements as this on renovation that do not negate what seem from the full canon to be Milton's theological positions. The importance of renovation in understanding Milton's Samson has already been pointed out by Albert C. Labriola, "Divine Urgency as a Motive for Conduct in *Samson Agonistes*," *PQ* LIX (1971): 99–107; see especially p. 105.

9. See John M. Steadman, " 'Faithful Champion': The Theological Basis of Milton's Hero of Faith," *Anglia* LXXVII (1959): 12–28, and Ann Gossman, "Milton's Samson as the Tragic Hero Purified by Trial," *JEGP* 61 (1962): 528–41. Labriola, "Divine Urgency," distinguishes between the earlier, biblical "intimate impulse" and the "rouzing motions," and concludes that they "betoken an exercise of free will to do good," unlike the temptations of the past, reprised in the three central episodes of the poem as "good temptations."

10. See, among others, Fredson Bowers, "*Samson Agonistes*: Justice and Reconciliation" in *The Dress of Words: Essays on Restoration and Eighteenth Century Literature in Honor of Richmond P. Bond*, ed. Robert B. White, Jr. (Lawrence, Kans., 1978), pp. 1–23; and Anthony Low, *The Blaze of Noon: A Reading of "Samson Agonistes"* (New York, 1974).

11. Catherine Belsey, *John Milton. Language, Gender, Power* (Oxford, 1988), p. 56.

12. As *Paradise Lost* makes clear, Providence is only a guide. God has "provided" for exigencies, and as Adam and Eve leave Paradise, he has provided hope and example in the saints of Books XI and XII and most specifically in the Incarnated Son—

> O Prophet of glad tidings, finisher
> Of utmost hope! now clear I understand
> What oft my steddiest thoughts have searcht in vain,
> Why our great expectation should be call'd
> The seed of Woman: Virgin Mother, Hail,

High in the love of Heav'n, yet from my Loyns
Thou shalt proceed, and from thy Womb the Son
Of God most High; so God with man unites.   (XII, 375–82)

The descendants of the Grand-Parents—such as Samson and the Israelites—should understand that Providence is the *uniting* of God with humans, but the Chorus, representative of those descendants and Milton's political contemporaries, ignore the "uniting" and take solace in God's provision when he no longer hides his face, but reappears to overcome their enemies.

13. In the background may be the philosophical development moving from a concept of God's revelation to that of God's manifestation. The Chorus would seem to credit God as a God of revelation, such as dominated religion prior to around 1670, a doer of miracles: God "to his faithful Champion hath in place / Bore witness gloriously." The deistic God seen and known through what he has wrought, through nature untrammeled by humankind's alterations, may lie behind Samson's finding of strength and action again. While authentic achievement comes from the unifying of God and human, it predisposes a new finding of direction and strength (mental as well as physical) which are inherent. Such manifestation of Godhead within the person is an adjunct of the deistic development that led to the pantheistic (and transcendental) concepts of the Romantic period. Milton's belief in God's revelation, as in his early rendition of Passover Psalm cxiv, may have been undergoing modification as he wrote the dramatic poem. Such modification is not different from the substruction in sonnets XV or XVI that Fairfax or Cromwell must act, not rely on the hope that Public Fraud will be cleared from Public Faith or that Liberty of Conscience will naturally follow with the advent of Peace.

14. *John Milton: Complete Poems and Major Prose*, ed. Merritt Y. Hughes (New York, 1985), p. 532. In treating this poem, it would be wise for the reader to review Hughes's epitome of the critical aura surrounding Dalila (pp. 532–34) and its "gross exaggeration of the dramatic evidence and of Dalila's importance in the drama as a whole."

15. Michael Lieb, *The Sinews of Ulysses: Form and Convention in Milton's Works* (Pittsburgh, 1989), chap. 7, "The Theology of Strength," pp. 125–27.

16. William Riley Parker, *Milton's Debt to Greek Tragedy in "Samson Agonistes"* (Baltimore, 1937), p. 127.